THINK ABOUT IT

By E. Leon Barnes

INTRODUCTION

Great books come in all shapes and sizes. Many of my favorites are intense studies on one subject that dives deep into that topic and tries hard to look at all sides of the subject. This isn't that kind of book at all. Instead it is a lot of short articles on all kinds of topics that all relate to one another in that they all have to do with living the life God calls on us to live. They are articles I've written at different times under different circumstances. Sometimes it is a time when I'm intensely concerned about something and writing is a way to get some feeling of release. At other times it is a much more relaxed setting when I'm just wanting to write about something that seems interest to me at the moment. I'm hoping that some of these will touch your heart where you are at the time you read it. Unlike the book that needs to be read from page one to the end all in order, this is one you can just as easily sit down and read from one segment at one time and another at some later point and it all make sense and fit where you are.

If you read it and find something that touches your heart, pass it on to someone else that might be benefitted by it. If something you read doesn't hit you right, read another one and see how it works for you. Of course it would be a pleasure to hear from anyone as you read especially if you found something in the book useful.

I pray that God will use the book to do good for anyone that goes to the effort to read it.

Leon Barnes
PO Box 870
Little Rock, AR 72203
leon@arcentralchurch.org

You can check my blog at "leoninlittlerock.com" or follow my materials on Facebook, Twitter or LinkedIn.

INDEX

All God's amazing creation was good and even "Very good." God had planted a garden eastward in Eden and prepared it for the man, Adam to inhabit. Adam must have been amazed at the beauty, and marveled at the animals God had created. But God made him intelligent from the beginning so he must have wondered quickly, "Why do all the animals have a mate that is different but like them, but I don't?" God looked at the situation and declared, "It's not good for man to be alone. I will make a helper suitable for him." You know the story. God had Adam name the animals as they filed by, I suspect to demonstrate to him that none of these would be that suitable companion for him. Then God performed the first surgery, taking Adam's rib to make Eve the perfect match for Adam just as he was the perfect match for her. God made a presentation of Eve to Adam who in amazement declared, "This is now bone of my bone and flesh of my flesh. She will be called woman for she was taken out of the man." It isn't clear whether the rest of the statement is from Adam or from God about marriage. "That is why a man leaves his father and mother and is united to his wife and they become one flesh. Adam and his wife were both naked and they felt no shame." (Genesis 2:23-25)

I want to focus on one thing from this story that I think has been misunderstood too often. God said he would make a helper that was suitable for Adam. What does that mean? Is a helper a servant, a slave or an equal partner? It is enlightening to look at the uses of this word "Helper" or other similar uses such as "Help". Look at just a few to get a good picture. In Psalms 10:14 it says, "But you, God see the trouble of the afflicted; you consider their grief and take it in hand. The victims commit themselves to you, you are the HELPER of the fatherless." In Hebrews 13:6 it says, "The Lord is my HELPER; I will not be afraid. What can mere mortals do to me?" Add to that the fact that the Holy Spirit is our helper in our times of weakness according to Romans 8:26. Jesus even promised to send us another helper the Holy Spirit.

Push the thought a little further and look at the times when God challenges us to be a helper of others. In Acts 9:36 Dorcas was described as one who was always doing good and helping the poor. When Paul gave the qualities for a Widow indeed in I Timothy 5:10 he said she must be a woman "who is well known for good deeds, such as bringing up children, showing hospitality, washing the feet of the Lord's people, helping those in trouble and devoting herself to all kinds of good deeds."

When I take the time to look at these different passages of Scripture that use the word "Helper" or "Help" something jumps out to me. Notice the helper was one who was reaching down to help someone who was in need. The Holy Spirit helps us in our weaknesses. God is a very present help in time of need. The widow was to help the hurting.

Rather than the idea of a "Helper suitable for him" meaning that God made the woman to be subservient to the man the word God uses indicates that she is going to be one who is capable and powerful to help him in the areas of need, weakness and struggle. Does that mean she is above the man? No, I don't think that is the point. But to think that God made Eve to serve as Adam's maid misses the point entirely. They were partners together to fulfill the work God had for them. Both were made in the image and likeness of God according to Genesis 1:26,27. The man and woman were made to fit each other, physically, mentally, emotionally and spiritually. When we think that either the men can do fine without the input of the women or the women think they can do fine without the input of the men we miss the plan God had from the beginning. Each supplies the very things that the other needs to be whole.

It is quite easy to find someone who will lead you through some sort of personal renewal. Offers abound from those who will help to rebuild the muscle tone you've lost through years of inactivity. There are those all around who can help you restore your skin tone and begin a renewal of a fresh and healthy appearance to others. Everywhere you look there is some kind of offer for training. It may be yoga, biking, zumba or a new name attached to some old idea. If Paul were here to give his assessment of them all it would be that they are all "Worth a little." His assessment of all bodily exercise was that it had a little value but that godliness was valuable in all ways and all things.

This month at Central we are focusing on God's Spiritual Harvest. We hold up the different mission efforts that we are supporting as a church in trying to bring people to God around the world. It is a wonderful thing to pray about, think about and make plans on how we can do more to carry the message of salvation to people who don't know God around the world. Think about how important it would be today if we had the cure for the Ebola Virus but hadn't really done much to get that cure out to the people who needed it. It would be considered a horrible crime for us to hold back the cure to such a major illness, no matter how much it might inconvenience us in getting that cure out to others. Sin is a far more horrible disease than Ebola. It is more contagious and more deadly. We actually have the cure for man's sin problem. In Romans 1:14-16 Paul said, "I am obligated both to Greeks and non-Greeks, both to the wise and the foolish. That is why I am so eager to preach the gospel also to you who are in Rome. For I am not ashamed of the gospel, because it is the power of God that brings salvation to everyone who believes: first to the Jew, then to the Gentile."

There are worlds of good things a church can do to make for a better world. We can provide homes for the homeless, offer adoption for the orphan, care for the widow and attention for the lonely. All of these are good things and if tied to sharing with those who are hurting and struggling the gospel of Christ that can save the lost soul then such good works become all the more important and valuable. But if our kind actions that help people out of struggling situations don't also share with them the message of the gospel we have only offered superficial help for a tragic problem.

In I Corinthians 9:19-22 Paul wrote these words about his passion to share the message of salvation with those who were lost. "Though I am free and belong to no one, I have made myself a slave to everyone, to win as many as possible. To the Jews, I became like a Jew, to win the Jews. To those under the law I became like one under the law (though I myself am not under the law), so as to win those under the law. To those not having the law I became like one not having the law (though I am not free from God's law but am under Christ's law), so as to win those not having the law. To the weak I became weak, to win the weak. I have become all things to all people so that by all possible means I might save some." If we could drop back a few years in Paul's life we would find an arrogant, self-assured young Jew who was on fire for the law and who belonged to the religious group knows as the Pharisees. At that point he was sure he was right and that all who failed to live by the law radically were hell bound. Now he is a humble servant, so longing to get the saving message of the gospel to people that he will do everything he can to get on their level, talk their language and feel their pain in hopes of leading them to Christ and salvation.

The massive question that haunts me every time I read this passage where Paul described his passion to win some for the Lord, is how far am I willing to go to be able to share the saving message of the gospel with a lost person? How much am I willing to give to support those who are ready to go to some foreign country to share the gospel? What will I risk to tell someone of the love of God and the sacrificial death of Jesus on the cross so they can be saved? If I were the one lost, how far would I want someone to go to get me the message of salvation?

Dear God in heaven, put a burden on my heart every day for those whom I will see or contact that don't know you that I will go way out of my way to be able to share the good news of Jesus with them so that some may be saved. Through Jesus I pray. Amen.

A SCAPEGOAT

Have you ever felt like you were being used as a scapegoat? In just about any scandal that takes place either in business or in government someone becomes the scapegoat and get's fired from their job for whatever the wrong was that was done while all the others who were guilty of the same thing or worse go free and are able to either correct the problem or continue as if nothing has happened. Watch and see if in the latest scandal with the IRS if there isn't some poor soul that was way down the food chain that get's fired and becomes the scapegoat while all the others that were far more important in the situation plead ignorance and go on as though nothing has happened.

Like so many ideas we tend to talk about people being made the scapegoat without any recognition of where the whole idea originated. I doubt that most of the people who will talk about a person being made the scapegoat in the IRS scandal have the slightest notion that they are talking about something that is discussed in the Bible and that has a Bible connotation. Back in Leviticus 16 God was giving instruction to Moses for the priesthood, especially to Aaron and his sons on how to conduct themselves on the Day of Atonement. Aaron was instructed to take a bull that was without blemish and offer it first for his own sins so that he would be prepared to offer the sacrifice for the people. Unlike Jesus who would later offer himself as the sacrifice to God for the sins of the people, and who didn't need to first offer a sacrifice for his own sins and then for the sins of the people, Aaron needed the offering for himself and every other priest until Jesus would have the same need.

When Aaron had made the offering for his own sins then he was to take two goats and bring them both before the Lord. One was chosen as an offering on the altar for the sins of the people. It was prepared and offered as the atonement for the people once a year. Then Aaron or the high priest who was one of his descendants was to come out from the offering of the atonement and lay his hands on the other goat that was to be the scapegoat. He was to confess the sins of the people over that goat and all their sins were to be placed on him. Then the goat was to be taken by another Israelite out into the wilderness where it would be released. It was to carry the sins of the people upon it as it served as the scapegoat so that Israel's sins could be forgiven or overlooked by God. The scapegoat was meant to take on the guilt of the people so they could go free before God for another year.

When Jesus went to the cross for us he was the perfect fulfillment of the atoning sacrifice for the sins of all mankind. He also serves as our scapegoat to take on him the sins of the whole world so we can have complete forgiveness and atonement for our sins. Because Jesus willingly took our place and offered himself as our atonement we don't need to have other scapegoats among us that we place the guilt on for our failings so we can somehow evade blame and go on acting as though nothing is wrong or needs to be changed.

It is seldom ever the case that one volunteers to be the scapegoat for some crime or wrong that is done. Too often it is someone who we think will never be noticed or whom it would be better to offer than for the whole church or whole company or whole agency to be harmed. Imagine the scene, as people are unhappy with what is going on in some high-level government activity. Word begins to leak out that something is happening that isn't right. Can you even imagine the person at the top of the agency, such as the IRS accepting the blame for wrong that has been done? No, the search begins for someone that is in a low level position that can accept the blame delivering those higher up from other criticism. A scapegoat is found and they are fired so that everyone is supposed to place the blame on them and life can return to the normal way and the poor person who is the scapegoat not only loses his job but also will likely be branded for life so that they can never find a meaningful job again. He takes one for the team but is then regarded as no longer part of the team they sacrificed to save.

With Jesus it is the one at the top, the perfect one, who is God and man, who raised his hand when the assignment was being made and volunteered to be the one. What a savior! But he isn't giving himself for our sins so we can continue as though nothing happened. He instead made it possible for us to change and bury our guilt so we can have a fresh start with God at any time. Thank God for the scapegoat!

ALL IN

As we've watched the Olympics the last week and a half, I've been amazed both at watching the drive of those who have appeared in the Olympics once or twice before and are still giving their all to being good at their sport and the new comers just getting started. At the first when the announcers were talking about Michael Phelps and his competing there were comments indicating he hadn't been training as hard as he should have been. But as the week moved on and he kept adding more gold medals that comment ceased to be made.

But I was particularly impressed with the ones who were there for the first time. Some were as young as fifteen and were winning in their areas. When they interviewed the mothers of some of the young ladies it became obvious that the young people who were competing hadn't been doing all the work to get there on their own. This had been a family commitment from early in their life.

When Gabby Douglas won the over all in Gymnastics it was wonderful. Her smile and excitement were a treat to see. But it was also interesting to watch the whole program to see that many from the USA won in different areas, but not in all and some of the ones who were real winners in one part of the games were not successful in others. I thought of something a high school teacher used to say to us. "It is important for us to learn both how to win and how to lose in life because no one wins every time and we grow more during the losing than we do in the winning." I can't say that I remember many things said to me during high school especially from teachers, but for some reason that statement has stuck in my mind now for about fifty years.

Think of every person who has even been able to qualify for the Olympics and you see a picture of commitment. They were willing to give up many of the things most young people in their age group were doing to be where they are today. They couldn't spend lots of time involved in video games because they were out doing and training to do the sports, instead of living in a pretend kind of world. Every time I watch such events, I'm moved to consider my commitment to the things that matter in life. The failure of being uncommitted haunts just about every aspect of life for us.

When we grow up with only casual interest and devotion to God the result is that we don't grow in our faith and most of the time it ultimately leads to our giving up our charge to live, as God wants us to live. Only the committed remain to serve when others around them are falling away or giving up.

It has been said that you can look at the commitment of parents for God and most of the time their children will be less committed and it will continue that trend from generation to generation until there is no commitment at all. Jesus lived on earth the life of total commitment. He said, "My food is to do the will of Him who sent me." Paul picked up on that heart and would say, "For me to live is Christ and to die is gain."

What are you totally committed to in your life? A husband or wife who isn't totally committed to the marriage and being the marriage partner God calls on them to be, will never have the marriage they could have had. The lack of real commitment is evident when partners are so concerned about what the other partner is doing wrong that they can't even see changes they need to make in themselves.

A parent who is only partially committed to bringing their children up in the way they should go will be more concerned with having their personal time and space than in the growth and development of their children. Often I see parents who are so committed to having fun that they ignore the most important things in life to get to do the things that they enjoy. There will never be any gold medals for parents who leave off the most important to do the much less important.

The very name, "Christian" is intended to convey the notion that we belong completely to Jesus Christ and our life is centered on following His lead in all aspects of life. Christians who grasp who they are take on more and more the image of Christ all the time. Too often we take our eyes off Jesus and put them on someone that we are impressed with and take on more the image of that person than of Jesus. We all need to keep the sentiments expressed by Paul in 2 Corinthians 3:18 clearly in mind. "And we all with unveiled face, beholding in the mirror the glory of the Lord are being transformed into the same image, from glory to glory, even as by the Spirit of our Lord." Keep your eyes of Jesus and draw closer to him always and God's Spirit will mold you into His image. Amazing! Stephen Covey, who died a few weeks ago, said that one of the habits needed for successful living is to "Keep the main thing, the main thing."

BE GENTLE

Sin has horrible consequences. Even when God forgives sins they still leave stains that affect everything. David the king of Israel demonstrates as well as anyone can how one can be a good person in so many ways and still make horrible mistakes that lead to massive family problems. He lusted for another man's wife, had sex with her and when she became pregnant he had her husband killed to try to hide the sin. He took her as his wife but tragedy followed.

David repented of the sin when God sent the prophet to confront him. He didn't deny it or try to minimize it. He declared "I have sinned and committed this great wickedness against my God."

But family problems haunted him from that day forward. One son lusted for his half sister, raped her and then threw her out. That girl's brother murdered the one who raped his sister. Then Absalom the one who killed his brother later determined to take the throne from his father. He slowly stole the hearts of the people making great promises of how he would help them in their troubled times. Then the time came when he believed he had the masses on his side and he had himself declared the king. He led an army against David, his father to take his throne. David and his people ran for their life. As the army of Absalom came out in battle array against David and his army, David divided his men into three groups under Joab, Abishai and Ittai. He first said he would go into battle with them but they convinced him that would be a mistake. As David prepared to send his men out to battle his son he gathered his three generals close with this charge, "Deal gently for my sake with the young man Absalom."

I suspect the generals were all thinking, "David, what are you talking about? He is trying to kill you! He wants your throne! This is an army going out to meet another army. How can we be gentle and fight for our lives and yours at the same time." The writer of 2 Samuel makes note of the fact that the people heard what he said. But it intrigues me that the generals didn't say anything back to David. They went out to do their job instead. They were hardened military men who likely felt far more anger toward Absalom than David could possibly muster.

How do you think you would feel if your own child was trying to kill you? I feel certain there were people there who were thinking, "David, it's too late for gentleness now." Probably there were family members who were thinking that this was the real problem that David had been dealing gently with his children all along, even when they needed strong correction he had been gentle in his response. The Scriptures tell the story of what happened but don't offer any judgment either from God or others on how David was bringing up his children. One thing is obvious; it is much easier to judge how another person is doing as a parent when you haven't been there. Probably many even in that day said nothing because they were struggling with some of the same kind of problems in their own home. Also, it is extremely difficult to correct your children for things that you either are doing or have done yourself. Imagine how it would have gone if David had heard that Amnon was lusting for his sister Tamar and had gone to him to correct him. Don't you think Amnon had heard the stories of how his father the king had allowed his lust to lead him to commit adultery with another man's wife and even have him killed to hide it? I suspect David knew that if he corrected it would be thrown back into his face. He avoided the confrontation.

One huge lesson we should get from this story is that our own failings must not keep us from dealing with the problems and sins of our children. When we do that we simply multiply our mistakes. I have talked with many parents who have gone through a divorce and now their children are acting up. They need a strong hand. But the dad is afraid to say much for fear of losing all contact. The mom says little because she is afraid they will side with the dad. A step dad often tries to step up only to be slammed by everyone. It was way past time for David to "man up " and admit his failings but say to his children that it was not an excuse for them to follow that bad example. Our children need a parent, not another buddy to go along with all that they do.

How did the battle go with the generals of David and Absalom and his army? Absalom's mule ran under an oak tree with thick branches and his head was caught in the branches. His mule ran out from under him and he was left tangled in the tree. When a soldier told Joab that he had seen Absalom hanging Joab led his men to the place and Joab thrust three spears into his heart. The men followed suit and Absalom was killed. Was it gentle?

When the messenger was sent to tell David his men had won in battle, David's question was "Is it well with the young man Absalom?" When the second runner informed him of Absalom's death David's cry was "O my son Absalom, my son, my son Absalom! I wish I had died instead of you, O Absalom, my son, my son!"

When I read those words, I ache for David. It is vital that we learn from him that a moment's sin leads to a lifetime of regret. It is vital that we learn our own failings must not become an excuse for not correcting our children and being the parent they need. It is vital that we learn that it can become too late for a gentle response.

BE

Last night I was reading the Gospel of Mark and began thinking about what made Jesus so different in his teaching from the religious leaders the people were used to hearing. It is obvious they were drawn to Jesus and wanted to hear every thing he had to say. They came, even though they often went away confused as to the meaning of some of his stories. I've often thought about the fact he spoke with authority as mentioned several times by the gospel writers and that was certainly a big difference. They wanted to use the rabbi's before them as their authority. Jesus went all the way to the thorn of God to gain his authority. He backed up the authority by casting out demons, by feeding multitudes with a few slices of bread and some small fish, by telling the storm to settle down and it obeyed. But there was more than just the authority that was different on Jesus. He was different from them by the way he taught. He so often dealt with big issues by telling simple stories out of their daily life and giving a spiritual meaning they hadn't considered before. But that still didn't seem to be what was so drawing about Jesus.

I think one of the huge differences between Jesus and the religious leaders of his day and of religious leaders of all time is, that he placed greater emphasis on "BEING" than on "DOING". In emphasizing "Being" he often refused to draw out the implications of different lessons he taught. Nothing demonstrates the point better than the beatitudes recorded in Matthew 5:1-12. He challenged us to be humble, be sorrowful, be gentle, be hungry, be pure in heart, be merciful and be a peacemaker. He made it clear that when we are each of these, we will be persecuted by the world. Often the persecution will come from the religious crowd, as it did with Jesus from the Pharisees, Sadducees and Scribes. Pilate nailed the reason as well as anyone. When they brought Jesus to him demanding that he be crucified, he knew that it was because of envy they had brought him. I wonder if you had stopped any of the crowd who were leading the march against Jesus, including the high priest himself, and asked, "Are you envious of Jesus?" what their answer might have been. Envy is seldom a thing that we are willing to admit, even to ourselves.

In many ways it is almost funny to think of these religious leaders being envious of Jesus. They had the places of authority. They had all the titles, the fancy clothes and fine offices. Jesus could honestly say, "Foxes have holes, birds have nests, but the son of man has no place to lay his head." He lacked the right education from their point of view, the right heritage, the right kind of disciples and the right authority. Their puzzlement was, "Where did this man get this knowledge?" They asked, "Who gave you this authority?" But in spite of all the things that might have hindered Jesus, the crowds came to hear and see him wherever he went. They brought their sick and hurting to him and they were healed. He welcomed the distraught, the rejected, the outcast and the afraid. When they left, their lives were changed. Even with him pleading with each not to tell others what he had done for them, they went out wherever they were and told anyone who would listen about Jesus and what he had done for them.

What in the world should we learn from all of this? We should learn that being is more important than doing. Religion is something you do. Jesus calls us to BE something different so we can be the salt that brings flavor to life, the light that gives direction, the leaven that causes the dough to rise. Our Christianity can't be based on just the fact we attend all the services and take communion each Sunday. It can't be just that we give ten percent each Sunday. It must be that we ARE His disciples, following His example in every aspect of our life. When we ARE disciples it will draw others to ask, what makes the difference in us?

Isn't it strange that Jesus told the people he healed not to tell anyone and they told it anyway and he tells us to go and tell what he has done for us and we often are as silent as the tomb?

BLESSED ARE

The Bible is literally filled with those proclamations of blessedness. It has always been a challenge for us to grasp many of those beatitudes in Scripture. When translators replaced the word "Blessed" with "Happy" it became even more confusing. How could someone who is mourning be happy at the same time? The truth is the word is not easy to put into an English word that has the full meaning of the Hebrew or Greek word that was used by Biblical writers. It is overwhelming joy, fullness, success, and completeness. Every time it is used it is a declaration of God's blessings and joy with a person in that situation. One may be "Poor in spirit" or "Mourning" yet God wants us to know that in such a state we are blessed by Him. God loves, accepts and rejoices with us in those times when all else in life seems to go against us.

Today a particular beatitude is on my mind. It isn't one that usually comes us since it wasn't one on the

Sermon on the Mount. It is one of the seven beatitudes in the Book of Revelation. In chapter fourteen and verse 13 John says, "And I heard a voice from heaven saying, 'Write, 'Blessed are the dead who die in the Lord from now on!' 'Yes,' says the Spirit, 'So that they may rest from their labors, for their deeds follow with them."

We all know that death comes. We know that most of the time it comes as a surprise to us. We all know those who suffered for a long time, especially in old age and finally reached the time of death with relief. In such times it is easier to feel the blessedness of one dying in the Lord. It is in those times when death hits us as a shock, when the person was young and seemingly healthy that death comes as an uninvited guest that moves in and refuses to leave. When that person that dies is a faithful and devoted servant of God it is easy to see how the person who died is blessed in the Lord. They are able to go home to be with the Lord and with the redeemed of the ages. They are able to join loved ones that died in the Lord in days past, often unexpectedly. They can rest from their work on this earth and have the rewards for the deeds they did in this life.

But what about all those who loved them dearly who are left behind? How are they to rejoice and feel blessed in such times? What about the partner that has walked by their side and leaned heavily on them for years? How are they to feel the blessings of the Lord? What about the children who looked to their parent for guidance and for an example of how to deal with life or even the grandchildren who will miss the loving smile, the hugs, the excitement and the acceptance of a grandparent? How are they to feel the blessings of the Lord in such times?

In the short run it is near impossible to feel much of anything. It seems so unreal that one who was vibrant and so alive is now gone. In moments of sanity you are glad they were devoted to God and you have confidence in their being with the Lord. You can rejoice that their situation is better. But that doesn't help much with the emptiness or loneliness that you feel. In many ways the greatest comfort comes from family and friends who hold on tight and are there with you sharing your struggle. But if those who come try to give pious platitudes that are supposed to make us feel better most of us will be glad when they leave.

There are some things that will help to bring blessedness into the life of those who hurt and feel the loss intensely. Like Job who had all his children taken in one day and reacted by tearing his garments and falling on his face to worship God, we can turn to God in devoted personal worship. The absolutely worst thing one in grief can do is allow the hurt to build a wall between them and God who loves and comforts in those times of great hurt. I'm not talking of the sanctimonious worship that declares it is all right. I'm talking about the worship the pours our heart out to God with integrity that says to Him what we really feel and what we are really going through. Read the Psalms and feel with David the agony that often asked God, "Why?" I've found that one sees things in the Psalms in times of grief that were never obvious before. It seems to me that it serves as the best prayer manual for times when we don't know what or how to pray. As God said the one who died would now rest from their labors it is good advise to the ones struggling with their loss to rest as well. Too often we try to drive ourselves on and become ill as a result.

There is a reason why the 23rd Psalm has always been such a basic part of funerals and family reading when one has died. It is truly one of the most powerful teachings ever on facing the death of one we love. "Yes and even though I walk through the valley of the shadow of death, I will not fear evil, for you are with me. Your rod and staff comfort me. You prepare for me a table in the presence of my enemies. You anoint my head with oil. My cup runs over. Surely goodness and mercy will follow me all the days of my life and I will dwell in the house of the Lord forever." Through the beginning of the Psalm David talked about the Lord as Shepherd and what "He" does. But when he reached this segment it turned to "YOU". When we stop seeing God as the "HE" and begin to talk to Him personally as the one who blesses, it helps us face whatever comes.

BROKEN POTS

On several occasions I've being attempting to move some pot or vase for Linda only to drop the whole thing or some part of it to see it shatter across the floor. Several years ago we were living in an apartment and Linda had either purchased or someone had given her, a beautiful teapot that she wanted cleaned and placed in a higher spot in the kitchen. I took it down carefully and she cleaned it, I should have stopped then, but I wanted to be helpful so I said, I would put it upon this place she had decided it should be. Sure enough as I lifted it to that spot, the top of it, slide off, crashed to the floor and shattered into small slithers of broken pottery.

In 2 Timothy 2:20-21 Paul makes this comparison, "In a large house there are articles not only of gold and silver, but also of wood and clay; some are for special purposes and some for common use. Those who cleanse themselves from the latter will be instruments for special purposes, made holy, useful to the Master and prepared to do any good work."

What are the special pots in your house? Which ones are treasured and which is worth so little, if it is broken no one really considers it a loss? God led Paul to describe us as God's children as those clay pots. In God's house some are for special use and some are used in the very ordinary things of life. In growing up I remember one large pot that was there to gather scraps of food that would become lunch or dinner for the hogs we were fattening for slaughter. If you looked around your house, which would be the pots that are special, either because of their value or where they come from or who gave them to you?

When I read Paul's description of the clay pots that were part of the different homes I wonder if I'm one of the pots for special use or just one that is used every day in some common task? Have you ever broken one of those valuable pots and then tried to repair it so that the one who owned and loved the pot wouldn't notice it? If it is one of those pots that sits up somewhere in the house but has no real use in daily living it might sit there for years and no one notice that it has cracks all around it. It can easily happen that after gluing it back together and sitting it up that it sits there for years until someone else tries to move it and it falls apart leaving them thinking they were the ones who did something to break it. They become terribly sorry and apologetic to the mother of the house for what they did. What do you do then? Do you step up and admit that you broke it several year's ago and it had been glued back into place? Or do you breathe a sigh of relief thinking, "Now no one will find out what I did?"

Since Paul said we are those clay pots in God's house, which kind of pot are you? Are you one of the pots that you set up on a shelf to admire but as far as being worth anything involving work, it isn't worth much? Are you one of those pots that don't look like much but it is the one that is reached for every day to perform some kind of work or service? It always seems there is one pot in the house that is just the right size and make up to use in just about everything you start to do. Are you the broken pot that has been glued back together and is still being used on a regular basis?

I suspect that most of us are among the broken pots because we are guilty of sin and failure in life. The remarkable thing about God and his kingdom is that He majors in using broken pots to accomplish his work. Think about the apostle Peter. He was definitely a broken pot. He had failed Jesus over and over again, but the Lord kept gluing him back together in the forgiving power of his blood and giving him a new mission. Paul was definitely a broken pot. Look at all the ways he had royally messed up as God's servant. But the Lord glued him back together and put him back into the service.

If you are like me and often feel you are a broken pot and wonder if even Jesus can glue you back together again so that you can be used, I've got some good news for you. Jesus loves broken pots. He collects them. If you look around the room you will see cracked and broken pots all over the place. You will see Matthew the former tax collector still working. There is Mark who forsook Paul and Barnabas when the going got rough. There is James who couldn't turn loose from the Old Law even after it had been completed. There is Timothy who was so timid he had trouble taking a stand. Apollos had a hard time with baptism. The list just keeps growing. If you keep searching you will find your jar in the room. The only question really is if it will be one in use and glued back together or will it be one of those on the high shelf that looks nice but no one knows what it's use might be?

"Lord let me just be one of your broken pots that you put back together and keep using!"

BUT YOU

I believe every word of Scripture, but that doesn't mean that every Scripture means the same thing to me. Some seem to jump off the page to shout, "This is for you. Don't miss it." That is true with just about the whole book of 2 Timothy, but I'd have to say that chapter four is the highlight of the book for me and the first few verses are especially meaningful. Paul had just told Timothy that the Scriptures furnish God's man completely with every good work. Then he challenges him to "Preach the word; be prepared in season and out of season; correct, rebuke and encourage with great patience and careful instruction." He goes from that to discuss the difficulties that Timothy is facing and will face in his work. There is coming a time when people won't endure sound teaching but will want things that make them feel good. Then verse five, it seems to me, is the key verse of the whole book. "But you, keep your head in all situations, endure hardship, do the work of an evangelist, discharge all the duties of your ministry."

Circumstances in life are often challenging. Even in church, among Christians there will be problems and difficulties. Sometimes it seems that the problems and challenges multiply because they are in church. But whether the difficulties we face are at church, at home or on the job, there is always the "But you." Instead of our joining in with the problems or the problem people, we can set a different course, have a different attitude and be part of the solution instead of part of the problem. I think it is natural for us when we are doing something that we feel is the work of God that He has called us to do, that we shouldn't face criticism from other Christians for our work. It seems to me that Timothy had such an attitude. He thought that since he was sent by Paul and by the Lord to do the work of the Lord in Ephesus, why was he facing so much opposition? Look at what Paul, by the inspiration of the Spirit, challenged him to do in such times.

First, "Keep your head in all situations." That is powerful advice for all of us. Under pressure the real us tends to come out. Instead of using circumstances as an excuse for bad behavior, we need the "but you" attitude that keeps our head in all situations. Second, "Endure hardship." Every picture Paul painted for Timothy of the work he was involved in, somehow involved difficulty and endurance. He compared his work to a good soldier in chapter two, to a hard working farmer and to an athlete competing in the games. Every illustration involved endurance. Third, "do the work of an evangelist." The word "evangelist" means "a carrier of the good news." This word is only found three times in the Bible but the uses help tremendously in showing what is meant by the word. In Acts 21:8 Philip is called an evangelist. He had been preaching the gospel of Christ for many years now in Caesarea and had brought up his daughters to tell the message of the Lord to others. In Ephesians 4:11 Paul listed different gifts from the Holy Spirit as apostles, prophets, evangelists, pastors and teachers. He said about the work of all these gifted servants that it was to equip the saints for the work of ministry for the building up of the body of Christ. His work as an evangelist was to work alongside those who were pastors and teachers so the church was built up and each person found their place to serve. In our text in 2 Timothy 4 it is obvious that his work was to preach the word of God clearly and powerfully that lives might be changed. Fourth, "discharge all the duties of your ministry." More than likely Paul was telling him not to try to fulfill everyone else's ministry but to do his well.

Circumstances may be difficult, you may feel that others around you aren't doing their job as they should, people may not seem to be listening to what you say and it may seem the whole world is headed in the wrong direction. "But you" demonstrates that we don't have to jump off into the pit of despair. We can keep on doing what God calls us to do no matter what may be happening with others.

May I challenge you to observe the "But you" in all of God's word? Instead of just going along to try to get along always be the one that stands up to do your work with no excuses.

CALL HIM "IMMANUEL"

In the supposed world of scholarly thinking the statement is often made that Jesus was never referred to as "God" in the synoptic gospels, which were simply the writings of the early church trying to settle their beliefs into the life of Jesus. The claim is it was only when the Gospel of John was written that the claim for Jesus deity along with his humanity was made. Usually these same writers will make the claim that John wasn't written until late in the second century by someone pretending to be John the apostle. There are tons of things wrong with such notions but the problem is that they are being taught every day in the halls of higher education by those religious professors who want to help those ignorant young people coming from Christian homes get things right about Jesus and the Bible.

Isaiah the prophet foretold the birth of the Messiah in Isaiah 7:14 by saying a virgin would conceive and bring forth a son who would be called Immanuel. Worlds of discussion has gone on about the meaning of the word "virgin" in this text while the main point isn't the virgin but the one being born that was called "Immanuel" which means "God with us." Micah the prophet speaking of that same birth said it would happen in Bethlehem and the one born would be from of old, "Yes from everlasting." (Micah 5:2) In Isaiah 9:6-7 the prophet spoke again of that birth. "For to us a child is born, to us a son is given, and the government will be on his shoulders. And he will be called Wonderful Counselor, Mighty God, Everlasting Father, and Prince of Peace. Of the greatness of his government and peace there will be no end. He will reign on David's throne and over his kingdom, establishing and upholding it with justice and righteousness from that time on and forever. The zeal of the Lord Almighty will accomplish this."

In Matthew chapter 1, which is part of the first of the synoptic gospels, the birth of Jesus is discussed. It is pointed out that he is a descendant of Abraham, thus fulfilling God's promise to Abraham. His mother was a virgin and the child was the result of the Spirit of God coming upon her so that she became pregnant. She gave birth to a son and she and his step father, Joseph called him "Jesus, because he will save his people from their sins." Matthew then referred to the prophesy of Isaiah and said that Jesus was the Immanuel he promised and that the word means, "God with us." It's Matthew that records the baptism of Jesus by John the Baptist and how the Spirit descended on him in the form of a dove and God the Father spoke from heaven saying, "This is my beloved son, in whom I am well pleased." Do you get the idea from that text that Matthew was picturing Jesus as God and man?

Matthew pictured the Spirit driving Jesus into the wilderness in chapter 4, to be tempted by the devil. He fasted 40 days and Satan approached with three powerful temptations. In the very first of those, he said to Jesus, "If you are the Son of God, command these stones to be made into bread." He will continue that charge with the other temptations saying, "If you are the Son of God". Each time Jesus handled Satan and his temptations to drive him away. Isn't it interesting that Satan, then later the demons Jesus would cast out, all recognized him as the Son of God and deity yet scholarly professors keep telling our young people no one, including Jesus ever thought of him being deity until much later. According to them, he only thought of himself as a man.

If your child goes off to a great college somewhere and calls to tell you they are taking a religious course about Jesus, the Bible or Bible History, don't be encouraged or comforted. All too often the greatest attacks on faith from higher education don't come from the science department but from those religion classes that we thought would really be good for them. It would be wise when you learn of your young person taking such a class to do some checking on that professor and what they do believe and teach. Some religion professors in public universities are people of great faith who will help everyone who sits in their class come to know Immanuel better. Many won't help but will undercut their faith.

This week I've read two books from two religion professors from different elite universities. One was tremendous and helped me see things about Jesus and the gospel I hadn't seen before, building my faith. Another, in the name of scholarship and honesty attacked the deity of Christ, the inspiration of Scripture and the integrity of the gospel writers. Both have numerous books on religious topics.

Jesus is Immanuel. He is with us. He prayed to the Father to send the Holy Spirit to abide with us forever.

Because of Immanuel we never face life or death alone. Praise the Lord.

CALLED

"Doesn't she have a real calling?" It is interesting that we tend to think of a calling in terms of some special ability, usually that is public, such as singing, playing an instrument or speaking before a crowd. When the Bible talks about a calling it is more often about character than ability. In 2 Peter 1 we are challenged by Peter to "Make our calling and election sure" right after the discussion of adding the Christian graces in our lives. He noted that those who continued to add these graces would never fall and in doing so we make our calling and election sure. In Ephesians 4:1 Paul offered one of the strongest challenges with regard to our calling when he referred to himself as the prisoner of the Lord and urged us to "live a life worthy of the calling you have received." But notice what he immediately talked about as to how we live a life worthy of our calling. "Be completely humble and gentle; be patient, bearing with one another in love. Make every effort to keep the unity of the Spirit in the bond of peace."

Most of us will struggle in life trying to figure out what our calling is when it relates to spiritual gifts or abilities. But it is really quite easy to recognize our calling as it relates to the character God wants us to possess. It intrigues me to think of every discussion of godly character that we are to grow in as a Christian ends up looking like a description of Jesus as he walked on this earth. He lived out the humble spirit or attitude even as God in the flesh. Remember how he described himself as "Gentle and lowly of heart" when he invited us to come to him for rest. It is amazing that the one perfect person who ever walked on the earth was also the least judgmental toward others but was constantly pictured as having compassion on others which meant that he put himself in their place and saw things from their point of view.

Think about how often we wish people would just come to where we are and look at things from our vantage point. We feel certain that if they could just see things from our point of view then they would agree with us on just about everything. Yet we seldom have the same desire to walk over to the other person's point of view and look at things from their vantage point.

Try for a day to see things from the following different vantage points and see if it changes any feelings about anything:

1. In your mind go back to Hitler's Germany and picture yourself as a Jewish father trying to keep your wife and children safe from the soldiers arresting people and taking them to gas chambers just because of their race.

2. Imagine being the young girl who is sexually abused almost every day by her stepfather and wonders why her mother doesn't see it.

3. Imagine being the elderly man who is ignored, abused and mistreated by the very family he gave his life to bringing up and protecting when they were young.

4. Imagine being the young girl kidnapped by someone claiming to be a friend who sold you as a sex slave to men old enough to be your father.

5. Imagine being the Christian in Africa who is fearful every time they meet that some Muslim group will attack them and burn their building around them.

6. Imagine being the black mother of a young teen boy or girl and afraid they may be targeted by someone simply because of their race.

Jesus looked out at the crowds of people around him and felt compassion for them because they were like sheep without a shepherd. Instead of trying to get us to come to look at others from his point of view, He came down to our point of view and looked at life through our eyes. He thus became the savior of the world.

"Father, help me to see my calling and be the person you are calling me to be each day."

CHOICE

"It's your choice." "No, it's not your choice. God does the choosing. The question is are you one of His chosen ones?" One of those discussions that seem to be eternal is the whole question of where God's sovereignty ends and where man's freewill start. Does the Bible teach that humans have freewill and can choose for themselves with regard to salvation and commitment to God? Yes it does teach that we have freewill and can choose with regard to salvation. Does it also teach that God is sovereign and that he both draws people to him and chooses people for His own? Yes it does teach the sovereignty of God and His choosing. So, how do both these fit together?

Focus on some of the text that speaks of God's choosing for a moment. In Acts 2:23 Peter said that God delivered Jesus to be crucified by his predetermined plan and foreknowledge. Yet in the Garden Jesus prayed for the Father to let this cup pass and then yielded saying, "Not my will but yours be done." When Peter took out his sword to fight for Jesus life, Jesus told him that he should put up the sword since he could call twelve legions of angels to deliver him if he wanted to. In John 10:17-18 Jesus said, "For this reason the Father loves me, because I lay down my life so that I may take it again. No one has taken it away from me but I lay it down on my own initiative. I have authority to lay it down and I have authority to take it up again." Jesus had the choice about going to the cross and being raised, yet it was by the predetermined plan and foreknowledge of God.

The reality that we have the freewill to make our choice for God or not is pointed out over and over again in Scripture. On Pentecost when the crowd heard Peter preach they were cut to the heart and cried out "What shall we do?" Notice Peter didn't say, "Nothing, it has all already been done for you." He said, "Let each one of you repent and be baptized in the name of Jesus Christ, for the forgiveness of sins and you will receive the gift of the Holy Spirit." In verse 40 it says that Peter continued to plead with them and exhorted them saying, "Save yourselves from this crooked generation." In Jesus great invitation he pleaded, "Come unto me all who are weary and burdened down and I will give you rest." (Matthew 11:28-30) In the great commission Jesus told us to go and make disciples in all the nations or all ethnic groups, baptizing them into the name of the Father, the Son and the Holy Spirit. Mark's account is "Go into all the world and preach the gospel to every creature. He who believes and is baptized shall be saved. He who does not believe shall be condemned." It is obvious from these that we have a choice about our salvation. The fact we are challenged by Peter to keep growing and add the graces in 2 Peter 1:5-11 and that by doing so that we make our calling and election sure and that we will never stumble if we do, demonstrates that choice goes on even in remaining among the saved. The notion that if one is once saved they can never be lost would remove our choice once saved and is a false teaching. We retain choice throughout our life. Peter went on in chapter two, verses 20-22 to tell of ones who had escaped the corruption in the world and then returned to the old life so that their latter end was worse than the beginning and it would have been better for them to have never known the way of God. Choice is clear and available for all people all the time.

What about God's choice then? In Ephesians 1:3-7 Paul pointed out that all spiritual blessings are in Christ and then says, "Just as He chose us in Him before the foundation of the world, that we would be holy and blameless before Him, In love He predestined us to adoption as sons through Jesus Christ to Himself, according to the kind intention of His will." God chose us. Jesus said in John 6:44-45 that no one could come to him unless the Father who sent him draws him. In Romans 8:29-30 it says, "For whom the Lord foreknew he also predestined to be conformed to the image of his son so that he might be the firstborn among many brethren. Those he predestined he also called, those he called he also justified and those he justified he also glorified." So it is clear that God chooses us for salvation and for life with him.

It is also clear that God's choice is that all people be saved. He had Jesus to die on the cross to demonstrate His grace to all people (Hebrews 2:9). His grace appears to all people teaching us to deny ungodliness and worldly lust (Titus 2:11). In 2 Peter 3:9 it says, "The Lord is not slow about His promise, as some count slowness, but is patient toward you, not wishing for any to perish but for all to come to repentance." He doesn't will for any to be lost.

Think for a moment. If you are a parent do you choose the kind of life you want your children to live? Do they always follow your choice or do they make choices of their own? I know we aren't God and aren't sovereign. But God's choice for us isn't a forceful one that takes away our choice. His choice is that all would have the chance of salvation and it is his choice that we determine for ourselves whether we will give our life to him and continue to live and grow in his will.

CLOSET CHRISTIANS

Have you heard of anyone coming out of the closet lately? Usually when we think of someone coming out of the closet it has to do with them revealing their sexual orientation to the world when they have kept it hidden for a long time. Recently a professional basketball player revealed to the world he was gay, thus coming out of the closet. But that isn't what I'm referring to at all.

Let me set the stage for the point I want to make with a short story found in John 19:38-42. Jesus had been crucified for the sins of the world. "Later, Joseph of Arimathea asked Pilate for the body of Jesus. Now Joseph was a disciple of Jesus, but secretly because he feared the Jewish leaders. With Pilate's permission, he came and took the body away. He was accompanied by Nicodemus, the man who earlier had visited Jesus at night." Thank God these two men who were both members of the Jewish Sanhedrin and were secret disciples of Jesus were willing to go to the trouble and risk to get the body of Jesus and bury it in Joseph's tomb. But did you note the word used of his discipleship? He was a "Secret" disciple. Just like the person who lives one kind of life in the world before others and lives a wholly different life in secret, some disciples treat their faith, their devotion to God, their Christianity the same way. They are disciples but secretly.

What is desperately needed in the church is for a ton of disciples to come out of the closet. I suppose that being a secret disciple is better than not being a disciple at all. But it is so far from what God intended for discipleship that I'm not sure it is better than not being a disciple at all. Secret disciples are completely selfish in their attitude. I'm sure that most of the time it is the same motive that Joseph and Nicodemus had. They were afraid of the Jewish leaders. Usually if we hide our discipleship it is out of fear of someone or something. Often it is the fear that others will look at our lives and think that it doesn't look like someone who is a disciple of Jesus. We may fear someone making fun of us or that it may change his or her attitude about us.

Whatever the motivation, as long as our discipleship is secret it can't serve as an influence to lead anyone else toward God. We can't be the witness for the Lord to tell others what great things he has done for us. We can't stand up for Him or for His principles in the world or our secret might just come out.

Christianity as a whole is the very opposite of selfish living. It is all about our influence and encouragement of others in what is right. When we come out of the closet with our faith it sets us up for others being able to come to us as they did to the Lord Jesus to be with someone who will listen to them and care about their needs. Think of the fact that one of the most common phrases used about Jesus during his earthly ministry was, "He had compassion on them." In Matthew 9 when he looked out at the crowd and saw them like sheep without a shepherd, he had compassion on them and immediately said to the twelve as they stood around him, "The harvest is plentiful, but the workers are few. Pray to the Lord of the Harvest that he will send out laborers into his vineyard."

Compassion for the world is one of the real marks of a disciple. But if we really feel compassion then we need to be praying for the Lord to send out more workers into the vineyard to lead more of those who are hurting and struggling in life to our Lord and Savior. But it is the height of inconsistency to pray for more workers in the Lord's field if we aren't willing to be one of them. We should be praying Lord send out the workers and start with me.

Think of the places and situations in your life where you have kept your faith in the closet. Is it at work or in the neighborhood? Is it when you are involved in some form of recreation? Is it in some business dealings or in the family situation? Get out of that closet and let your discipleship shine. The world needs the influence of real disciples who aren't afraid to take a stand for Jesus. By the way, if you are going to live more like a Pharisee than Jesus, it might be better just to stay in the closet.

COME AND SEE

Why do people come to a church where they have never been before or where they really don't know much of what is going on? Without question the number one reason is someone who is a member there invited them. It's just like it was when Jesus called Phillip saying, "Follow me" and Phillip immediately found Nathaniel and invited him to come to Jesus. When Nathanael raised the objection, "Can anything good come out of Nazareth?" Phillip didn't try to argue with him or accuse him of prejudice against Nazarenes. He said, "Come and see." When Christians invite people to come to worship with them, many will come. But whether they come again or not often depends more on how people treat them when they are there than on anything that actually goes on during the worship itself. Sure it matters what the singing is like and how the preacher preaches the word of God. But in all the studies that are done it is amazing that people tend to remember more how friendly people were to them than anything else.

In a recent study of why people decided to come back again after visiting a church the point was made that what happened in the first few minutes before services began and what happened the first few minutes after the services were over had a tremendous amount to do with whether or not people returned. We tend to focus more on what happens before the service begins in having greeters to meet and try to help any guest know where everything is and what they need to do and having workers on the street to help those who arrive. Even there it is of greater importance what we all do in meeting people around us who are guest and letting them know how glad we are that they have come than any special effort can accomplish.

At the conclusion of the service in most churches we tend to look for folks we know who have something in common with us to visit and see what has happened in their lives over the last week. It is great that we build friendships among Christians and enjoy being together. But if we are really interested in building the church and reaching people for the Lord we need to take a different approach and change the culture that has been true for most of us for a long time.

What if we established the five-minute rule to say that during the first five minutes after services instead of people spending time visiting with those they already know to look for someone they don't know and visit with them. It would be especially good if in meeting and visiting with people whom you've not met before to ask if there is anything they would like for you to pray with them about. If they say that there is then take the time right then to bow together in prayer and pray for the particular needs of that person. Imagine what a change there would be in the whole culture of the church if 3 minutes after services you looked inside and everyone was pretty much still there and there were people all over the crowd meeting others and visiting with them about their life, but also many in the crowd with their heads bowed in prayer to God for those they had just met.

Culture in a church is always hard to change. But it does change one person and one family at a time. You can be the one in your section of the crowd that starts to change the way things go before and after church. Why not today adopt a section of the worship center and declare to your self you are going to meet anyone that sits in that section and get to know him or her. Look for someone that may be alone or look like they don't really know other people around them. You can become a world-class soul winner if you work the area around you each week.

I know that many are saying already, "But Leon, I tried that and when I introduced myself to the person that looked new to me I learned they had been members here for five years already." Sure, we've all had that to happen. And it will happen again if you really work at meeting people. But if they've been here five years and you haven't met them or gotten to know them, it is surely time to do so. It just might lead to us building a relationship with that person to help us both grow up for God. Don't just be someone in the crowd. Be salt and light. Be leaven to get inside them. Be the friendly face that people remember as someone who really cared about them.

It is interesting how we tend to react to any news of what the Supreme Court, the President or the legislature does with either glee or frustration. Our longing is that all decisions and laws would be in harmony with our belief system. But it is difficult for us to separate our belief's spiritually from our political views. Since the court ruled that companies such as Hobby Lobby aren't required to provide coverage free to their workers on abortions and some forms of birth control, we tend to feel great about it all. I certainly agree with Hobby Lobby on not being forced to pay for abortions if that was part of the whole thing. I'm not certain that their information is correct with regard to some of the forms of birth control being "Abortion light."

At the same time we tend to be bothered tons about the immigration situation with children coming into the country from South America by the hundreds without any means of support or assistance in this country. Most seem to be clear that we should ship them back home and be done with it all. It is always amazing how easy it is in our minds to determine what is right as long as it is in the abstract dealing with people we don't know or even know much of anything about.

A few years ago our daughter and family became friends with a large family of people from Haiti that had come to this country after the earthquake had destroyed so many lives in that area. The children who came didn't have any choice about the matter. They were brought with the full consent and assistance of our government. Now the children are adults and Americanized. They want to get jobs and be productive citizens providing for their own. But the same government that was so welcoming and helpful to get them here won't allow them to get jobs or work visa's to do so. Since I now know two of the young ladies and one of them lived with our daughter and family for a year or so, it is amazing how unfair I feel the treatment is and how utterly crazy it seems that anyone would say, "Let's send them back where they came from." The point I want to get across is this, It is easy to make decisions and feel strongly that you are right on that decision as long as we are dealing with abstract cases. When it comes to people we really know and care for our minds tend to change. ' I can say that the people I know are different from the others or I can recognize that personal involvement changes our thinking.

I'm for religious freedom and don't believe the government should pass laws or make regulations to force people to do what would violate their conscience. But I can see already what will happen next. There will be people and companies that decide that every part of the law and regulation that they don't really want to do will suddenly violate their conscience and their religious beliefs. There is a simple test to determine how much a thing required is a violation of our belief, would violate my conscience. The test is what will you do if the law isn't changed? Will you still abide by your conscience and face the consequences or fines, jail or execution? When Peter and John were arrested for healing the man who had been cripple for 38 years and was laying at the gate of the temple each day begging for money, the religious leaders demanded that they stop preaching in the name of Jesus and performing these miracles in his name. Do you remember Peter's response? "Whether it is right in the sight of God to give heed to you rather than to God, you be the judge; for we cannot stop speaking about what we have seen and heard." (Acts 4:19-20). They were beaten and let go. They went away rejoicing that they had been allowed to suffer in the name of Jesus. When they were rearrested for preaching Jesus, They were threatened with death and given strict orders not to continue teaching in this name. They could easily have just remained quiet with the plan to go on preaching. But God led Peter to speak up and say, "We must obey God rather than men." (Acts 5:29) Their religious conviction was strong enough they were ready to take the punishment and even face death if necessary rather than violate their conscience.

It is very easy to say about any law or regulation that we don't feel right doing it. It is easy to say it violates my conscience. But the real challenge is, what now? Suppose the ruling of the court had been the opposite and they had ruled that businesses and agencies must make these provision for birth control methods that are similar to abortions, what would the companies have done then? Would they continue to operate anyway and pay the fines? Would they close the doors and walk away? Would the owners be willing to face jail or execution for violating the law before violating their conscience? Religious belief that is strong enough that you are ready to suffer and even die rather than violating is the real thing. These come and go beliefs that will change rather than lose tons of money aren't real at all. These are conveniences to take a stand that won't matter a whole lot if I lose.

DADDY

Through the years I've been called by lots of names, some good and some not so good. In high school a friend started calling me "Mugzy" for some reason and it stuck with many people. Fortunately when I left home the name was lost in the process. When I get calls from someone wanting to sell me something it is usually "Ernest" that is the name and I always know it is someone who doesn't really know me even if they try to pretend they do. I've been called "Preacher" lots of times along with other such words. But there has never been a name that meant more to me than being called "Daddy". Now the word "Papa" has come to be an extension of "Daddy" and has much of the same feeling to it.

Daddy was the word I grew using for my dad and never even thought of using any other word. In growing up there were many things about my own dad that I wanted always to be the way I would be a dad myself. Of course there were things that I promised myself I would never do in the same way. Like the rest of you I found myself saying and doing many of the same things I thought I never would. Dad was an easy person to respect but was not the touchy feely kind of dad. He left that end of bringing up children to mother and my older sisters.

Let me share a few thoughts on being a dad that matters in your children's life. I know that great dads come in many different shapes and sizes and are of all kinds of temperaments. The picture of a great dad changes with every generation. We seem to run from one idea to another as we try to fill in the gaps of what we saw in our own father's work from the past generation. But there are some things that must be there in every generation to be God's man as a dad.

The clearest statements of Scripture on being a father were written by Paul, who so far as we know never had any children. Yet it was the Holy Spirit who was guiding his words not just the experience of his life. Look at the two statements he made. Ephesians 6:4 "Fathers, do not provoke your children to anger, but bring them up in the discipline and instruction of the Lord." It should be noted that he makes this charge in connection with the quote from the Ten Commandments of "Honor your Father and Mother so that your days may be long in the land." The other is in Colossians 3:21 "Fathers, do not exasperate your children, so that they will not lose heart."

It is intriguing that most of his charge is about what not to do instead of what to do. Don't provoke them to anger and don't exasperate them. He even explains the result of failing to follow the charge on exasperating them by saying it will lead to them losing heart. What are some of the ways we may provoke our children to anger or exasperate them? By the way, he isn't talking about making them angry for a few minutes by telling them they can't do something or by having them to carry out some responsibility. He is talking about developing that kind of anger that becomes permanent and changes their whole future. That temporary anger usually turns into gratitude when one grows up. The anger he refers to only turns them away and makes one bitter when they grow up. To anger or exasperate comes when we show favorites as Jacob did with Joseph and produces jealousy between our children. It comes when our discipline is unfair and doesn't fit the crime. Too many fathers only know one way to discipline and use it for every problem. That is foolish. Discipline in relation to the wrong done. We exasperate when we constantly point out what is wrong or negative in our child and predict for them a horrible future.

What about training and discipline that brings them up in the Lord? Training is different than telling. It has to do with showing by your own life as well is giving the instruction. It takes time, presence and effort to train or discipline. To discipline anyone involves discipleship. A disciple is a learner, a student or apprentice. If we discipline we must be teaching and showing what is to be done. To punish without instruction or training isn't discipline but cruelty to vent our own anger and frustration.

Remember our goal is to "Bring them up" for the Lord. If I teach them to make millions of dollars and be admired by the world, but don't show them to way to live for the Lord, I have missed the point of God's plan. Don't be satisfied with teaching them how to hit a home run or be the star of the show. Teach them about Jesus, forgiveness, and grace. Show them the joy of godly living and being on fire for the Lord. Then you will have really blessed your child.

DEAR LORD, FORGIVE

It's been a long time since I've heard this song. We used to sing it on Sunday evenings as a closing song quite often when I was preaching in Mississippi a little over forty years ago, but I've not heard it much, if at all since then. I'm not sure about the name of the song. It seems like it was "An Evening Blessing" or "An Evening prayer". Here is what I remember, "If I have wounded any soul today, if I have caused one foot to go astray, if I have walked in my own willful way, dear Lord forgive. Forgive the sins I have confessed to Thee, forgive the secret sins I do not see, guide me, keep me, and my teacher, be. In Jesus name." I'm not positive I've got all the words just right, but that is what I remember.

The song was obviously written as a prayer to be prayed at the end of the day when we are looking back on what we have said and done through the day. It is a powerful message for us. We are all beings of influence. Our lives, our words, our attitude and our way of seeing things all have tremendous affect on the people we deal with each day. Most of the time when I think of my influence on someone else my mind quickly runs to the people I am around the most, such as family and those that work with me in the office. We certainly have lots of influence in those areas. But it is likely the influence we have on the occasional acquaintance that we think least about and may, at least at times, have greater affect.

We can easily shout the message, "Don't judge me!" But the truth is people are judging you and your actions all the time. They are checking to see if you are for real. Is the faith you talk about demonstrated in your actions toward others? Think of a situation where your light is shining and your saltiness can be felt. You are in the grocery line at Kroger or Wal-Mart. You have three items and are in a hurry, so you get in the express lane. In front of you is a mother with a small baby and two toddlers demanding her attention. She has a pretty full basket and you know for sure it is more than the maximum allowed for that lane. Your reaction will be noticed. Will you be irritated at the woman and the children and make some snide remark? Everyone else in the line will notice your reaction to the woman, the children, and the checker. If you show compassion and try to help the woman it will show as well. Which direction will your light shine? What about the hospital parking lot where you have gone to visit a friend who had surgery. The parking lot is full but you notice someone getting into his or her car to leave. You stop to wait for them to back out so you can get their spot and you wait, and you wait. It seems they will take all day getting their seat belt on, the key in the ignition and just backing out. After you wait for what seems to be forever, they back out and back in your direction. You back up to give them room to get out and just as they get out someone pulls in from the other direction and steal the parking spot you have been waiting for all that time. How will you handle it? Your light will be shining. You will have influence by how you react.

Consider some principles God has given us in such times. In I Peter 3:8-9 God had Peter to write, "To sum up, all of you be harmonious, sympathetic, brotherly, kindhearted, and humble in spirit; not returning evil for evil or insult for insult, but giving a blessing instead; for you were called for the very purpose that you might inherit a blessing." Or what about Jesus teaching in the Sermon on the Mount in Matthew 5:43-45 "You have heard that it was said, 'love your neighbor and hate your enemy.' But I say to you, love your enemies and pray for those who persecute you, so that you may be sons of your father who is in heaven; for He causes His sun to rise on the evil and the good and sends rain on the righteous and unrighteous."

Influence matters. Our actions matter greatly. You never know who is watching to see how real your Christianity really is. Your actions will either draw people who watch, closer to the Lord or drive the further away. I often reach the end of the day needing forgiveness for the times I failed to show the right influence in treating others with kindness and respect. God help me do better today.

DEFILING GOD'S TEMPLE

There were few things more disgusting to the Lord during the Old Testament era than the desecration of the temple. Even when Jeremiah was pleading with Judah to turn back to God and avoid the Babylonian Captivity that was coming upon them one of the main problems was how they had defiled the temple with idols of all sorts in the temple. When Daniel was given visions of the future as the captivity was coming to a close Gabriel foretold how there would be the abomination of desolation when the temple of God was defiled and the daily sacrifices ended and God's temple was run over by the heathen ruler.

What made the temple so significant to God was that it was where His presence dwelt among the people. It was the place where they would come to meet God. When the Old Testament covenant was abolished it was just a matter of time until God allowed the Romans to trample the temple underfoot and destroy it forever as the place to meet God and worship Him. God had planned for the day when the temple wouldn't be a building where people came to offer sacrifices and go through all kinds of ritual to please God. The temple of God was to be the church of the Lord. In Ephesians 2 after describing how we are saved by the grace of God through our faith Paul explained that in Christ the wall between Jews and Gentiles had been torn down and that God was making of two different kinds of people one body through the cross. He described the church as the whole body where people are saved and become part of God's family and are being built together into God's holy temple. The church is the place to meet God, to worship him and to serve him regularly. This is referring to the whole body of Christians who make up the body of Christ. In 2 Corinthians 6 Paul again described the church as a whole as God's temple where we worship and serve him. He pointed out one was inconsistent when they were unequally yoked with the unbeliever and tried to join the temple of God with the temple of demons.

In I Corinthians 3 Paul turned from the discussion of the church as a whole body to the local congregation of the Lord's people, in Corinth. He noted that ministers of the gospel are only servants through whom one believes and that we plant and water but God gives the growth. He had been discussing problems in the church like division, immaturity and jealousy. In that connection he reminded them that they were the temple of God and that if anyone defiled the temple of God, God would destroy him, for the temple of God is holy, which temple you are. Too often this verse has been used to talk about things we may do such as smoking or overeating that harm our physical body and defile the temple. But in this text he isn't talking about our physical bodies at all. He is noting that the local church, even the church in Corinth with all its problems was the temple of God and if one did anything that defiled or tore down the temple of God, God would destroy them. His point was that when we fuss, divide and do or say things that tear down the local church we are defiling God's temple and God would destroy us for it. That certainly didn't mean there could be no criticism of the church because Paul often was critical of what the local church was doing and pleaded with them to change. But when we become self-centered and think only of our place and importance, we defile God's temple and will be destroyed for it.

In I Corinthians 6:18-20 Paul made one more application of the concept of being the temple of God in our era. He was pleading with them not to become involved in immoral relationships because in doing so we took the temple of God and joined it to a prostitute. Our bodies are the temples of the Lord that is holy. We've been bought with a price and ought to glorify God in our body, his temple that is his. The Spirit of God lives in us as Christians making our bodies the dwelling place of God.

So our body where the Holy Spirit dwells is God's temple. The local church where we are members of the Lord's body is God's temple and the place where God dwells. The church as a whole body is the temple of the Lord. God dwells in His temple and we worship and serve him there. To defile or pull down the temple of God, whether we are talking about our physical body, the local church or the church as a whole is a deeply serious matter and will bring the wrath of God just as surely as the introduction of idols into the temple worship during the Old Testament did upon Israel. Be careful how you speak of and how you conduct yourself in the temple of the Lord. What an amazing privilege to be God's temple or to belong to it! What a foolish action to do things that pull down God's temple because of some personal agenda or hurt!

DISAGREEING, DISAGREEABLY

All of us have times when we disagree with something that is being said by someone we love and respect. In such times we may choose, for the sake of the friendship simply to overlook the area of disagreement and work at keeping that subject from becoming a topic of conversation again. But if it is a matter of great importance to you, something that you feel will do harm to your friend to believe as he does, you are much more likely to state your disagreement. Probably all of us have had times when someone corrected us about something and we were grateful for the correction. At the same time, I would guess that others have corrected all of us and it was extremely painful to us. It is a real advantage to have people around us that are willing to disagree with things we say so that we don't go off half prepared for what may happen next. The leader who surrounds themselves with "yes" men and women will always end up making tragic mistakes that might have been corrected quite easily if those around them felt they could be corrected.

In 2 Timothy 2:22-26 Paul instructed his young friend, Timothy on how to disagree with others with the right attitude. "Flee the evil desires of youth and pursue righteousness, faith, love and peace, along with those who call on the Lord out of a pure heart. Don't have anything to do with foolish and stupid arguments, because you know they produce quarrels. And the Lord's servant must not be quarrelsome but must be kind to everyone, able to teach, not resentful. Opponents must be gently instructed, in the hope that God will grant them repentance leading them to a knowledge of the truth, and that they will come to their senses and escape from the trap of the devil, who has taken them captive to do his will."

Notice the different aspects of Paul's charge to Timothy and thus to us as well. First, get away from youthful desires that are evil. You need maturity rather than childish rivalry to grow stronger. One's pursuits should be for righteousness, faith, love and peace. Often we have disagreements because we are pursuing the wrong things to begin with.

Second, Paul told him not to have anything to do with foolish and stupid arguments that produce quarrels. There are so many areas even in our spiritual life that to disagree about them is foolish, since they don't make any difference anyway. Don't take a chance on offending a friend over something that is of no value before God. Think of areas where fellow Christians have disagreed but which have nothing to do with Christian living or commitment to God. A good example of this type disagreement is over the age of the earth. Some, who think of themselves as fighting off liberal ideas, demand that we believe the earth is young and creation of it happened no more than ten thousand year ago. Others strongly believe the earth and all of creation happened millions of years ago. Neither have a Bible basis on which to stand. Scripture just says, "In the beginning God created the heavens and the earth." Nothing in Scripture demands that we understand the beginning as being between 6,000 and 10,000 years ago. Creation happened in the beginning, whenever that may have been. To argue about such a topic is a foolish and stupid argument, which makes no difference at all as to what the future will be for us as God's children.

Third, Paul said to be kind when you correct someone instead of quarreling with them. Along with kindness be able to teach, and don't be resentful. If we are going to disagree with someone over an important point then we need to take the time to research the topic so our answers are reasonable and clear.

Fourth, Paul told him that he needed to correct the opponent with gentleness, hoping that God will grant the person repentance that leads them to know the truth. If we kindly approach another person about an area of disagreement and clearly explain what we disagree about with a humble or gentle spirit it will make a difference. But notice our correction of another ought to be with view to bringing them to repentance that leads them to the knowledge of the truth. Often the problem we face in correcting someone is that the goal is just to get him or her to see things the way we do. The goal should be much deeper. It should be to get them to repent of wrong and become right with God.

Finally, notice that when we disagree with the right spirit, God may work through the words of disagreement to produce repentance. Just as when we plant and water the seed hoping for growth, we must be clear that if growth comes it will be God's doing. When Paul was in Philippi he and his friends went out to the riverside to try to find people who were already interested in God and his will. There they found a group of women praying. Perhaps they were praying for God to send them someone who could help them know God's will. As Paul taught the gospel to them God opened Lydia's heart for her to grasp the good news and she was obedient to the faith.

Disagreeing with another person always carries difficulties. But when done right it can change lives for good.

DOES IT MAKE ANY DIFFERENCE?

This past week Hillary Clinton made all the news programs with her testimony before Congress with regard to her office's handling of the attack on the Embassy in Lybia, which left the Ambassador and three others dead. When a Senator asked about the way the administration had gone on talk shows to declare it was because of a video that made disparaging remarks against Mohammed, that this had happened and noted that it was obvious from early on that this wasn't the case, her response was to angrily shout back to the man, "What difference does it make, at this point, whether it was a coordinated attack or just some men who went walking and decided to kill some Americans. Four men are now dead." I think I've seen the video of her response now twenty or more times. It obviously took the heat off of her for a moment and got her on TV for a time in a rather positive way.

Focus on the question itself for a moment. What difference does it make at this point? The implied answer is that it doesn't make any difference. In some ways that is certainly true. No matter what the reason, it won't change the fact that these men were murdered. They will still be just as dead when we are informed of the truth of what happened and know who messed up that led to their death. But it might make a world of difference in how we handle such situations in the future. It might make a world of difference to other people living on such foreign soil. It would certainly make a difference in whether someone is punished for their failure to act in a reasonable and defensive way to save the men's lives.

The question, "Does it make any difference?" is vital in many issues of life. When looking at some teaching in the Bible or some practice in church and someone makes the statement, "I don't think this is the right way to do things. I've been in the church for 40 years and this doesn't pass the taste test to me. Let's reexamine what we are doing." Then we must decide if the action is something that is right or wrong or does it make any difference? Some things are insignificant and don't really have any affect on the rightness or wrongness of a matter. For example, one might object to some song that is being used in worship to God and declare this isn't a good song. They might point to the beat of the song and say it sounds more like a bar song that one used for worship. Or they might say that it is teaching the wrong thing and leading people astray from God. How do we then decide if the complaint is worthy of our thoughts and demands action or if it is foolish nitpicking over things that make no difference in our devotion to God?

In order to know whether it makes a difference we must look at what God has clearly said in Scripture with regard to our singing. He has declared that we should sing and make melody in our hearts to the Lord, singing psalms and hymns and spiritual songs together (Ephesians 5:18-19; Colossians 3:16). He even referred to our singing as a means of teaching and admonishing one another. So if the song in question teaches something that violates what the Bible teaches then it is wrong and must not be used. It would be exactly the same as if a teacher or preacher said things that were wrong and led people in the wrong direction. But if one objects to a song because they don't care for the beat of the song or something of how it is being sung or even when it is being sung, that would be a completely different matter. If it doesn't affect the message or meaning of the song then the only question is if it is teaching what is right.

Consider it in this light. A man in a restaurant observed a waitress putting some powdery substance into a man's drink. He called for the manager to come to the table. Then he pointed to what was done and said, "I think she put some kind of poison in his drink." Suppose she said, "No, it was sugar that he wanted for his tea." If the contents of the glass were tested and indeed it was just sugar then the waitress is exonerated. But if they found that the substance contained not only sugar but small amounts of rat poison as well, then the whole matter changes and her conduct is

51

criminal. In spiritual matters the test is always, "What does the Bible teach on the subject?" It isn't ever the right question to ask, "Is this what we have always done?" Or "How do you feel about what is being done?" It isn't even, "What does the church think on this topic?" The church isn't the authority and there is no pope in the church talked about in the Bible. So the only appeal that can be made is to the Scriptures to see if an action violates what the Bible teaches or is it insignificant or making a law where God hasn't made one.

Does it make any difference? It depends on the question and on what God's word teaches on the subject.

DON'T BE SURPRISED

As time changes, our attitudes toward different things that happen in our life change as well. From the beginning of Jesus ministry he made it very clear that living for Him would often bring trials and challenges. Even in the beatitudes his concluding blessing was, "Blessed are those who are persecuted for righteousness sake for theirs is the kingdom of God. Blessed are you when men persecute and revile you and say all manner of evil against you. Rejoice and be exceedingly glad for great is your reward in heaven for so persecuted they the prophets also." Each time Jesus sent out the disciples on their limited missions he warned them of the persecution that would follow them. He even told the apostles that they would be brought before kings and authorities to be questioned and they shouldn't worry about what they would say in such a time but it would be given to them by the Holy Spirit both how and what to say.

By the time Peter wrote the first of his letters to followers of Christ, it had become peaceful enough that when Christians were mistreated or persecuted they felt it was somehow wrong and that such a thing shouldn't be happening to them. The primary point of Peter's whole letter is that you will suffer as a Christian and you need to live right through those times. In I Peter 4:12-14 he reaches his point of emphasis in the book. "Beloved, do not be surprised at the fiery ordeal among you, which comes upon you for your testing, as though some strange thing were happening to you; but to the degree that you share the sufferings of Christ, keep on rejoicing, so that also at the revelation of His glory you may rejoice with exultation. If you are reviled for the name of Christ, you are blessed, because the Spirit of glory and of God rests on you." He will go on to challenge them not to suffer for evil done in their life but to suffer as a Christian and instead of being ashamed of it, one should glorify God in the suffering.

Suffering was so tied to Christian living in the first century that they recognized that one who would bear witness for Jesus would naturally go through some persecution or suffering. One thing that demonstrates this point is that the same word translated "Witness" in the New Testament is also translated "Martyr". Today, when I hear that some fellow believer in Christ has been injured or killed in some country because of their following Christ it is disturbing and it just doesn't seem right. Often in such times Christians long for the government to step in and destroy those murderers who would try to kill people just because of their being a Christian. But it is obvious when we turn back to the New Testament that such an attitude is completely wrong. Certainly I don't want those who follow Christ to be killed anywhere. But I do know that it is often the blood of the saints that leads to the greatest work and growth in the kingdom. Oddly it isn't usually during the times of peace and tranquility that the kingdom grows the best.

Remember in the Book of Acts the church was growing rapidly in Jerusalem but wasn't moving out of Jerusalem. Jesus had told them to start in Jerusalem, and then go to Judea, Samaria and the farthest corners of the earth. But they seemed to be stuck in Jerusalem until the martyrdom of Stephen in Acts 7. Acts 8 opens with the explanation that some of the brethren buried Stephen and that Saul was breathing out threats against the church everywhere. Then in verse 4 it says that as the disciples were scattered from Jerusalem, they went everywhere preaching the word and as one illustration of this effort, he said that Philip went down to Samaria and preached Christ to them. From there the church would literally spread throughout the world.

Persecution comes in all kinds of ways. Notice Jesus tied to the point on persecution to people reviling you, and speaking all kinds of evil against you, falsely. It doesn't have to be execution for it to be persecution. Jesus also said, "Woe to you when all people speak well of you." As followers of Christ we should stir up some commotion by our teaching of salvation through Christ alone. Our difference should set us apart and at times make those we are around uncomfortable because we don't join in with every joke or activity they try.

Peter does conclude in chapter five of his book with a clear message of how we should handle the persecution. His answer is "Humble yourself under the mighty hand of God, that He may exalt you at the proper time, casting all your anxiety on Him, because He cares for you. Be of sober spirit; be on the alert. Your adversary, the devil, prowls around like a roaring lion, seeking someone to devour. But resist him, firm in you faith, knowing that the same experiences of suffering are being accomplished by your brethren who are in the world." (I Peter 5:6-9)

DON'T QUENCH THE SPIRIT

In the Bible it is often the case that huge, powerful points are made in very short order. In I Thessalonians 5:16-22 Paul laid out seven commands that are extremely important for all time. In time I want to look more closely at each of these commands but it seems appropriate to me to begin with one in the middle. It is this command, "Do not quench the Spirit."

It is common in Paul's writings to talk about the work of the Holy Spirit in the Christian. He often made the point that the Spirit is given to us as a deposit on the blessings we will receive in glory. He prayed for the Ephesians that they would be strengthened by the Holy Spirit within them (Ephesians 3:14-20) and challenged them not to "Grieve the Spirit" by their actions. Earlier in this letter to the Thessalonians he had pleaded with them to move forward with their walk in pleasing God and in being sanctified in Christ. After pointing out that such sanctification leads to purity in my life morally, he said in I Thessalonians 4:8 "So, he who rejects this is not rejecting man but God who give His Holy Spirit to you." To the Galatians he pointed out that the Spirit leads us and we walk in the Spirit. In doing so the Spirit bears fruit in our life regularly.

But what does it mean to "Quench the Spirit?" Our first thought with quenching anything is with regard to pouring water on a fire. If the campfire is burning bright and we are ready to leave it is normal to take a bucket of water and pour it on the fire, quenching it. But we also realize that it is common for someone to quench our spirit. You see it more easily in a child or teenager. Often it is a parent who is the quencher. The child is going along in life when they make some mistake and there before the Lord and everyone else they rip into the child with criticism that often goes beyond the event to say that you "Always" do things like that. I've seen it happen so many times on the ball field. A young boy is playing out in the field and misses a ball hit near him. As he picks himself up he hears the screams of his dad or of a coach shouting what he should have done and what was wrong with his actions. At that point you see the spirit of the youth being quenched. The fires are being put out. Their zeal for the sport or for trying are lessened and often completely destroyed by the critic who couldn't do better but is certain he knows the right thing for the child to do.

But how does that help with understanding "Don't Quench the Spirit?" It is pointing to the fact the Holy Spirit of God is not only in us, but also actively in us. He dwells in the Christian, but isn't dormant. When the Spirit guides, leads or strengthens us or opens our eyes to see someone in need or who longs for a friend or help in some circumstance and we push back with excuses for not reaching out to help the person in need, we are resisting the Spirit. If we continue in such action we will quench the Holy Spirit and His work in our lives. When the Spirit brings us into contact with a person who asked us some question about our spiritual life or faith and we push it aside or make some silly response we are quenching the Spirit's work in us. Think about the fact that Stephen challenged the Jews in Acts 7 for always resisting the Holy Spirit and Paul pleaded with the Ephesians not to grieve the Spirit. Now he commands us not to quench the Spirit. Notice the process begins with our becoming a follower of Christ who is baptized into Him and receives the Holy Spirit as a gift. When the Holy Spirit works in us to bring about growth through the study of His word and we fail to follow that lead to grow we are resisting the Spirit. When we continue to do things and fail to do what we should in our commitment to God, the Holy Spirit is grieved; His heart is broken by our failures to follow His guidance. When that action continues and we see the doors God is opening for us on every side but we refuse to enter them and refuse to live the pure and sanctified life in Him we are then quenching the Spirit. If we constantly pour the water of sin on the fire God gives with His Spirit we quench the Spirit completely and He stops opening the doors for us and leaves us without the fruit of the Spirit and without the strengthening of the Spirit. We lose His guidance of the Spirit and are left to find our own way that is tragic. DON'T QUENCH GOD'S SPIRIT IN YOU!

DOUBTING DOUBTS

Honest Christ followers still question their faith in the Lord. It's not all the time. Many times we can feel and see the presence of God in our lives and recognize ways that He is at work with and in us to bring us to a better place. In those times we tend to become comfortable with faith and wonder why anyone would ever doubt God and His existence. During these times you may say or here lots of others talk about how blessed they are by God and even wonder what is wrong with people who have doubts in their life.

But those aren't the only times that most of us face in life. We also go through the dry, lonely days when we can't see or feel God's presence at all. When we pray it just doesn't seem that anything happens. We may read the Bible extensively in such times, wishing to find that answer that will set us back on that right course where we know that God is not only in existence, but involved in our life. Much of life is spent in the throws of doubt and despair.

One of the most impressive things to me about the whole Bible is that God put it together in such a way that people's fears and doubts are obvious in life, even the ones who have at times expressed such great faith, at other times lay out clearly their doubts and fears. Have you read Job lately? I've found as the years have passed that I need to read Job again every few months. The lessons there are far too easy for us to forget in an age of pop psychology and the "Happy, happy, happy" mentality. If you listen to the authorities on TV or even the preachers that are featured there you would think that the main goal of life is to be happy and that anything that doesn't make you happy quickly should be gotten rid of. How utterly foolish! Such an attitude leaves one who is going through a difficult time in marriage believing the answer is to get out and find someone else that can make me happy. The surprise comes when in a few months or years they go through a difficult season in the new marriage. Real purpose, meaning and fulfillment in life comes when you work through the hard times and get closer to each other than ever before.

Think of Job the man who God had James to write about as an example for us of faith and patience before Him. Yet when I read the Book of Job I find it difficult to see the patience in the way we use the word. He did everything, but take his calamity lightly. Remember what he went through. He first lost everything he owned which was a considerable amount since he was the richest man in the East. Then all ten of his children were killed by a tornado at one time. At this point the Book of Job says that Job tore his garments, put on sackcloth and ashes on his head and fell before God to worship saying, "The Lord gives and the Lord takes away. Blessed be the name of the Lord." That is great that he reacted that way to begin with. It wasn't long after that that the second wave of trouble came from Satan with God's permission. This time Satan struck his body and he had horrible boils from the top of his head to the bottom of his feet. In agony he sat each day in a pile of ashes with a broken piece of pottery scraping the wounds. It was at this point that his wife felt it was too much to bear and she encouraged him to "Curse God and die." He said, "Shall we receive good at the hand of God and not evil?" He told her that she was speaking like one of the foolish women by telling him to do such a thing. Friends came to help and sat silently with him for a week. Finally both Job and the men begin to speak. His words were ones of agony, despair and frustration with God. He couldn't understand why he a man of faith and dedication to God would go through such a thing. His friends, who were all still healthy and hadn't gone through any real loses felt sure they had the answer. They knew that it had to be because Job had committed some horrible sin since God didn't punish people who hadn't done anything wrong. If we serve him we will be blessed. So if we suffer it must be because we have done something wrong.

Imagine Job sitting day after day in the ashes, scraping, crying out in frustration, wondering why this was happening to him and his closest friends constantly saying, "If you will just acknowledge your sin and repent God will forgive you and you can be restored to your old position."

Job knew he hadn't committed any sin to bring this about. He refused to ask God to forgive something he didn't believe he had done. But the boils, the ashes and the pottery were still there, day after lonely day. Where is God when you go through such at thing? Surely he will step in quickly and give him relief.

I don't know how much time went by. By looking at all that happened it would seem that it went on for months and may have been over a year in time. The rich man is now a beggar. Those who once went to him to borrow money had turned against him now. How do you think you would have reacted? Probably we would have reacted a whole lot like Job. Likely you would have complained, fought for relief, and have become somewhat obsessed with the whole matter of dealing with the pain and fear.

Read Job, especially Job's speeches and feel his doubt, frustration and concern for the future. The man sought out for his wisdom became an object of derision. But through it all Job held on to his faith and shouted his personal faith on the days it was strong to God. He was sure that he would see his redeemer outside his body at some point in time. God recognized his faith and blessed him all over again. He had twice the stuff in the end than in the beginning. But the scars of loss stayed with him. He couldn't forget the people like him who were in trouble and didn't understand it. What is most amazing to me is that in the end of the whole thing God calls Job to him and explains to him that in all his questioning and times of doubt he was still the one who was pleasing to him. The friends were intent on defending God from any attack but in the process committed graver sins and mistakes. They needed Job to pray for them.

Doubting your faith isn't bad if it leads you to reexamine your faith to see why you believe what you believe. Just remember to not just examine your faith but your doubts as well. If you starve your faith and feed your doubts you will come to have no faith and only doubts. But if you doubt your doubts and feed your faith you will tend to have a strong faith.

ENTERING THE KINGDOM

Jesus is the king over his kingdom and the most important commitment anyone can make is to enter the kingdom of Christ and live under his direction. Since Jesus is king it makes all kinds of sense to listen to what he said about entering the kingdom he would build. Seven times in the gospel accounts he made a declaration about how a person could enter the kingdom. Let's see those statements and then draw some conclusions.

1. Unless you are born again you can't enter the kingdom – John 3:3
2. Unless you are born of the water and Spirit you can't enter the kingdom – John 3:5
3. Unless your righteousness exceeds that of the scribes and Pharisees, you will never enter the kingdom of heaven – Matthew 5:20
4. Not everyone who says Lord, Lord, will enter the kingdom but the one who does the will of my Father in heaven – Matthew 7:21
5. Unless you turn and become like a little child you won't enter the kingdom – Matthew 18:3
6. It is easier for a camel to go through the eye of a needle than for a rich man to enter the kingdom of God – Matthew 19:24
7. If your eye causes you to sin, tear it out. It is better to enter the kingdom with one eye than have both and be thrown into hell – Mark 9:47

When you look at the list all together, do any of them surprise you? Sometimes it seems to me that many have a mental picture of Jesus so wanting people in the kingdom that he will accept anything we might offer him. In life we often see different organizations start with very high standards that one must follow to be a member of the organization. But when few people want to meet the standards it is often the case that the ones who launched the organization will lower those standards to get more people in. In an environment such as that it would be easy to think of Jesus and His kingdom in the same light. But if you have seen Jesus and His kingdom like that, please wake up and realize Jesus is compassionate, loving and full of grace. But he is God and His standards won't be dropped to get people in who aren't really committed to Him or His kingdom. Remember at the end of Luke 9 when three men in order came to Jesus wanting to be in the kingdom at a little lower standard. One wanted to come but Jesus knew he didn't grasp what it would be like, so he said to him, "Foxes have holes and the birds of the air have nests but the son of man has no place to lay his head." The next wanted to follow but needed time to go home and bury his father. Jesus said, "Let the dead bury the dead. You come follow me." The third wanted to come but wanted to go home and tell the people farewell before leaving. Jesus said, "He who puts his hand to the plow and looks back isn't fit for the kingdom of God." Jesus isn't so desperate for people to come into His kingdom that he will lower the standards for people to come in.

Focus on the necessities to get into the Lord's kingdom as declared by Jesus the king. It requires a new birth of water and the Spirit. That involves a whole change in us. We become new creatures before him. Getting into His kingdom isn't a matter of some minor adjustment in life but a complete turn around. To make such a change will require having the humble heart of a child that is broken hearted because of the sin or failure in life that hurt their mom or dad. It requires righteousness beyond the scribes and Pharisees, who loved the law and were constantly looking for ways to add burdens to others and for excuses for their own failures. They had fallen in love with the law of God, but failed to fall in love with God the law spoke of. If I'm going to be in the Lord's kingdom, I can't make money or things in life a god along with him. He must be so far ahead of such things that there is no comparison. Our treasures must be in heaven and not down here.

Jesus invited all who are weary and burdened to come to him and enter his kingdom. He said when people that had been invited in rejected the invitation and made excuses he would send his servants to invite those outside the accepted group to all kinds of people. But when they brought in all sorts of people, remember there was a man there when the Lord came out, who wasn't dressed in a wedding garment and Jesus confronted him as to why he was there without the wedding garment. He was thrown out of the party. Jesus invites all people. But to enter one must follow the plan Jesus laid out putting on the wedding garments of true conversion, a childlike spirit, a willingness to obey and a commitment to put Him before everything else in this world. I want desperately to be in Jesus kingdom forever and reign with him far beyond this world and time, don't you?

FORGIVE ME

Two of the hardest words for us to say are "Forgive me." Most of us are ready and willing to forgive others when they come to us with the request "Forgive me." But for some reason it is a different thing for us to ask the other person to forgive us. Many times it is easier to go before a whole church and ask the people to forgive some wrong than it is to go to one person, look them in the eye and humbly ask them to forgive us. Yet one of the most powerful things any person can do is to go directly to the person we may have wronged in some way and ask for their forgiveness. It will break down more barriers than just about anything we can possibly do.

In 2 Corinthians 12 Paul had talked about his being carried into paradise, whether in the body or out he didn't know. He had discussed with them his thorn in the flesh and his reaction to it by the grace of God. Even though he had asked three times for the Lord to remove it, God had clearly answered, "No". But God had also told him that he would give him the grace he needed to handle the thorn. He pointed out that His strength was made perfect in weakness and that He could actually use the weakness of Paul to reach people that wouldn't be reached by His strength. After that discussion he turned to the point of why he had refused to allow them as a church to support him financially. He had clearly pointed out in his first letter to them that it was right for those taught the word to support those who taught them. But he refused their support. He at the same time was receiving support from the church in Philippi, which had far less money than Corinth. But there was something about the church there that caused Paul to not be willing for Corinth to give him money. Notice his words in verses 11-13 as it relates to our point on asking others to forgive us. "I have become foolish; you yourselves compelled me. Actually I should have been commended by you, for in no respect was I inferior to the most eminent apostles, even though I am nobody. The signs of a true apostle were performed among you with all perseverance by signs and wonders and miracles. For in what respect were you treated as inferior to the rest of the churches, except that I myself did not become a burden to you? Forgive me this wrong!"

Had Paul wronged the church by refusing to allow them to support him financially? No, but if they took it to be a slight he was willing to ask for their forgiveness. The reality is that just about any wall between people can be dissolved rather quickly with the simple words, "Forgive me." Think of all the times when our emotional walls start up, whether in a marriage, or in family relationships or even in wrongs done to us as a child, we build the wall one wrong at a time. As months and years go by we have the wall so high that all we can see or feel about the other person is contempt. At this point just about anything the other person says or does is wrong and just adds another brick to the wall. You are likely thinking, "Yes I have a wall like that and as soon as the person who wronged me ask I will forgive them, but they haven't asked and don't even seem to realize they have done wrong." I understand but here is what I would ask of you. Go to the one who wronged you and humbly, honestly ask them to forgive you. "But I'm the one that has been wronged. Why would I ask them to forgive me?" In spite of all the ways we have been wronged there is one thing sure, we have done some things wrong ourselves. Be the mature one. Take the first step. You might even choose one way you know you have been wrong. Ask to be forgiven. Follow that quickly by adding, "And I forgive you." Jesus prayed for the Father to forgive the ones crucifying him. Surely you can just forgive the one who has wronged you. Does that remove all their wrongs? No, but it takes the load off your back and tears the wall down. Do this honestly, humbly and see if it isn't life changing!

FORGIVENESS AND CONSEQUENCES

Forgiveness is a powerful thing. It is always an act of grace. You can't earn or deserve forgiveness from God or man. The very point of asking someone for forgiveness is that we have in some way wronged that person or God. If you were to approach your wife after you have just made a huge blunder, saying, "I know I wronged you a few minutes ago but you must forgive me. After all I forgave you last week when you messed up so you owe me forgiveness this time" how do you think it would go? We never get forgiveness from anyone based on our merit. When we approach a person asking them to forgive wrongs that we have done, we are asking for mercy and grace that will release them from the sin and its guilt.

Forgiveness is a wonderful thing. Jesus during his earthly ministry often gave forgiveness to people before they even asked for it. People would come to him for healing like the man who was carried by four men to Jesus' presence wanting the Lord to heal him who was cripple. The Lord saw the faith of the men who carried the handicapped man. He spoke to the man, "Your sins are forgiven." The religious leaders around him were frustrated because he said to the man "your sins are forgiven." They were saying, "Who does this man think he is? Only God can forgive sins. Who is he making himself out to be?" Jesus knowing their thoughts confronted them directly, by asking which is easier to say, "Your sins are forgiven" or "Arise, take up your pallet and walk. But in order that you may know that the son of man has power on earth to forgive sins I say, 'Rise, take up your pallet and walk." The man was cured immediately.

Jesus also taught us to be ready to forgive others. He said in the model prayer "Forgive our sins as we forgive those who sin against us." In Luke 17:1-5 Jesus told them that if one sins against them seven times in a day and turned to say, "I repent" forgive him." God longs to forgive us of our sins. Jesus even in being crucified by a religious mob, first cried out to God, "Father, forgive them. They don't know what they are doing."

It strikes me that those of us who follow Christ should be praying this same prayer for those in places like Iran or Venezuela or Libya who often declare their hate for the United States. Even in times when the radical Muslims attack the people of this country with the attempts to destroy the things and people who represent this nation, the right response isn't revenge but forgiveness. We ought to stand for the truth of Jesus and his word, but have the heart of mercy all the time in representing our Lord and Savior.

But, isn't it true that we reap what we sow? Don't people still have to suffer the consequences of their sins even when they are forgiven? The story has been told of Robert E. Lee the general who led the confederate army during the uncivil war that after the war and his signing of a peace treaty at Appomattox that he was visiting a widow whose husband and two sons had been killed in the war. She was angry and bitter toward the people in the North and the leaders of their army. General Lee said to the woman, "It is time to forgive all the wrongs and find peace in your own heart." She angrily answered that she was scarred as deep as one can be scarred and that she could not forgive the things they did to cause such a scar. General Lee pointed to a large oak tree in the front yard of the house. It had been lightning struck years before and that had created a large scar on the tree. But the tree had grown over that scar and now a large hump was there where the lightning struck. But the tree had continued to grow and thrive. Lee pointed to the scar and said, if you are to give tribute to your husband and sons who died, you need to be like the tree and allow yourself to grow over the scar, too heal from the wound and thrive in life again.

Sin leaves a scar. It leaves a sore or tender place on us. Even when sin is forgiven there are still consequences of that sin. Think of a drunk driver hitting an innocent young person who had just gotten their drivers permit. The drunk driver may repent and be forgiven. But it won't change the injuries given to the young driver." Even forgiven sins have consequences in this life. They won't keep one from heaven, but they will still leave scars and hurts in our lives.

GIVE ME ONE OF THOSE

Have you seen that commercial where the guy had bought some insurance and felt so empowered by it that he was out in the park watching a man juggling chain saws, with them running, of all things, and he keeps saying to the juggler, "Give me one of those, I can do it, give me one?" It doesn't make me want to buy any insurance but it is a memorable commercial.

Here is what I like about the commercial. It seems to me that it is a great insight into human nature, whether or not the makers of the commercial recognized it. One person has spent his life practicing to do something that requires a ton of skill and years of practice to accomplish, giving up many of the other pleasures and opportunities of life to learn that skill.   But another person comes along who thinks because he stayed in a particular motel last night he can do the same thing. It reminds me of the twelve year old boy holding a basketball, watching an NBA game in which a seven foot, three inch center takes the ball and with a smooth hook shot from ten feet out drops the ball into the basket to get nothing but net. The young man looks at it and declares, "I can do that. Just come out in the yard and watch me."   What do you do in that situation?   Do you encourage the young man and say, "I'll bet you can do that. Why don't you go out and practice the shot a few times and then I'll come out and watch you?" Do you try to explain to him that this man is two and a half feet taller than him and that he has been practicing that shot every day for a hundred times for years now? Do you tell him he might be able to do that in time to come if he will put in the work and sacrifice to do it that the one who made it has done?

Many years ago I remember being with Brother Gus Nichols who knew the Bible as well as anyone I've ever known and could quote huge chunks of Scripture word for word. A lady came up to him, as we were standing there and said, "Brother Nichols, I would give my life to be able to know and quote the Scriptures the way you do." His answer has been drilled into my mind ever since. He said, "Well, that is exactly what I have done." She looked puzzled and Brother Nichols looked like he was in deep thought.

What is it about us that we want the finished product in our lives without spending the time and effort to get there? I may be wrong but I think it is often because we have given encouragement and the person has taken it seriously. When the three year old gets up on the hearth of the fireplace and starts waving his hands and singing songs we sing at church and the parent says, "You sound just like Chad" we know she doesn't mean that as reality. But he doesn't. If he grows up constantly being told how great he is at song leading, when he has never gotten any training, never worked to learn how and never given the time, effort or time in prayer to God to develop something more than some of the Mechanics, he will be deceived.

The same is true if the little boy is doing his preaching on the hearth and is told he sounds just like Leon, "Except for speaking faster". It is certainly meant to encourage. But too many grow up thinking they can do any job without going through the time or effort to really learn how to do the job well. Most of all they haven't spent the time on their knees before God developing a relationship with him so that they aren't just trying to give another speech like they did in a class at school.

When we tell the young child that they are great at some sport or talent all the time and convince them that they are the best that has ever been at that sport or activity, we always mean it to encourage and build up the child. But I wonder how many times we really convince them, "I don't need training. I don't need to listen to the coach. I don't need to work at it. I'm good just like I am." The result is that another person with tremendous ability becomes a worthless player stuck at the 5th grade level because in their mind they have already arrived.

Maybe we should say to the person who is trying to do a job but not there yet at all, "You really have ability. With training and help, along with some hard work you really could be good at it." We then plant into the mind of the person, this isn't easy and it can't be done just based on ability, but requires lots of effort and training on my part. The results will be far healthier whether we are talking about spiritual efforts at church or playing ball or doing some work.

GNATS AND CAMELS

It isn't usually some big thing that causes problems, in our homes, churches, businesses or governments. Most of the time it is something everyone admits is of very little importance but it has become the focus of what everyone thinks and says. Spend a day listening to married couples describe what is causing them problems in their marriage from day to day. You will hear them talk about things that were once endearing or funny but now those same things are ripping the heart out of the marriage. Businesses often crumble even though they have been great companies building precision parts. Most of the time when that happens it is the result of some minor matter that has been turned into a huge problem. Even in government it is often some unintended action or word that is used that erects a wall between different groups in the office. Think of the election going on in Wisconsin today. The governor has been recalled and a special election is being held which will either result in him being turned out of his office or his being re-elected to the office he has already won, once.

No wonder Jesus took the same thoughts and applied them to the Pharisees and teachers of the law. "Woe to you, teachers of the law and Pharisees, you hypocrites! You give a tenth of your spices – mint, dill and cumin. But you have neglected the more important matters of the law – justice, mercy and faithfulness. You should have practiced the latter without neglecting the former. You blind guides! You strain out a gnat but swallow a camel." (Matthew 23:23-24)

Notice some important lessons on life from these verses from Jesus. First, these verses demonstrate that one can be very religious and still not be right with God at all. Religion and righteousness don't always go together. God looks at the heart of the individual not his rank or title in the church. Second, sometimes the ones, who seem to be the most religious of all, are just acting. Jesus called them "Hypocrites". We use that word often for someone who isn't sincere or one who wants to look religious but doesn't really live the life God calls him or her to live. In the first century the word "Hypocrite" was commonly used for a person who was an actor. The actors often wore mask to help to portray someone or something. The one who put on the mask was called a hypocrite. They weren't really as they seemed but were good at pretense.

Third, some things even in worship and praise to God are very important and other things aren't very important. We need to be aware of which commands of God are considered by Him to be vitally important. Remember when Jesus was asked, "What is the first and great commandment?" He answered quickly that it was to love God with all our heart, soul, mind and strength and the second was to love one's neighbor as yourself. Here in this text Jesus laid out some things that were not very important like paying tithes of the herbs one used in the kitchen. The principle of tithing was important in that one needed to practice giving of the first and best of what they have to God for His work. But when the command loses it's meaning and becomes more of a ritual than an honest desire to give to God of what is valuable to me it becomes of very little importance. Some of the things that Jesus regarded as of great importance were, justice, mercy and faithfulness. The basic notion of justice in the Bible is that it is to take care of the people who aren't able to take care of themselves. It was to stand for right treatment of people no matter what their race, color on national origin may be. Mercy is acting out the grace that is in my heart. Mercy puts legs on grace. It is doing the merciful and gracious things for others who can't repay my actions. Faithfulness is the act of being full of faith. It is being dependable and true. Think of what it means to be a faithful wife or faithful husband. It is the one whom you can trust, even with the greatest treasures of life.

These blind Pharisees had gotten their spiritual values all mixed up and were putting great value on things that had little value and putting little value on the things God put great value. That turned them into blind guides. These are the people who strain out a gnat and swallow a camel without even a sputter. When I was growing up on a farm we would milk the cows and bring it in to Mother who would strain it through a piece of cloth to get bits of trash or gnats out of the milk. Imagine the picture Jesus is painting with his words. Here is the Mother of the house being very diligent to strain out all the small particles in the milk which might harm the family but at the same time she allows a full grown camel to go right through the strainer and into the milk. This was intended to be a funny scene that taught a powerful lesson. Don't get so caught up in getting every small matter right while ignoring the most important matters in living for God.

GOD IN THE STORMS

Why are there storms, tornadoes, hurricanes, earthquakes and tsunamis? If God were a good and loving God as we preach, why would he allow or produce such storms in the world? Surely an all-powerful God could make a world without all the storms. Doesn't God see the devastation in the Philippines today? I suppose that such questions have been raised since the beginning of time. I always think of the story of Elijah when he was running from the evil queen Jezebel and went to Mount Horeb to meet with God. God spoke to him on the Mount, but it wasn't what he had expected. God's question was "What are you doing here, Elijah?" He pleaded that he was the only one left serving the Lord and he wasn't doing any good so please just go ahead and take my life. God asked him to come out on the ledge of the mountain and there was a mighty storm, but God wasn't in the storm. There was a fierce wind but God wasn't in the wind. There was a horrible fire, but God wasn't in the fire. Then he heard a whisper. It was God saying, "What are you doing here Elijah?"

I don't think there is any single answer as to why there are storms on the earth. It is certainly true that God did at times send massive storms on people usually because of sin and rebellion in their lives, such as with the flood or with the drought brought on Israel when Elijah prayed for the rain to stop and it stopped for three and a half years until he prayed again for it to rain. But to conclude that every storm or every tragedy that happens in life is because of the sin of people would be a horrible mistake. When God brought on the storm he made a way for the righteous to be protected in the storm. In the flood, Noah and family were saved in the ark. In the destruction of Sodom, Lot and his family were given an escape. When the drought was brought on Israel God made a means for his people to be taken care of.

Generally, the reason for storms is that we live in a world that was fine-tuned by God for human, animal and plant life. In order for that form of life to flourish in the earth, there must be storms of different kinds to provide the elements for life and growth. Could God remove the storms? I have no doubt he could. But at what expense would such action come? It is similar in many ways to the question, "Why doesn't God stop the evil in the world? Couldn't a good and All-Powerful God make us where we didn't hurt each other or attack one another? I have no doubt God could make us in such a fashion. But the expense of doing so would be the removal of man's freedom of choice. If we are no longer able to choose whether we will live for God or for ourselves then we cease to be the humans made in the very image and likeness of God.

The world is changed by storms of all kinds. But when a forest burns there will be benefits for the land and even the animal life that come down the line. When an earthquake hits, it is devastating. Yet the lava flow will bring benefits to the land in the years to come. I suspect there aren't any storms that hit and even do massive damage that one couldn't look back some years later and see benefits and blessings that came from it. Does that make it good for the people who are hurting right now? Certainly, it does not. Their situation is horrible and they need the help of caring people from all around the world. God is in the help that people send or bring to the hurting people.

Two things we ought to remember about God when we wish for him to intervene and stop the storms of life are these: First, God doesn't just see things as they are today.

He is able to see back to the beginning and beyond and he is able to see what the blessings and hurts will be in the future from any problem or hurt in life. Second, we should remember that while God is good and loving, that isn't all of God's nature. To choose any one aspect of God and so focus on that aspect that we can't see any other sides of God's nature results in worshiping an idol of our own making rather than the God actually revealed in nature and in Scripture. God is a God of amazing grace and love. But he is also a God of justice, or order and power. He is a God who set up the laws of nature that makes the world operate and that at times produces the storms. What if God intervened in the laws of nature every time he saw problems and hurts coming on people? We would never know what to expect in anything. The order we depend on would be destroyed. Cause and effect would be removed. I wouldn't know from one time to the next what would happen when I did the same thing over and over again. We wouldn't know what to avoid or what to hold on to. Medicines would no longer work since cause and effect would be gone. The very order and dependability of the creation depends on God leaving the laws of nature in place.

Doing some things result in even more or greater problems and that is true even if it is God that is involved.

GOD IS STILL IN CHARGE

There is no doubt that today's election is an important one, from top to bottom. But I do think that many are viewing it as more important than any election really is. I'm for voting and seldom miss the opportunity to cast that vote. Most of the time I even go early to vote just to make certain nothing hinders me from casting my vote. I have no doubt that I'll have chosen some that others will agree with me about and they will be elected and I have no doubt that some of the choices I made, the majority won't agree with and they will be defeated. As important as the election may be and as much as things will change depending on who is elected, especially as president, it won't be what determines the future of the nation.

One of the reasons God gave us the history of the Nation of Israel in the Old Testament was to demonstrate to us that He is in control. He often uses the worst of leaders to accomplish His purpose in the world. If you read the stories in I and II Samuel I and II Kings and I and II Chronicles it is amazing how God sizes up the different leaders that reigned in Israel. About each person it will tell how old they were when they became king, who their parents were and how long they reigned in the land. But then it will also say something to the effect, "And he did evil like his father Ahab." Or "And he did good like his father David and God prospered the nation during his reign."

But life in the nation depended more on the people and their life for God or for some idol they had erected as their personal god, than it did on who was king. Sometimes we follow the Israelites of old when we blame every bad thing in the nation on the one who is leading at that time. But there are other great leaders in the nation besides the one or two who sit as President and Vice-President. If the people are holy, righteous and good then we can overcome the worst of leaders. But if we are selfish, egotistical and cold hearted toward those who are hurting then even the finest of leaders won't make us a great nation. Israel was great when they were godly. They were weak and subject to all kinds of bondage when they turned a deaf ear to God and set out on their own courses. In truth God often raised up ungodly leaders to teach his people the effects sin had on them.

But God raised up spiritual leaders in the land that never held an office and never ran for an election. But their preaching, teaching and life made a huge difference in what happened in the land. Elijah lived during the lifetime of Ahab, one of the worst kings that Israel ever had. He was married to Jezebel and together they made a horrendous team, whose selfish pride hurt the whole nation. But it was Elijah who prayed and God shut down the rain on the land for three and a half years. It was Elijah who prayed again to start the rain back. It was Elijah that confronted the prophets of Baal and had 450 of them put to death. He was the one who foretold the horrible deaths that both Ahab and Jezebel would have. And it all happened just as he said.

We've reached the time in our nation that more and more people think that the whole future of the nation hangs or falls on who is the president. The truth is that the whole nation rises or falls on the blessings or withholding of blessings from God Almighty. If we as a nation continue our run from Him and from His will in our lives then no matter who becomes president the nation has nothing to look forward to except ruin. Think of all the mighty nations that have existed in the world and how many of them felt they were invulnerable. But now we only read of them in the history books. Just about every one of those nations died, not from a military defeat but from the crumbling morals and godless living of the people who lived there.

Today and tonight as you watch the election returns, take some time to remember the prayer Jesus taught his disciples to pray. "Our Father in heaven, hallowed be your name. Your kingdom come, your will be done, on earth as it is in heaven. Give us this day our daily bread and forgive our sins as we forgive those who sin against us. Lead us not into temptation but deliver us from the evil one. For yours is the kingdom, the power and the glory forever. Amen." Certainly I am praying for this nation and its future and would encourage everyone to do the same. But I'm praying more often and with greater fervor for the will of God to be done on earth as it is in heaven. At the same time, I pray, "And God, start with me. Your will be done in my life as it is in heaven." I have almost no control over what happens in the world but I have lots of control over what happens in me. So, as we work to clean up the world and the nation, let's not forget to clean up ourselves.

GOD WITH US

Where is God in it all? One of the most powerful concepts ever revealed in Scripture is God's active presence among us. When the Messiah came into the world as a man it was God's promise that he would be called "Immanuel" meaning God with us (Isaiah 7:14). It is fashionable to picture God as far away, uninvolved in life and waiting for us to call on him to do something of personal benefit to us, to act. Do you remember what God said of Himself when He appeared to Moses in the burning bush? Moses asked for his name so that he might be able to tell the people of Israel when he went back to lead them out of Egypt. God said, "I am who I am. God tell them 'I am' has sent you." One of the greatest promises of God is His divine presence in our lives. When Jesus gave the great commission he promised he wouldn't leave us to do the job alone but said, "Lo, I am with you always even to the end of the age." The writer of Hebrews shouted the message, "He will never leave nor forsake us so that we may boldly say the Lord is my helper. I will not fear what man can do to me." Every time God called a person for a big job, bigger than the person felt they could do, it was followed by the promise, "I will be with you." Read Joshua chapter one and see how many times God said to Joshua, that He would be with him so that he didn't need to fear but be strong and courageous.

Even in those times when we feel so alone and that no one really cares what happens to us, God is there. Elijah had performed a mighty feat when he stood down the prophets of Baal and led the people of Israel to stop halting between two opinions and to choose God. He had prayed for the rain to come again and God had delivered. But when Jezebel promised to kill him as he had done to the prophets of Baal, fear gripped him. He ran away and sat down by the tree, alone, burdened down and afraid. He was so low that even his prayer is depressing. He told God he was the only one left trying to do right and that he just wanted the Lord to take his life and bring him home. God reminded him more than once of the 7,000 people he had who had not bowed the knee to Baal but Elijah was hard to convince. God sent him to Mount Horeb where the Ten Commandment law had been given and there spoke to him in a still, small voice saying, "Elijah, what are you doing here?" He again made the cry that he was alone. No one else cared for God or His will. Again God challenged his understanding and gave him a fresh mission. He served effectively for the remainder of his life when God would take him straight to heaven in a chariot of fire. God was with him all the time. He even sent ravens to feed him and gave him sound sleep to recover.

I love the story of Daniel and how Daniel declared God's action in our lives. When Daniel and his friends were captured and brought to Babylon, they were given the kings food to prepare them for work as advisers. Daniel refused to eat the king's food and ask for vegetables instead. In Daniel 1:9 it says, "And God gave Daniel favor and compassion in the sight of the chief of the eunuchs." In verse 17 it says, "As for the four youths, God gave them learning and skill in all literature and wisdom and Daniel had understanding of all visions and dreams." When the king had a vision that others couldn't interpret, God gave Daniel wisdom to interpret it. When Daniel spoke of God's giving him the interpretation in Daniel 2:20-23 he said, "Blessed be the name of God forever and ever, to whom belong wisdom and might. He changes times and seasons; he removes kings and sets up kings; he gives wisdom to the wise and knowledge to those who have understanding; he reveals deep and hidden things; he knows what is in the darkness, and the light dwells in him. To you, O God of my fathers, I give thanks and praise, for you have given me wisdom and might, and have now made known to me what we asked of you, for you have made known to us the king's matters."

God hasn't left us alone. He isn't sitting leisurely by in heaven waiting to see what will happen. He isn't resting until the end of the world. He is active and involved in our world and our lives. But I must know that God often acts in the world as a result of our prayers. He thus challenged us to pray for kings and all who are in authority that we might lead a quiet and peaceable life in all godliness. When did you last pray for God to act in Nigeria to save the Christians and those who might come to him? When have you prayed for the people in Iraq who are being murdered because they refuse to submit to the terrorist? When have you prayed for God to act in Iran or Syria or any other place where our brethren are being hurt and killed? We fuss, and complain but too often forget we serve a mighty God who can remove kings and lift up kings.

GOD'S DRAW

There is an air of concern everywhere one goes, about the future of the church and of Christianity as a whole. More books come out each day discussing why people have left the church. Surveys and studies are being done by every church consulting group in the world it seems on why so many young people are turning from faith and going away, many of them never to return to faith. The most recent thing has been to note the number of people who attend church on a regular basis has declined drastically over the last 20 years. Every new book or consulting group has an answer on what should be done to solve the problem. Of course many of the same folks had an answer years ago on what needed to be done and churches around the world tried to follow that advise only to see the decline accelerate. Perhaps it is time to go back to the one book that speaks for God on the matter and see what God gives as answers to the problem.

John the apostle in giving us his story of Jesus on earth on four different occasions pictures Jesus talking about being "Lifted up" from the earth and the things that would happen as a result. I want to focus on one of those for a moment and bring another up with it. In John 12 Jesus was entering his final week on this earth before being crucified. He had been marching toward Jerusalem and now John spends the second half of his book telling of that last week in Jerusalem. In verse 20 there is a signal that things are changing when some Greeks among those who are there for worship festival approach Philip with the request to see Jesus. Philip went to Andrew who went to Jesus with it. But John seems to drop the story in the middle of it and picks up instead with what Jesus said and did when he heard from Andrew. In Verses 23-24 he said, "The hour has come for the Son of Man to be glorified. Very truly I tell you, unless a kernel of wheat falls to the ground and dies, it remains only a single seed. But if it dies, it produces many seeds. Anyone who loves their life will lose it, while anyone who hates their life in this world will keep it for eternal life."

Jesus then said, "Now my soul is troubled, and what shall I say? 'Father, save me from this hour? No, it was for this very reason I came to this hour. Father, glorify your name!" (Verses 27) God the Father broke into the whole conversation by speaking from heaven as thunder, "I have glorified it and will glorify it again." Jesus noted the voice was for their benefit and said, "Now is the time for judgment on this world; now the prince of this world will be driven out. And I, when I am lifted up from the earth, will draw all people to myself."

Back in John 6 when Jesus was picturing himself as the bread of life and pleading with people to eat of that bread, in verse 44-45 he declared, "No one can come to me unless the Father who sent me draws them, and I will raise them up at the last day. It is written in the prophets: 'God will teach them all. Everyone who has heard the Father and learned from him come to me."

To be lifted up Jesus had to go through death. As a seed he had to be planted and die to be regenerated in life. The Father lifted him up as he was crucified, as he was raised from the dead and as he ascended back to the Father. He was lifted up when he sent the Holy Spirit on Pentecost and the church was established. He is lifted up today when we speak clearly the word of God teaching people about Him and pleading with them to "Follow Jesus".

Too often in church we become so consumed with lifting up ourselves or our church or our actions or our worship or our whatever. In doing so we lose sight of the whole plan and mission of the church given by God, "Unto Him be glory in the church and in Christ Jesus throughout all ages, world without end." (Ephesians 3:21) The huge problem of lifting up people is that people always let you down. The very one we think was the hero yesterday will become the problem tomorrow.

If Jesus is the focus and lifting him is our goal, it doesn't matter which age group you are in our how your group is supposed to look at things. It won't matter what race you are and whether or not your group is getting its rightful place. It won't matter what sex you are and whether or not you are getting credit for all you do. It is all about lifting up Jesus. When that is done, as it should be, God will draw people to him. He will do it through our teaching and preaching of His word. But we can never manufacture the draw by our own abilities. When we substitute our abilities for God's draw we ultimately lead people to ourselves and away from the Lord. Lift Him up in everything you do. See what God can do with His draw.

GOD'S SIDEKICK

Lone Ranger had Tonto. The Cisco Kid had Poncho. Batman had Robin. McGarret has Danny. Heroes we can think of have a sidekick that works alongside him or her and helps them in their mission. When you look at the life of Jesus on this earth he had the twelve around him and of them he had Peter, James and John that were closest to him and of them he had a special relationship with John. When Jesus ascended back to the Father and the apostles set out on the mission to carry the gospel to the entire world they still had pairs that worked together. Peter and John seemed to be a team. Paul and Barnabas, which turned into Paul and Silas and Barnabas and Mark, were teams as well. Whose team are you on?

In 2 Corinthians 6:1-2 Paul said, "As God's co-workers we urge you not to receive God's grace in vain. For he says, 'In the time of my favor I heard you, and in the day of salvation I helped you.' I tell you, now is the time of God's favor, now is the day of salvation." In most relationships Paul was the dominant partner. If you spoke of Paul and Barnabas or Paul and Silas or even Paul and Timothy, it always stared with Paul. But notice when he thought of his relationship with God and carrying out the mission the Lord had given them; he pictured himself as God's sidekick rather than the other way around.

Too often in life, I think we try to turn it around and make God the one that is our sidekick there to assist us in our every endeavor. We tend to think that we can set the mission and pray for God to come alongside us and carry out the mission. It is certainly true that God pictures the Holy Spirit of God as our helper. Jesus even described him as "Another helper" which is more literally translated "Another helper of the same kind as I am." We should think of God being there to assist us in doing the things he calls us to do. When he called servants like Joshua and challenged him to be strong and courageous it was tied closely with the point, "I'll be with you." He would help Joshua do a work that was far bigger than Joshua's personal ability to accomplish. But it is important to notice that God was calling Joshua to do the work He had set for him. It was God's mission and Joshua was the partner with God in accomplishing the mission set for him. In that mission God would help him every step of the way. It was vital that he know that God wouldn't send him out on such a work without providing for his strength and courage.

In 2 Corinthians 6:1-2 Paul paints a picture of being a sidekick with God. God's mission was to get the message of grace to the people so that they could accept his graceful offer to the salvation of their soul. It was God's mission, God's message and God's offer. He called Paul to become a "Co-worker" with him to fulfill the mission by getting the message to the people so they could take advantage of God's offer for salvation.

Imagine Paul walking down the street one-day and a man stopping him to ask him what he was doing these days? They might even say, "The last time I saw you, you were a Pharisee working for the Jewish leaders in Jerusalem." Paul might respond, "I'm working with God these days, carrying his message of grace to all people, trying to convince people that this is the day of salvation, not some future time when it seems more convenient." He might even have explained himself more fully by saying, "When I worked as a Pharisee I was following the agenda of the religious leaders, the rabbi's who were of the same sect as me. But now I've given up my agenda and am following the Lord's. I live each day trying to discern his will and doing it instead of trying to convince him to follow my will."

There were times when people who were "Co-workers" with Paul developed an agenda of their own and had to separate to go in their own way. "Demas has forsaken me, having loved this present world." In 2 Timothy 1:15 he mentioned Phygelus and Hermogenes who had deserted him. In I Timothy 1:20 he told of Hymenaeus and Alexander who had suffered shipwreck with regard to their faith and Paul had handed them over to Satan to be taught not to blaspheme. One of the worst mistakes one can make is to try to convince one not to leave who has already determined they have an agenda they are going to follow no matter what God's will is.

When we are God's co-workers our desire is simple. Find God's will and do it. Matters like, who gets the credit or will anyone know what I did, suddenly become meaningless. If it is God's work he is the one to be glorified not us. Notice Paul's prayer in Philippians 1:9-11, "And this is my prayer: that your love may abound more and more in knowledge and depth of insight, so that you may be able to discern what is best and may be pure and blameless for the day of Christ, filled with the fruit of righteousness that comes through Jesus Christ – to the glory and praise of God."

GODLESS CHATTER

"Death and life are in the power of the tongue." Words can make such powerful differences in the lives of people all around. "Sticks and stones may break my bones but words will never hurt me." That sounds good. But who is the person who hasn't been hurt or helped by words? Wars are started and ended by words. The longest lasting relationships usually begin with the right words. While it is certainly true that words will never take the place of action, it is equally true that action will never take the place of a well-chosen word. The gospel, which is God's power for salvation to all who believe, is couched in words. God decreed that the message would spread through the foolishness of preaching.

When Paul was in the Roman dungeon awaiting his final appearing before Nero when he would offer up his life as a sacrifice to God, he wrote his young protégé Timothy both to ask him to come to be with him in these final hours and days of his life on earth and to encourage Timothy in taking up the mantel that Paul would lay down as he died for his faith. In chapter two of this letter of 2 Timothy he reminded him of things he had taught him earlier and told him to pass those things on to faithful men who would be able to teach others also. (Vs. 1-6) But I want to focus on his message to Timothy down in verses 14-16. "Keep reminding God's people of these things. Warn them before God against quarreling about words; it is of no value, and only ruins those who listen.   Do your best to present yourself to God as one approved, a worker who does not need to be ashamed and who correctly handles the word of truth. Avoid godless chatter, because those who indulge in it will become more and more ungodly."

"A word fitly spoken is like apples of gold in pictures of silver." But a word misspoken may do untold harm to the one who listens to it. In church it is too often the case that we get caught up in words that will do absolutely no good to anyone who hears it. No wonder Paul would warn his young friend to warn the church about quarreling over words. What kind of things were involved that would lead to Paul making such a challenge to Timothy?

There were those whose words teaching false ideas or doctrines. He went on to tell of those who were teaching that the resurrection was already past and were upsetting the faith of some. It is obvious in looking at the whole book of 2 Timothy that a lot of the misuse of words had to do with genealogies and fusses about things in the law. Likely there were discussions going on about what was just the right way to say everything about God's will.   Just as today people developed code words to show to those of the in crowd that they knew the language and fit in with the right group.   If you couldn't say things just right or get the pronunciation just right you were not part of the accepted ones. Paul's response to it was that all of this kind of thing was of no value. Instead he said that it brought ruin to those who heard it.

Lots of things that we get all hot and bothered about, as Christians must absolutely break the heart of God. He longs so much to bring people to salvation that he would pay the price of giving his one and only son to become one of us, live among us as a man and take our sins upon him to allow God to punish our sins on his own son so that we can have the forgiveness of sins. He went to every extreme to be able to offer us salvation. Yet in church, the body of Christ, we too often get completely away from that driving force of reaching one more person for Jesus and get caught up in silly arguments over things that make absolutely no difference while people who are lost wait for someone to care enough to share the gospel message with them.

Can you imagine what it will be like in judgment when folks stand before God and actually expect to please God because they didn't or did clap? I suspect that Jesus again weeps over all such trivial pursuit that goes on in the name of faith. Notice Paul's plea to Timothy was to give every effort to be acceptable to God as a workman that has no need to be ashamed who handles correctly the word of God. When we handle the word correctly it won't be as a hammer to hit folks with that don't see everything the way we do. It will be as the powerful word able to save our souls as we humbly receive its message, looking intently into it as a law of liberty and continuing in it every day (James 1:19-25). God's word is powerful and sharper than a two-edged sword. Our fusses over insignificant words are empty, silly, ridiculous and worthless. Let's stay with the powerful words of the Lord.

GUILT, CRIME, INNOCENCE

Yesterday I watched much of the funeral service for the young man who was killed in Ferguson, Missouri by the policemen. It is heart breaking any time a person is killed and especially when it is a young person whose life seems to be before them. I hurt for the parents as they struggle to deal with the loss. I also ache for the policeman that is being accused of murder by preachers who want to stir up the crowd more than they desire justice. I don't know what all happened that day. I don't know if the young man was trying to give up, running away or if he was attacking the policeman and was shot as the policeman tried to save his life. In reality neither do any of those who were shouting for the policemen to be arrested and charged with murder know what happened, yet. I want to know. If it was some sort of racial attack I fully agree that the policeman should be charged with murder.

But here are some absolutes that need to be considered. The race of the boy or the policeman has nothing to do with whether it was murder or self defense. If the situation had been reversed and it was a black policeman and a white young man it wouldn't change one thing about the nature of the incident. Nor would it have changed the nature of the incident if both had been black or both had been white. Justice depends of what actually happened which in this case will now be very difficult for anyone to decide because it has been turned into both a political and a racial action.

Another absolute is that most of the destruction and rioting in that area had nothing to do with what happened to the young man. Instead angry, self absorbed, ungodly preachers and thugs came in to take advantage of the situation so they could get their names in the news and appear on camera. Thieves used it as a chance to break in and steal from storeowners who had served the very neighborhood in which the boy lived. Why do you suppose these self-styled leaders in their fancy suits and perfect hair don't show up when some drug dealer is using kids to sell and deliver and take their drugs and when their actions lead to the murder of not just one but many other young people in that area and every other area of this country. Do we really think it is worse to see the policeman shoot someone than a drive by vengeance killing in the same area?

When scenes like the one we've seen in Ferguson take place it will have results for a long time and very few of the results, if any, will be good. If you were a white policeman would you feel secure going into that neighborhood tomorrow?   For that matter, do you really think any policeman will feel like they have the support of the people or will the fear that whatever they do, even if it is defending the people in the area will work our correctly? Such mob action will lead to a reluctant, hesitating police force in the area. One of these days there will be a policeman, either there or some other place in some other city where they've seen and heard about Ferguson, will see a crime, will observe a young person with a gun, but will hesitate to do anything because of fear of what might happen. The result will likely be that either the policeman is shot or some other person, such as a storeowner or a battered wife. Police brutality and abuse should be condemned anytime anywhere. But be sure that you know the facts and the actions of the policeman were actually out of line. Also, if we want the police to be there to defend us and stop crime we had better be coming out in support of them when they do the right thing.

Race relations in this country or any other cannot improve as long as there are charlatans who thrive on the publicity they get from shouting racism. To treat people differently because of their race, color, education, income or accent is dead wrong. God made us all in His image and likeness. When we love our neighbor as ourselves it will change every community. Racism is equally awful whether it comes from blacks toward whites, whites toward blacks, Arabs toward Jews or Jews toward Arabs or any other groups. People are individuals and must be judged for their own actions. Even God doesn't judge us as a group. He will judge each person one at a time for the deeds done in the body whether good or bad. (2 Corinthians 5:10)

HARD TO PLEASE

What kind of gift receiver are you? An easy to please gift receiver is one that accepts a gift of any kind and fusses over it profusely. "This is just what I was hoping for." "I've always wanted one of these." Are you that kind of person who when you receive a gift you immediately put it to use either by wearing it, using it or putting it in a prominent place? Perhaps you are one of those people that are very hard to please as a gift receiver. When you receive a gift it just seems impossible for you to pretend you like it in some way and not show how deeply disappointed you are that you didn't get something else for which you had been hoping and praying diligently.

Let's face it our human nature doesn't always give us what we are looking for. Sometimes we look at whatever has been given to us and wonder why in the world someone who loved us would have given us something like that. In Matthew 11:16-19 Jesus said that was the way the people of *Israel had been with regard to his coming into the world. John the Baptist had sent his disciples to ask Jesus if he was really the Messiah or should they look for another. Jesus had given them the proof they needed and sent them back to John. He then bragged on John to the crowd and told what a great man of God he was. Then he said, 'But to what shall I compare this generation? It is like children sitting in the market places, who call out to the other children, and say, "We played the flute for you, and you did not dance; we sang a dirge, and you did not mourn.' For John came neither eating nor drinking, and they say, 'He has a demon!' The Son of Man came eating and drinking and they say, 'Behold a gluttonous man and a drunkard, a friend of tax collectors and sinners!' Yet wisdom is vindicated by her deeds."*

The picture Jesus painted before them is a powerful illustration. He pictured children playing on the streets of the city. They sang a happy song but no one danced, then they sang a sad song but no one cried so now they don't know what to do. If they had been our children they might well have said, "We've tried everything and they still won't play with us so we don't know what else to do." Some people are just hard to please. Jesus and John the Baptist were completely different from each other, yet they both preached and taught the same thing. But John came as one who abstained from everything questionable. He was a Nazarite and neither drank wine nor any other strong drink. He stood out from the crowd as one that did none of the things they had identified with the people in the world. Yet Jesus came as one that still taught the same message that the kingdom of God was coming and they needed to repent of their sins and be baptized, yet he participated with them in drinking wine and eating whatever was set before him. It had been God's purpose to send both men into the world to represent the cause of the Lord and demonstrate that people could be very different from each other and still both are right with God.

One of the peculiar things about our human nature is that we tend to want more from people than what they are willing to fulfill. Whatever a person is willing to give it just doesn't seem to us to be quite right for what we think it should be. In church we tend to try to make Jesus into one more like John who stands off at a distance and has few close friends around him. When others try to join them his words seem harsh and may seem to push people away. Yet people are obviously drawn to him and to his message.

Jesus pictured the people of that day being like children because whichever way the person was that God sent with his message it wasn't what they wanted. It often seemed that we would rather remake Jesus into something a little more like John and perhaps a little like Paul and then we will claim him as our Lord and Savior. Some things he said and did just don't seem like what a good Christian would do. But then we are pressed to remember that a Christian is to be like Jesus not the other way around so when the molds we have don't fit what Jesus actually said and did, it is the mold that needs to be broken, not Jesus. He is God's perfect picture of the Father and His will for us. He is the word made flesh so that he both lived the message and proclaimed it.

HEAL THEIR LAND

I love prayer services and believe we ought to have many, many more of them. I believe when we stopped calling the mid-week services at church "prayer services" and started calling them "Bible studies" or now there are multiple names used, it was largely a mistake. There needs to be times when God's people come together to pray and demonstrate their dependence on God both as a group and as individuals. It is obvious in the Book of Acts that when problems arose there was a natural reaction of the Christians getting together to pray about it. In Acts 4 when Peter and John were called before the religious tribunal to give account for healing a handicapped man and they were beaten for their actions the church got together immediately to pray about it. In Acts 12 when James had been executed as the first apostle martyred and Peter was arrested with view to executing him as well, the church gathered in a Christian home to pray. When Peter was released he knew immediately where to go to find the brethren.

I'm very thankful for movements going on today like "One Cry" that is calling on people of faith to pray for the country that there will be a turning back to God and to following him. But it discourages me to see us take Scripture applying to the nation of Israel and apply them to this country as though the United States were God's chosen people today. How often have you heard 2 Chronicles 7:14 quoted as motivation for us to pray for this country? Listen to it. I think you will recognize it quickly. "If my people, who are called by my name, will humble themselves and pray and seek my face and turn from their wicked ways, then I will hear from heaven, and I will forgive their sins and will heal their land." If you look at the context of this verse it is at the dedication of Solomon's Temple when the Lord appeared to Solomon and challenged him and the Nation of Israel to be faithful to Him and when they messed up and sinned to return to Him knowing He will forgive and bless again.

Now, here is my question. What does this verse have to do with praying for this country and God healing our land?

You might respond by saying, "Well, how would we apply this beautiful text if it doesn't apply to our country today?" God's chosen people today aren't a country. They are His people from all countries, nationalities, backgrounds, languages, ages and sexes. The spiritual Israel today is the church that Jesus established almost 2000 years ago after he had ascended back to the Father and sent the Holy Spirit on the apostles on the Day of Pentecost in Jerusalem. Three thousand people that day became the initial followers of Jesus Christ and would later take the description of "Christians". It would be great to pray as God told Solomon to pray there in 2 Chronicles 7:14 and really as He describes all through this chapter to Solomon. But pray it as the church, as Christians for those who are Christ followers. We need it. Just as Israel had turned away from God's plans and taken ones of their own, too often the church has followed the same route. The very people that Jesus prayed for in John 17 that we would all be one as He and the Father are one so the world would believe that God had sent him has splintered in a thousand directions. Certainly, the people of God and the church as a whole needs healing that only God can provide.

So, we need prayer meetings. We need to have them at church, in homes and anywhere else that we can. God hears the prayers of those who honestly cry out to him in faith and repentance. If we repent and turn to Him, he will truly heal our land. It just won't be the United States but the church of the living God. Does that mean we shouldn't be praying for the United States? Certainly not! Paul told Timothy that of first priority was to pray for all people, for kings and all who are in authority that we may be able to live quiet and peaceable lives in all godliness and holiness, because God wants all people to be saved and come to the knowledge of the truth. (I Timothy 2:1-5) In Romans 10:1-3 Paul said, "My hearts desire and prayer to God for Israel is that they might be saved." It would be great to pray that kind of prayer for this nation or any other. It is important that we pray the right prayers for the right ones as we go to pray.

I GIVE UP

Do you remember as a youngster having a friend hold you down or tickle you or even twist an arm until you say, "I give?" No doubt it is short for "I give up." Usually declaring I give on those occasions meant some sort of defeat. But that isn't always the case. Think with me about some areas we all need to learn to "Give up."

I need to give up controlling the universe, even if it is just my small part of that universe. In our arrogance we often feel that we can make things happen the way we have planned it no matter what anyone else may think about it. But it only takes 75 or 100 times when we are sure we have everything under control and them falling apart, for one of multiple reasons for us to begin to see we aren't in control. Only God has control of the universe and the only person I can change in the world is me. If I'm wearing myself out trying to change someone else or force him or her to do what I think they should do it will only lead to frustration.

I need to give up on demanding that other people share my same dreams for the future. How many of you ended up marrying the person your parents dreamed you would or going into the profession they hoped you would go into? If we didn't follow all the same dreams and goals they had for us then why do we think our own children should follow our dreams and goals? When we get the idea that the only right way of doing a thing is the way I do it, then we will never be satisfied with the work of any other person. That will mean I never mentor another person and never help a young person learn or grow because none will do the job the way I want it done. Give it up and realize you didn't create the world and don't have any good advice to offer the God who did.

I need to give up on forcing someone else to be sorry for the wrongs I feel they have done to me. Even God Almighty found it difficult to get Israel to repent of forsaking him and going after the other gods of the land. He punished them with captivity, famine, pestilence and bondage, yet they kept going back to their ways of idolatry each time and turning away from him. If God couldn't get people to see their sin and repent of them we aren't likely to get the job done either. We can show compassion, love and acceptance. But no one can force another person to see their errors so they can be restored.

I need to give up on revenge. God said, "Vengeance is mine. I will repay says the Lord." His challenge to us is to "overcome evil with good." Notice Paul's instruction on the matter. "Do not repay anyone evil for evil. Be careful to do what is right in the eyes of everyone. If it is possible, as far as it depends on you, live at peace with everyone. Do not take revenge, my dear friends, but leave room for God's wrath," He went on to quote from the book of Proverbs "If your enemy is hungry, feed him; if he is thirsty, give him something to drink. In doing this, you will heap burning coals on his head." (Romans 12:17-21) Think of the huge load it takes off our backs if we simply leave all such things in the hands of God.

I need to give up on earning my salvation. "All we like sheep have gone astray everyone to his own way. There is none righteous no not one." Even as the devoted follower of Christ we still fail. John said, "if we say that we don't sin we only deceive ourselves." Grace is the means of our salvation. When I realize that I am saved by grace through faith I will also begin to see that "We are God's workmanship created in Christ Jesus unto good works." (Ephesians 28-10) Our works or service and commitment to God aren't to earn our salvation but to demonstrate our gratitude and appreciation for what God has done for us by grace. When I give up on earning my way in, I can relax and enjoy the blessings of God who loves us more than we can ever imagine and who wants all people to be saved and come to the knowledge of the truth.

It could well be that the single greatest word in any language, is the word, "Immanuel". When God promised through Isaiah the prophet that a virgin would conceive and have a son that would be called Immanuel it was a massive promise. God had a wonderful plan for humanity from the beginning of creation. When He made the man and woman in His image and likeness, "God blessed them, and God said to them, 'be fruitful and multiply, and fill the earth and subdue it; and have dominion over the fish of the sea and over the birds of the air and over every living thing that moves upon the earth." (Genesis 1:28) God placed them in the beautiful Garden of Eden where they were in charge. They could eat freely of every tree. The animals were all domesticated at the time. God only gave them one requirement for them not to do. "Don't eat of the tree in the middle of garden, the tree of the knowledge of good and evil." Of course, they failed God's plan and took of the forbidden tree.

God didn't then give up on humanity. They were driven from the garden and faced the trails and temptations of the world. God in his longing for us to be what he had planned for us to be called Abraham that through him and his offspring all nations might be blessed. Through his descendants God called the Nation of Israel to be his chosen people. They were challenged to be a royal priesthood and be God's blessed people through whom the messiah would come into the world. Israel failed miserably as the chosen ones. The mission given them of being the special people of God went completely astray. God promised through the prophets that there was coming a time when through Abraham's seed, and through David the man after God's own heart, a Savior, a Messiah would come. I suspect they thought of the messiah as being like the judges that God had raised up to deliver them when they repented of sins or like Moses the great lawgiver whom God called to lead them out of bondage into the Promised Land. God even promised Moses that he would raise up a prophet like him and the people were to listen to Him in everything.

When the angel of the Lord appeared to Mary and promised to her that the Holy Spirit would come upon her and she would become pregnant and give birth to a special child who would be the savior of the world, it was God fulfilling the promises to Abraham, Moses, David and to the world. They were to call his name "Jesus" meaning that "God saves". He was the messiah promised, the anointed one. He is Immanuel. Matthew explained to us that "Immanuel" means "God with us". God became one of us. "The word became flesh and dwelt among us and we beheld his glory, the glory of the only begotten son of the Father, full of grace and truth." (John 1:14-15) In Hebrews 2:14 it says, "Since, therefore, the children share flesh and blood, he himself likewise shared the same things, so that through death he might destroy the one who has the power of death, that is the devil, and free those who all their lives were held in slavery by the fear of death." Paul described what happened in Philippians 2:5-10 as Christ being in very nature God, didn't see equality with God as something to be grasped, but emptied himself and became a man and being found in fashion as a man he humbled himself and became obedient to the point of death, even death on a cross."

"Immanuel" God with us is the message that God came down and walked in our shoes, felt our pains, went through all of our temptations without sin and then took our sins on him to die on our behalf. When Jesus was about to go away he promised he wouldn't leave them as orphans but would send another advocate to be us always. God hasn't left us alone. His promise never to leave or forsake us gives us strength to go on no matter what may be happening in our lives.

Emblazoned on our foreheads and across our hearts needs to be the Message, "Immanuel". We aren't alone. God is with us always. He was with us in life, in suffering, in temptation and in His death on the cross. He was raised in power to give us resurrection power in living for him each day. Imagine what it means when we go to work each day knowing "Immanuel" God is with us. Think of when we go home each day to work with our family, Immanuel, God is with us. When we go to school to handle the problems and temptations there, Immanuel, God is with us. When Satan makes his greatest attack on us, Immanuel, God is with us. When we hurt so bad we can't express it, Immanuel, God is with us. Our battle cry is "Immanuel". Shout it as loud and often as you can. We are never alone as His people. IMMANUEL SAYS IT ALL.

IN STEP WITH GOD

Can you remember what it was like to walk with your dad when you were a rather small child? It always seemed to me that Dad took huge steps and as a child I had a hard time keeping up with his pace. It never seemed to me that I was in any way setting the pace for us to walk. When we think of walking with God it is vital that we keep clearly in mind that God is the one setting the pace and our job is to walk along with him in the direction and at the pace that he sets for us. Too often in life we want God to come alongside us and sanction the things we are already involved in doing. We don't want to change our pace or our direction to suit his but to come up with our ideas and dreams and have him pronounce his blessing on them.

Enoch walked with God. Abraham was God's friend and walked before him. Throughout Bible history there is a simple story line that at times people sought the will of God and determined to walk with the Lord in the direction and at the pace he wanted for life. In those times God richly blessed his people and promised his care in their lives. But those times tended to be short lived. Every time God's people followed that path it turned into wonderful blessings in their life. But always, there was a turning from that to walk in their own willful ways instead of with God.

The Book of Judges is a rather short presentation of what happened throughout the history of Israel as God's people and in truth is sets a pattern that is still followed in our own time. The people became selfish. They worshiped the idols of their own making, which meant that they really worshiped themselves rather than God. Each time the result was that they took a nosedive into sin, immorality and mistreatment of others. God would allow their enemies to come in and overtake them and turn them into slaves. They would cry out in agony to the Lord and he would raise up a person to serve as judge among them and lead them to drive the enemies out and lead them back to God and devotion to him. They would usually serve God throughout the lifetime of that judge but then when that judge died they would slowly drift back into sin, rebellion and idolatry and the same cycle would start again.

Here is the question that we each need to answer personally and we need to answer as a church. Are we making our own plans, developing our own dreams and visions and asking God to come alongside us and sanction our plans and bless them? Or are we seeking to find God's plans and God's will that we might come alongside Him and follow his lead, his direction and his pace. Let's be honest that what we view as success may not be the Lord's view at all. We tend to look at the numbers and God looks deeper to see who is being influenced for Him, who is growing in his service, who is reaching out in love to help a fellow traveler in their way?

Two powerful verses that most of us remember at least in part are Romans 12:1-2. "Therefore I urge you, brethren, by the mercies of God, to present your bodies a living and holy sacrifice, acceptable to God, which is your spiritual service of worship. And do not be conformed to this world, but be transformed by the renewing of your mind, so that you may prove what the will of God is, that which is good and acceptable and perfect." This whole picture is one that should drive our service to God. Our bodies are to be a living sacrifice or offering to God, not just some segment of our lives, but our whole selves. That is our worship and service to God when we offer ourselves completely to him. Instead of letting the world set our mold, we are clay in the hands of God the potter who molds us into his image and likeness. When we renew our minds to follow him, we are able to see and understand his will, to know what He wants from us. It is in that setting that Paul will go ahead to talk about our being part of the body of Christ and each person being gifted by God to serve him in some area of work. To know God's will is to understand where we fit into the will and what he wants us to do as his servants.

This week as you bow before God in prayer, instead of asking God to bless your plans and desires, ask him to let you see and understand his will for your life. Ask him to renew your minds and to accept your body as a living sacrifice to him. Ask God to reveal his will for your life and to guide you each day into his service. Pray that he will open your eyes to the hurts, fears and dreads of others that he might use you as a means of helping someone else. When we see his will and seek ways to walk alongside him to serve others it will be amazing how blessed we are and what fulfillment it brings into our life.

INDEPENDENCE DAY

On July 4th, 1776 the Declaration of Independence was finalized and sent to England. As a nation we would no longer be under the reign of the king nor accept the taxes that were passed on to us. The men who signed that Declaration paid an extremely high price for their courage. Many paid with their lives, others with their fortunes and others with their means of livelihood. It is amazing the price people will pay for freedom. Yet freedom either in the political realm or the spiritual realm is hard to hold on to. There is something about our human nature that longs for freedom for ourselves but will turn right around and begin to make laws that limit the freedom of others and of us. In the political realm the loss of freedom is usually tied to security. Slowly but surely people will give up one freedom after another so that they can feel secure. It is certain that some of these sacrifices are good for the country and good for the people but it is extremely difficult to draw the line. Even if one generation declares that they are willing to go no further in giving up their personal freedoms, the next generation typically will move the line over several feet further.

As we celebrate the freedoms of our nation it is a great time to spend some of your free time praying about the nation. Thank God for his love and care for this country and be thankful for every person who has sacrificed life, or liberty or fortune for the safety and good of the country. Also pray for those future generations that they will turn back to the many of the principles and freedoms of generations past. Most of all pray that we as a nation will have a real spiritual revival. Such a spiritual revival can't come from any act of congress or any plan from the President. Such a revival must come from people like us who start the revival on our knees. Pray for the President, for the people who surround him and for those who serve in Congress that God will give them wisdom to lead, judgment to make right choices and courage to stand for what is right. There is a movement going on across the nation called "One Cry" that is an effort to get all people of faith to pray for the country and especially that there would be a spiritual revival in the nation. In the words of one of the early reformers, I can't at the moment remember his name, it is time to draw a circle on the ground and get inside the circle and pray for God to begin spiritual revival in the nation and in the world beginning inside that circle.

As we celebrate Independence Day for the Nation, let me suggest we celebrate Dependence Day as the Body of Christ. Too often in our Spiritual lives we become far too independent, trying to make our own way and coming up with our own plans rather than leaning on the God of the Universe. Our God promises to never leave us alone. When Jesus was about to ascend his message to the disciples was to go and make more disciples and teach them to follow the things he had taught them but then he promised, "Lo, I am with you always, even to the end of the world." When he was getting close to the time of his crucifixion he said to the twelve and to us, "I won't leave you as orphans. I will send you another helper, the Holy Spirit who will be with you forever." He said the Spirit had been with them but would be in them. The Father promised, "I'll never leave you nor forsake you. So we may boldly say, the Lord is my helper. I will not fear what men can do to me." We aren't alone. To have God the Father, Christ the Son and God the Holy Spirit with us all the time and not depend on them for guidance and help is the greatest action of foolishness that one can imagine.

In my efforts to hear God's guidance in my life it is important to be careful that the Spirit I'm listening to is the Holy Spirit. In I John 4:1-3 the apostle warned, "Dear friends, do not believe every spirit, but test the spirits to see whether they are from God, because many false prophets have gone out into the world. This is how you can recognize the Spirit of God: Every spirit that acknowledges that Jesus Christ has come in the flesh is from God, but every sprit that does not acknowledge Jesus is not from God. This is the spirit of the antichrist, which you have heard is coming and even now is already in the world."

When the spirit I'm listening to wants to take away the freedom we have in Christ it isn't the Spirit of God. His law is a law of liberty and brings us freedom. (James 1:25; 2 Corinthians 3:17-18)

Have a great Independence Day and a great Dependence Day and life.

What was that about the best-laid plans of mice and men? The city of Little Rock had great plans for this past weekend's marathon. But it didn't quite work out to be that beautiful day in March that they had planned. Many of us had lots of plans for what we would do Sunday night and Monday but our plans changed rather quickly with all the ice that fell. It really doesn't matter what kind of plans we have, or how well they are laid out, interruptions come. How we handle the interruptions says a lot about our faith, maturity and character.

The apostle Paul was a great planner. He seemed to be constantly thinking of the next city or country that he would travel to and preach the gospel. In Acts 16:6-10 he and his companions traveled throughout the region of Phrygia and Galatia, "Having been kept by the Holy Spirit from preaching the word in the province of Asia." They travelled on to the border of Mysia and tried to enter Bithynia but the Spirit of Jesus would not allow them to. Finally they came to Troas, where Paul had a dream of a man pleading with him to "Come over into Macedonia and help us." Knowing something of Paul's nature, can't you imagine the frustration he felt when they kept going from one area to another and the Spirit kept telling them no, this isn't the place for you now? God had a bigger plan than what Paul or his companions had. When they followed the Spirit's lead and went into Macedonia it resulted in the establishment of the church in Philippi, which would become one of Paul's greatest supporters in every way.

When Paul wrote the Book of Romans he told them of plans to come to Rome and preach among them and then have them assist him as he went on to Spain to preach in areas where no one else had laid a foundation yet. It seemed like a wonderful plan that God would surely get behind. Paul would indeed reach Rome in the next few years, but not at all as he had planned. He had asked the church in Rome to pray for him as he went to Jerusalem to deliver a gift from the churches among the Gentiles, that it would be accepted and that it would help to tear down the walls between Jewish churches and Gentile churches. God had the Holy Spirit to warn Paul on the way to Jerusalem that it wasn't going to be a smooth trip. He would be arrested. His companions tried to convince him not to go but he went anyway and was arrested, sent to Caesarea, where he would be left for three years before appealing to Caesar. He made it to Rome as a prisoner, who was shipwrecked on the way. In Rome he would work from a rented house where he was constantly under the guard of Roman soldiers. There he constantly had people coming in to teach them the message of Jesus.

How do you react when your plans just don't go the way you had laid them out? We have several options on how we will deal with those interrupted plans. We can get angry and pout over the fact it isn't going like we thought. We can fuss and complain to everyone who will listen or even to a few that don't listen. We can feel like a failure that just didn't plan closely enough, so we go back and adjust the plans to make them even more detailed in hopes that nothing will go wrong this time. Or we could react by seeing the new opportunity that is before us because of the interruption of our plans.

Paul later wrote the church in Philippi about his ordeal. He knew of their concern for him and how it had worked out. He said, "What has happened to me has actually served to advance the gospel. As a result, it has become clear throughout the whole palace guard and to everyone else that I am in chains for Christ. And because of my chains, most of the brothers and sisters have become confident in their Lord and dare all the more to proclaim the gospel without fear. It is true that some preach Christ out of envy and rivalry, but others out of goodwill. The latter do so out of love, knowing I am put here for the defense of the gospel. The former preach Christ out of selfish ambition, not sincerely, supposing that they can stir up trouble for me while I am in chains. But what does it matter? The important thing is that in every way, whether from false motives or true, Christ is preached. And because of this I rejoice." (Philippians 1:12-18)

I want that attitude that I can see how God uses even the worst interruptions to bring about good and reaching others for him.

IS IT CATCHING?

"Wash your hands." "Don't drink after anyone else." "Don't touch that door knob with your hands, it's filthy. Use some tissue." "Do you think it's catching?" We live in a time and place that is deeply concerned about catching something, especially something that might make them ill. Several years ago when I was preaching in a different city I was amazed that there was a man in the congregation who refused to shake hands with anyone. I thought to begin with it was just me and that it was some kind of protest against my preaching. But I noticed he didn't shake hands with anyone else either. He was the first person I ever met who was so conscience of catching something that he refused to shake another person's hand. Today I see many more who have that same fear.

I was visiting with an elderly lady who was suffering with cancer and was in the hospital again after a long battle and she knew the end was getting close. I sat down beside her bed and took her hand and prayed for her comfort. When I finished praying she had tears running down her cheeks. Before I could say anything she said, "Leon, excuse me for crying. It's just that hardly anyone wants to touch me anymore. They stand at the foot of the bed and talk to me and some even pray for me. But they act like they are afraid to touch me for fear of catching what I have. Thank you for holding my hand." I thought of Jesus when the leper approached him saying, "Lord if you are willing you can make me clean. Jesus said, I'm willing and reached out and touched him." I suspect the touch meant about as much to the man as the healing.

In our fear of catching something, there are some things we need to consider. Some things need to be caught. Not all contagious things are bad. There are people who being around them makes me feel better about life. They give off a sense of enthusiasm about life and the opportunities we have each day. Some people are contagious with their compassion. They care so much about people who are in trouble or who are hurting in some way that their compassion is catching. I've got some friends that being with them for a while causes me to be more open, sharing and loving toward other people. Their spirit is catching. Being around others causes me to be more patriotic.

The truth is, God calls all of us as Christians to be contagious. Our faith and devotion to God should be so catching that just being around us leads people to want to know more about our faith and our savior. Isn't that what Peter was saying in I Peter 3:13-16? "Who is going to harm you if you are eager to do good? But even if you should suffer for what is right, you are blessed. Do not fear their threats; do not be frightened. But in your hearts revere Christ as Lord. Always be prepared to give an answer to everyone who asks you to give them a reason for the hope that you have, keeping a clear conscience, so that those how speak maliciously against your good behavior in Christ may be ashamed of their slander." Notice, Peter wants us to live in such a way that people can see the hope we have and will ask about that hope. It is important to notice that his charge is given in a time and atmosphere of suffering. If they kept the right attitude during times of suffering it would show their hope and lead to people asking about that hope.

Most of the questions people ask me in matters of faith aren't about my hope. They ask about certain doctrines or why we do some things we do. But answering those questions seldom leads a person to give their lives to God.

In Colossians 4:4-6 Paul dealt with the same point by telling us to be careful about our speech, make sure it is seasoned with salt so that we can answer people who ask questions.

I long to be so contagious as a disciple of Christ that people are catching the faith and hope that will lead them to making a full commitment to Christ. I pray that we will all become more contagious as disciples. The world is in deep need of hope and it depends on us to show them the way to the one who can give such hope.

IS THAT A SIN?

I didn't intend to be eaves dropping. But I was intrigued by the conversation of some people in Best Buy. I was waiting for someone and half-heartedly looking at some things when I walked close enough to this group of younger people in a rather animated conversation. I heard one say, "Well, that's not a sin" to which one of the others, replied, "Well it is too. The Bible says it is a sin." I didn't know what they were talking about but the mention of sin and the Bible peaked my interest. The one who first declared that whatever it was wasn't a sin didn't give any ground. He said, "No the Bible doesn't say it's a sin. I looked it up and it doesn't ever say that it is a sin for a guy and girl to have sex before they are married." The conversation continued, but I got a phone call in the middle of it and walked away so I could hear the one on the phone.

Later I began to think about that conversation. As the young man was saying he looked it up he was holding up his smart phone, indicating he had looked it up on his phone. Think of how that might have gone. I suppose he might have looked up the topic, "Sex before marriage". To which the Bible study site would have responded "No such phrase is found." He then reached the conclusion that the Bible didn't say anything about the subject of sex before marriage. It never dawned on him that there might be another way the Bible spoke of the topic without using the very words he had entered. What does the Bible say about sex before marriage? It says that "Fornication" or "Sexual immorality" is something that we should run from. In I Corinthians 6:18-20 it says, "Flee from sexual immorality. All other sins a person commits are outside the body, but whoever sins sexually, sins against their own body. Do you not know that your bodies are temples of the Holy Spirit, who is in you, whom you have received from God? You are not your own; you were bought at a price. Therefore honor God with your bodies." Earlier in the chapter he noted that one who had sex with a prostitute became one flesh with her.

God, as a blessing for marriage, planned sex. It involves more than just the physical act of sex. It is an emotional and spiritual bond that makes two people one. Sex before marriage is taking something God put in the marriage and turning it into something God never meant for it to be. He went on in chapter 7 of I Corinthians to say that in order to prevent sexual immorality let every man have his own wife and every woman have her own husband. Inside the marriage sex is pure, holy and right (Hebrews 13:4). Outside marriage, whether before marriage or with someone whom you never intend to marry, having sex is sexual immorality. In I Thessalonians 4:3 Paul wrote, "It is God's will that you should be sanctified: that you should avoid sexual immorality; that each of you should learn to control your own body in a way that is holy and honorable, not in passionate lust like the pagans, who do not know God."

But the real point of this article isn't about sex before marriage or outside of marriage. It is about understanding what the Bible says. To assume the Bible has nothing to say on a topic just because it doesn't use the words or phrases we use today is a gross misunderstanding. Think about it in this light. The Bible says nothing about cell phones or Facebook. But it says a whole lot that affects our use of them. It says we should treat each other the way we want to be treated (Matthew 7:12). It tells us not to be judgmental about others and correct our own sins before trying to correct someone else's (Matthew 7:1-5). It tells us to be honest and use integrity. It demands that our language be pure and notes that our words come from the heart demonstrate what is in our heart. (Matthew 15:16-20) It condemns slander of every kind. Gossip is pictured in the Bible as something that destroys friendships, hurts relationships and tears apart families.

One of the marks of the New Testament is that it doesn't specifically deal with every right or wrong that might be brought up. It is unlike the Old Testament that went through a whole litany of sins that people needed to avoid and in great detail pointed out the rituals they were to follow in matters such as worship to God. In the New Testament matters are typically dealt with in larger principles that must be applied to situations and circumstances we face today. Being a good Bible student demands a great deal of work, time and study. Be wise in what you say with regard to what the Bible forbids, or what it commands for us today.

IT CAN GET WORSE

When a person is horribly ill or is an invalid they often feel that things just couldn't get any worse for them than it is at that moment. I suppose it is normal for us to judge what we consider the worst of all situations by the standards of what we have seen or experienced for ourselves. But we need to always remember that our experiences, no matter how varied, are limited. While things may be the worst they have been in my own life or situation, it doesn't prove it is the worst of all times for all people.

In John 6:1ff there is a story of Jesus in Jerusalem in the temple area walking by an area called Bethesda, which had five colonnades around it. He found numerous sick and disabled people who were trying to get into the water, as it was moving. He focused on one man who had been handicapped for 38 years. He lay there every day trying to find the answer to his condition. Jesus approached him and asked a powerful question. "Do you want to get well?" He had been in this condition for a long time. Perhaps he had adjusted to his situation and was settled into a routine he had rather just stay with. Immediately he tried to answer Jesus without really saying "yes" or "no". He told how he tried to get into the pool when the water was stirred but someone always made it in before him. With that partial answer Jesus said, "Arise, take up your pallet and walk." The man was immediately healed and got up from where he had been laying, picked up his pallet and headed on his way toward home, I suppose.

As he walked on his way, some of the Pharisees who were the religious leaders of the day stopped him and asked why he was violating the Sabbath law by carrying his pallet around. He answered that the man who had healed him had told him to pick up his pallet and walk so he had obeyed the man. They wanted to know who this was that had given him that charge. But the man didn't know. Jesus had walked away after healing him, back into the crowd without waiting for more people to gather or for the man to fall before him in praise for what he had done. It was later in the day when Jesus found the man in the temple courts and said to him, "Don't continue in your sins, or something worse will come upon you."

He may well have believed that he had been experiencing the worst conditions in the last 38 years while he had dealt with his affliction. All those years of lying there among the ill, the handicapped, the hurting and the lonely had surely taken their toll on the man. To now have relief after all this time must have seemed like the best thing that could ever have happened. But Jesus points to both a better and a worse way that he can go from there. He can continue to live in sin and things will end up worse than ever for him. Or he can leave his life of sin and follow the Lord in his life and things can be better than he ever imagined on his best day of daydreaming about a better life. We don't really know if Jesus was contemplating the eternal realms beyond this time and world or if he was just thinking about life in the here and now. Either way the principle remains the same.

He had experienced some bad times, but not the worst they could be. He was now having some good times for a change, but not the best it could be. He could turn from the way of sin to God and have forgiveness of all sins in his life and have a healing that was a thousand times better than the physical healing he had by the pool.

It seems to be the case that Jesus saw in him what could be with his help. In truth he sees the same thing in you and me. Alone we mess up and fail. With his help we can turn things around and do good in the world. But with Jesus we are never just left where we are. We are always becoming something more with his help.

JESUS AND POLITICS

Would Jesus vote if He were in this environment today? Would He get involved in the political actions that go on daily? Did He say anything that related to the political world when He walked on the earth?

In a political season that already indicates it is going to be brutal with each side attacking the other and trying to make them appear as Satan incarnate, it is worth considering what our place, as followers of Christ ought to be. It is certain that Jesus had interaction with the political world. Think of some of the things He said and did that give a good example to us in the political wars of our own time.

First, when choosing the people who would be his ambassadors to the world he chose men of very different political views and as far as what is recorded he didn't enter into the discussion of their politics but challenges them to "Follow Me." Matthew as a tax collector would have been among the hated class of Jews that were completely antagonistic to the Zealot, Simon. But if their differences affected their work in the kingdom we hear nothing of it. That fact ought to help us to see that the church isn't tied to any particular political views. Our place is to worship and serve God with all our ability, serving as good examples to all and being good citizens of the country we are part of. When a church tries to align itself with one particular political view it will leave out those who differ from that view and may well lead to that person being lost to the cause of Christ.

Second, Jesus treated those tied to the government the same as He did any other person. He healed the servant of the Centurion and declared that he had not seen faith like his even among the Jews. He defended Zacchaeus the tax collector when He encountered him. The crowds were antagonistic toward him but Jesus said He was going to his house for dinner. When Zacchaeus declared that if he had taken anything from any one wrongly he would restore it four times over and would give half his money for the poor the Lord praised him. In that discussion is where Jesus said He had come into the world to seek and save the lost. In a day when many seem to hold contempt for anyone who works for the government we need to be reminded that the Bible tells us that those who are government officials are ministers of God sent to execute wrath on the sons of disobedience. Peter declared that we should honor the king and Paul told us to pray for kings and all who are in authority that we may lead a quiet and peaceable life in all godliness.

Third, Jesus in the Sermon on the Mount shocked the Jews by saying that if someone compelled them to go with them one mile they were to go two. The context of this statement is that the Roman Soldier had the right to compel a person who lived in a country conquered by Rome to take a load he was carrying for a mile. The Jews hated the obligation and often had markers to show exactly how far a mile was so that when they met the obligation they could drop the load and demonstrate their contempt for the soldier, the country and the obligation. Jesus challenged all to take a different attitude toward such service. We aren't affected by Roman soldiers coming to us demanding we carry their load, but we are often compelled to do things as citizens of the country that we don't want to do. Think of how we should apply this second mile principle. Instead of trying to get by on the least we can do, we ought to do the best we can to serve even when it is a law or obligation we don't like.

Fourth, when confronted about paying taxes to Caesar, Jesus took a coin and asked whose image was on the coin. They said "Caesar's image." He replied, "Render to Caesar the things that are Caesars and unto God the things that are God's." Priority always belongs to the kingdom of the Lord instead of the kingdoms of men. We are to seek first before anything or anyone else, the kingdom of God and his righteousness (Matthew 6:33). We must also remember that God controls all the kingdoms and nations of the world along with their leaders in His hand. When any nation turns to ungodly living God will bring them problems, tragedies and challenges that are given to bring them back to Him.

What would Jesus do with regard to citizenship in a country if He were on earth today? He would certainly be a great citizen who worked to make the world better by example and effort. He would stand against wrong living no matter who did it. He would condemn sin and sinful attitudes from the ruler of the country and for any other leader in the nation. But Jesus would keep priorities on the things that matter most in life. His primary interest is always in saving the people from sin and not the national pride of the people. We are wise when we follow His example and make everyone welcome in church and allow them to choose the side they wish politically but point out the wrong and immoral behavior of any leader to challenge all to right living.

I love many of the "Christmas songs". Many of them do an absolutely amazing job of presenting the good news about Jesus coming into the world to be our savior. Certainly there are some that have things in them that aren't exactly right. But if you listen to any of the "Christian stations" or even tune into some source of contemporary Christian music or the old songs done on the Gaither hour there are some things in any of them that aren't exactly right. Should we then refuse to listen to any of the singing because of an error in some of the songs? Wouldn't that be like someone saying we ought not to read from a translation of the Bible because it has some errors in it? How long would it take to realize there aren't any translations that don't have some errors in them? People make translations. I believe good, honest, scholarly people who intend to translate everything exactly right normally serve as translators, especially when it is a standard translation with large numbers of translators from varied backgrounds. But they are human and they make mistakes. So I think we ought to listen and sing the "Christmas songs" with gusto. If we see something in the song that is wrong then either change the error to truth, skip that verse or use a different song. But don't throw out the baby with the bath wash.

But where does the Bible ever mention anything about Christmas? Didn't the whole Christmas idea come much later and didn't it come out of the Catholic Church? Certainly the word "Christmas" isn't in the Bible and yes it is true that whole idea arose later and had its origin in the Catholic Church. Does that mean it is wrong to celebrate the birth of Jesus? Isn't it true that it is good to celebrate any aspect of Jesus coming into the world as one of us to make a way for our salvation?

Let's be clear there are many things that go on in the name of "Christmas" that are just plain wrong. To use the birth of Christ and some folks bringing him gifts as an excuse for spending money we don't have to give things that people don't need and usually don't have a place to put them anyway, is ridiculous. When we begin to put up all the different decorations we probably ought to find out what those things are saying to other folks. For one to use the Christmas celebration as their only time to go to church each year or even one of their two times since they go on Easter as well, is wrong.

But my real question is this: Why in the world would we refuse to talk about and celebrate the birth of Jesus at the time when people all around us are doing so? Why not tell the world what Jesus did and what it means to us while the topic is on their mind? Why not teach them what the Bible really says about Jesus birth and then tell about how he emptied himself of deity to become a man and then humbled himself as a man and became obedient unto death, even death on the cross? (Philippians 2:5-10) Why not point out that though he was rich, for our sakes he became poor that you through his poverty might become rich? (2 Corinthians 8:9) Why not tell people that Jesus didn't just come into the world as a baby in a manger, he grew up and became a man who taught us how to live and demonstrated that life for us and ultimately went to the cross to pay the price for our sins so we can be saved by his grace?

As a boy growing up in rural Alabama I was in a bunch of Christmas plays. I was a shepherd a few times, an angel at least one time (There were likely reasons I didn't play the angel more than once); I was Joseph a couple of times. Along the way I think I played every part except Mary and the baby Jesus. To be sure these were not big productions. I guess my mother made whatever costume was involved. But I know this; every boy and girl learned some things about Jesus and his birth we would not likely ever forget. I also know there were some parents who came to see their child in the Christmas play that never came to church otherwise. It is that very prospect that by doing things like a Christmas play that just might bring in a parent, or grandparent that would never come otherwise and who just might stay on for worship and hear the whole gospel story of that baby who became the Messiah, and made it possible for even me and you to be saved from our sins. In that way one just might be won to Christ.

How often will such an opportunity come to get that unbeliever there where they can hear the gospel preached by us ignoring Christmas or even trying to tell them how they are all wrong? Let's sing, "Joy to the world, the Lord has come, let earth receive her king."

KEEP IT IN THE FAMILY

One of the hardest lessons a child has to understand is what is appropriate to tell out in public and what should remain inside the family. I doubt there has ever been a parent that wasn't embarrassed at some point when their child blurted out something about life in the family circle that they didn't want told. Often that child is telling a teacher either in school or Sunday school about something in their home life. When the child comes home and tells everyone what they said, there are red faces, a feeling of consternation and a quick lecture on what should be shared with others and what should remain in the family.

It should first of all be clear to a child that if there were things going on in the family that endangers them or some other member of the family, keeping it secret would be wrong. But if it is just something foolish, and embarrassing to the family then the secret ought to stay there. No matter how devoted the family may be to God and each other there will be things that happen behind closed doors that they wouldn't want a child going out to tell. Sometimes it is because they understand that the child isn't mature enough to grasp the meaning behind what happened. Their innocent testimony may well be a misinterpretation of something that was not wrong and may even have been a special time in the family.

That same principle is true with regard to the spiritual family, the church. Think for a moment about some of the things Scripture says on this whole topic. Paul said that we should "Provide things honest in the sight of all people." He was concerned about what the world thought about the church and their honesty. When Jesus discussed the matters of greatest importance with the disciples before he was crucified, he said, "A new commandment I give to you that you love one another as I have loved you. By this all people will know that you are my disciples because you have love for one another." (John 13:34-35) In John 17:20-21 Jesus is praying his amazing prayer for the disciples. He had prayed for God to keep those who had been with him. Then he said, "I do not pray for these alone but all those who will believe on my name through their word, that they all may be one, Father, as you are in me and I in you that they may be one in us, so the world will believe that you have sent me."

Think of these matters for a moment. What people see and hear about the church and the love we have for each other will have a tremendous amount of influence on them. It may well determine whether they become Christians themselves or reject God's church all together. What will most impress people about the church won't be their teachings, their organization or even how well they take care of the poor among them. Most of all they will look at their unity and their love for each other.

Of course there will be times when one Christian has a strong disagreement with another Christian. Most of the time it will be a disagreement about something one of them believes is in the Bible that the other believes is a misinterpretation of the Scriptures. Sometimes it will just be a disagreement on some matter of judgment such as when Paul and Barnabas disagreed about whether or not John Mark should go back out with them on their second missionary journey.

Whatever the area of disagreement may be, if it is something that I feel is important enough to affect a person's relationship with God I need to confront the person who believes the wrong. Paul gave Timothy instructions on how to go about such confrontation in 2 Timothy 2:24-26. He told him to not be quarrelsome but kind to everyone, able to teach and not resentful. He told him to gently instruct the other person in hope that God will grant them repentance leading them to knowledge of the truth and will come to their senses and escape the devils trap. A tremendous illustration of how this is carried out in real life is when Apollos came to Ephesus to preach Christ. He was a great speaker and teacher who knew the Old Testament scriptures well. But he only knew about the baptism of John. Aquila and Priscilla were living there at the time and they took him aside and showed him the way more accurately. They didn't challenge him in front of the whole church. They didn't call a crowd together to tell them how they had confronted Apollos. They didn't put the whole matter on Facebook to arouse all kinds of attention and antagonism against Apollos. They wanted to save Apollos for the great work ahead, not take the fire out of his life.

When people attack some other church or fellow member of the body in a public way, one has to wonder if they are really trying to save the person or make a name for themselves. We need to love fellow Christ follower enough to correct them in love. When we do so many times we will learn that it wasn't the other person who was mistaken but us.

LEAVING, BEING JOINED

When God made Eve and brought her to Adam it was as a "helper suitable for him." Man and woman were made for each other. It wasn't that God makes a specific man or woman for each of us. I hear all too often that "I married the wrong person." The idea seems to be that if I had just found the right person then marriage would be wonderful.

Most of the time it isn't a matter of the person but of how we treat each other in the marriage. God doesn't have some specific one built in heaven to match your specific specifications. If things aren't going well at home it isn't because you messed up and married the wrong person. It is because the right persons aren't conducting themselves, as they should in the marriage relationship.

Imagine the scene when God caused Adam to go sound asleep and took a rib from his side to make the woman that he brought to the man. Adam looked at her and declared, "This is bone of my bone and flesh of my flesh. She will be called woman. For this reason a man will leave his father and mother and be joined to his wife and the two will be one flesh." Neither Adam nor Eve had a father and mother to leave so they could be joined to each other. But God gave Adam a formula for successful marriage that would apply to all marriages in all ages of time. Focus on the key elements of this declaration.

We are of the same humanity. She is bone of my bone and flesh of my flesh. Neither the man nor the woman is made of some inferior product and is beneath the other person. Remember when as children we heard that girls are made of sugar and spice and every thing nice and boys are made of spiders and snakes and puppy dog tales. It was cute, but not for real. We are made differently but of exactly the same materials. We share the place of being made in God's image and likeness and of Him longing for a relationship with us. As long as anyone thinks of his or her marriage partner as somehow inferior to him or her or superior to him or her, the marriage is in trouble. There are no senior or junior partners in marriage.

Leave father and mother. The ties between a boy or girl and their parents are often so strong that you can't even imagine loosening such ties. Parents, think, "this is my little girl" or "this is my little boy." I brought them into the world. What do you mean we have to loosen the ties between us? Far too often a marriage is destroyed because either the parents won't turn loose of the newly married one or the newly married won't leave father and mother. Why does it matter anyway? It matters because in marriage we need to look to each other for love, answers, assistance and partnership. If every time there is a problem she calls home to find out what daddy can do about it, then he feels like the third wheel in the relationship. If he calls home every time there is a problem to see what mom or dad says then she feels I'm still married to a little boy that doesn't have a clue how to be a man yet. What does it mean to leave father and mother? It means you lean on each other. It means you look to each other for companionship. It means you are working to try to please each other rather than anyone else, besides God. It means you don't call mom or dad to go through everything that is going on in your married life together. When you start telling them all that is wrong with the one you chose they will treat them more and more as an outsider in the family and as a loser in life.

Be joined to your husband or wife. It intrigues me that the word used by God means to be glued to another person. When you stick to each other it means you enjoy being with each other no matter what you are doing or not doing. When a man only seems to want to be with his wife when they are headed to bed for sex, it makes her feel like a sex tool instead of a marriage partner. If you are joined together you constantly work to strengthen the glue between you instead of trying to find a way to loosen its grip. Being joined is the development of a strong "Like" for each other. Love is wonderful and we all need to love and be loved. But the kind of love that matters so much in marriage is the love of liking another person and enjoying being in their presence no matter what we do. Every time temptation arises to unglue from each other and become glued to someone else, we should increase the glue with each other all the more. Get closer and don't let Satan get between you. By the way Satan gets between you by means of mom and dad many times. Sometimes he eases between you with some other person that you allow into the place in your heart that belongs to your marriage partner. Our joining is also tied to each other and walking hand in hand serving God.

When you build this bond in marriage the result is you can be naked and unashamed as they were. Their whole self, mind, body and soul was joined to each other. There were no walls that they allowed to be constructed between them as a dividing line. When we are completely open with each other it results in such strong personal ties that we go together for a lifetime.

LET BROTHERLY LOVE CONTINUE

Do you have brothers? Being part of a large family with three brothers and four sisters gives one a different perspective of the command to continue in brotherly love. While it is true that the Bible describes five different kinds of love, there are two words for love used commonly in the New Testament. One is the "Agape" love that God has for us all the time, which is unconditional and deals more with behavior than feeling. The other word "Phileo" is the root from which we get the word for "Brotherly love". Philadelphia is the word and from that word we get the name for the city of brotherly love. In I Peter 1:22 both words are used in the same verse. "Having purified your souls by your obedience to the truth for a sincere brotherly love, love one another earnestly from a pure heart." Even when Jesus was questioning Peter about his love after the resurrection, he and Peter used both words interchangeably.

So what is involved in "Brotherly love?" For me brotherly love is different at different points in my life. I went through a time as a boy when I had something of a "Love – hate" relationship with my brothers. Since I was the youngest, I often felt picked on and left out of the things they could do and I couldn't. I never remember a time that my love for them wasn't such that I would defend them and their actions if anyone said anything negative about them. The old saying is "Blood is thicker than water' meaning that our physical relationships while sometimes stressed are always tight. If anyone said or did anything to hurt one of my brothers or sisters it has always been painful to me as well.

So what does it mean to love our brethren? He isn't talking about our physical families but our spiritual families. When we are born again into the family of the Lord, God is our father, and Jesus is our older brother but all Christians are our brothers and sisters in Christ. God longs for us to develop that kind of family love for each other inside the body. I can easily remember the day when you went to church and heard people generally refer to each other as brothers and sisters. If felt strange to me when I started preaching at 18 and people would come up and call me "Brother Barnes." I would look around to see if my dad was somewhere around. "Brother" shouldn't become a title used for preachers or some few others but we should see each other as brothers and sisters in the Lord.

If we are brothers and sisters there surely ought to be the longing to be together as often as possible. I always look forward to going back to the area of my birth to get to see family and spend some time catching up with everyone. If we in church don't really enjoy getting together, beyond just the times we meet for worship then we are missing the whole idea. If my brothers or sisters are sick or hurting, I am anxious over their recovery and will certainly be praying for their healing. Shouldn't that be commonly true in Christ? But what if that sickness isn't physical but spiritual illness? How do we show brotherly love for someone in our spiritual family who has drifted from the Lord or has gotten involved in some sin in their life?

If we are family, we certainly won't just accept the fact that someone has gone away from the Lord or his family and turned to sin. We will do everything possible to help them come back to the right way. In Matthew 18:15-17 Jesus said, "If your brother sins against you, go and tell him his fault, between you and him alone. If he listens to you, you have gained your brother. But if he does not listen, take one or two with you, that the evidence of two or three witnesses may establish every charge. If he refuses to listen to them, tell it to the church. And if he refuses to listen to the church, let him be to you as a Gentile or tax collector." Later Jesus brother James said, "My brothers, if anyone among you wanders from the truth and someone brings him back, let him know that whoever brings back a sinner from his wondering will save his soul from death and will cover a multitude of sins." (James 5:19-20)

Imagine being in a family and a new baby is born. How will a family react? If that baby is a brother or sister won't we do everything to take care of them and help them grow up healthy and strong? In God's spiritual family we also have new babies born into the family. Our job should be to reach out with love and compassion to accept them into the family and grow and become strong in his kingdom. Brotherly love is needed by all of us. Think of ways you can demonstrate such love to a brother or sister in the Lord today.

LIFE ON MISSION

Jesus came into this world with a clear mission. He became one of us, taking on human flesh and growing up in a normal, hardworking, and somewhat poor family with brothers and sisters. He stated his mission best in Luke 19:10 as the people around him couldn't grasp why he would go to the home of Zacchaeus, the tax collector. His answer that explained his entire life of ministry was "I've come to seek and save those who are lost." When we see that, as Jesus mission it makes it clear why he would choose ordinary men to be his apostles who could identify with the people around them. It makes sense why he spent time with people having huge sin problems in their life, such as the woman at the well or Legion. In his healing of people's diseases he often said, "Your sins are forgiven you." It was the signal that while they had a physical problem that needed healing they also had a greater problem with sin that needed forgiving.

Notice his mission wasn't to make us happy all the time. It wasn't to make sure we were healthy, wealthy and wise. It wasn't to deliver us from every social problem men face. It wasn't to liberate everyone who felt mistreated. His mission went so much deeper than all that. He wanted to save us from our sins. If we are saved from our sins we can, with his help begin working on solutions to the other problems. If one is dying with heart disease or cancer it will be tough to get the doctor to turn his attention to the pain we have in our little finger. He will work on the cancer or heart problems with view to dealing with the minor things later when the big ones are taken care of.

Near the end of Jesus ministry he said to the apostles, "As the Father sent me into the world, so I am sending you." His last great challenge to them was to "Go therefore and make disciples in all the nations, baptizing them into the name of the Father, the Son and the Holy Spirit, teaching them to observe all that I have commanded you." He gave them a mission that would drive their lives and ministry until the day they left this world in death. Most would die as martyrs for their faith. All would go through tough times to get the good news of Jesus out to the world. If you read 2 Corinthians 11 as Paul discusses the things he had gone through in his ministry you get a feeling of what it was like for them in fulfilling their mission.

Often we talk about the mission of the church as being to make disciples in every nation by baptizing them and teaching them to live as Jesus taught, but too often we miss the point that this is the mission of every follower of Christ. It isn't just a corporate command that is the real responsibility of the preachers or elders or maybe some small group in the church that is specially gifted to carry out God's mission for us. Think again of Jesus command to the apostles. They were to go and make disciples whom they would teach to observe the commands of Jesus which included as a primary part of it to go and make disciples, teaching them to observe all things, which would include them going and making disciples. The process goes on and on so that we all are a people on mission for the Lord. It isn't that we have a mission that we choose to do every once in a while. It is that we are missionaries to our world. Just like with Jesus we must be part of the culture we wish to reach for the Lord. We are to be in the world without being of the world. You can't lift another person out of the well of sin by jumping in with them. But you must identify with them, love them and be ready to drop the rope and pull them out then teach them how to keep from falling into the well again.

The world is absolutely full of people who don't know God and who have decided they don't need God. We live and work around people every day who need hope in their life but have no idea where to get it. Think today of how you can build a bridge between you and those you know who are without Christ and without hope in their life. Show them that you care about them; listen to their concerns and worries. Begin talking about the difference God has made in your life. Start opening the door to bring someone else to life to the full with Jesus. Think of Paul words to the Romans, "I'm in debt both to the Greeks and barbarians, both to the wise and unwise, so as much as is in me, I am ready to preach to you the gospel of Christ. For I am not ashamed of the gospel, for it is the power of God unto salvation, to everyone who believes to the Jew first and also to the Greek." (Romans 1:15-16)

LITTLE THINGS

While it is foolish to make mountains out of molehills, to strain out a gnat and swallow a camel, or treat the insignificant as if it were extremely important, small things still matter. Compare two statements from Jesus in regard to small things. In Matthew 23:23 He said, "You Scribes, Pharisees, hypocrites who pay tithe of mint, anise and cumin, but have omitted the weightier matters of the law, justice, mercy and faith." In Luke 9:42 He said, "For it is the one who is least among you all who is the greatest." Later Jesus told several stories that explain how little things could make a huge difference. In the story of the master giving servants talents of gold according to their abilities, they were to use it while he was away. The one given 5 talents gained 5 more. The one given 2 talents gained 2 more. But the one given the one talent hid his because he was afraid. When the master returned he said to the first two, "Well done you good and faithful servant. You have been faithful over a few things, I'll make you ruler over many, enter the joys of your lord." Immediately after this story Jesus told of the judgment scene when he would separate the faithful from the unfaithful, the sheep from the goats. To those on the right he said, "Come, inherit the kingdom prepared for you from the foundation of the earth." He explained to them that they had fed him when he was hungry, given him drink when he was thirsty, clothed him when he was naked, visited him when he was sick and in prison. They didn't know they had done any of those things. He explained, "Truly I tell you, whatever you did for one of the least of these brothers of mine you did for me."

While it is foolish to make a big deal over the insignificant, we need to be very aware that God blesses us in big ways when we are faithful in little things. The poor widow only gave two small coins worth less than a penny, yet in the economy of Jesus she gave more than all the others. It is worth noticing that it was typically little acts of service to others or to God that He regarded as matters of major importance.

During Jesus earthly ministry it was often the things we would consider insignificant that made a difference in people's lives. He touched a leper before healing him. He took little children into his arms and blessed them. He washed the disciples feet. All such things demonstrated his faithfulness in his mission on earth.

When we are faithful to the Lord and His work in the smallest things he opens doors for us to serve in bigger areas and blesses us with bigger opportunities. In Luke 19 there is a story from Jesus that sounds very much like the parable of the talents in Matthew 25. But there are significant ways in which it differs. The master in this story is one who is being made king over an area. He is going away to be anointed as the king. While he is away he gave servants an amount of money, each the same amount and told them to use it while he was gone. When he returned after being made the king, even though the people hadn't wanted him as their king, he calls those servants to him. One man had taken the money and multiplied it ten times. The master commended his faithfulness and gave him rule over ten cities. The second had gained five and the master commended his faithfulness and gave him rule over five cities. The other took his and hid it out of fear for the master. The master condemned him as a lazy and wicked servant. He told the servants to take his money away and give it to the one with ten for to the one who has more will be given and from the one who does not have even what he has will be taken from him. In this story the king then called those who didn't want him as king and had them killed before him. But the point of the story was that how they used the money he gave them was a test to see how faithful they would be to him. He gave them authority in the kingdom to the same degree that they increased the money he gave them. God blesses us now according to how faithful we are with the small opportunities he places before us. But even more significant is the fact he will bless us in eternity based on our faithfulness in the small things he puts before us now. When we think we are too big or too important to do some small service that is needed in the body of Christ today, we are cutting ourselves off from the big opportunities God has planned for the faithful.

In the story of the king giving the money to the servants in Luke 19, one of the amazing points is the king saying take the money from the one who didn't use it and give it to the one with ten. The people replied, "Why him?" Why not give it to the one with five to make them more equal? The principle laid down there is one Jesus offered on other occasions as well. "To him who has, more will be given. But from him who does not have, even what he has will be taken away." The more we do with the small opportunities God opens for us, the greater the opportunities he puts before us.

LOOK AGAIN

Have you noticed how easy it is to get stuck in our thinking? If you've ever been in an automobile that is stuck you can see the analogy easily. When you are stuck in your car you just can't go anywhere and the more you try to get out the deeper you get into the mud. If we get stuck in a car or truck there is always someone with four-wheel drive or a wrecker service that can come and pull us out. But when we get stuck in our thinking it is much less likely that anyone will either try or be able if they try to pull us out of it.

So many people are nervous today about church concerns and what will happen in the future. Some are certain that if anyone changes anything from where we have been for 50 years then it will be apostasy from the faith. The reality is we always need to be willing to re-examine our beliefs on all matters over and over again all through the years. There are tons of things that I felt very sure of when I was 25 that I don't feel the same way about now. I still believe the Bible as much as I did then. But I've come to see that some of my ideas were based on either poor translations of God's word or poor application by me. Sometimes it was a matter of accepting the logic I had heard from someone else and just assumed it was valid but when I really began to dig into it myself, I realized it was wrong.

Was I right with God at 25 when I believed some things that I now see differently? Of course I was. Our being right with God doesn't depend on us being right about everything we believe or none of us would be right with God. Consider the fact that Jesus had been teaching the apostles night and day for more than two years and some of them more than three years, yet when he reached the end of his earthly ministry he said there were still many things that he had to say to them, to teach them, but they weren't ready for it yet. He promised to send them the Holy Spirit to guide them into all truth. Would you think that the moment the Holy Spirit came upon them on the day of Pentecost they were immediately corrected about everything? If so that would mean the Holy Spirit was a far better teacher in one day than Jesus had been in three years.

Consider Peter preaching on Pentecost and saying, "Whoever calls on the name of the Lord will be saved." And then later saying after telling them what to do to be saved, "For the promise is unto you and to your children and to all who are afar off, as many as the Lord our God shall call." Can you read that and not realize he was saying the gospel was for all people? Before Jesus ascended he told them they would be witnesses in Jerusalem, Judea, Samaria and the uttermost parts of the earth." But in Acts 10, some ten years after Pentecost and the Lord's ascension message, when God called Peter to go preach to the family of Cornelius the Gentile, he had to perform a miracle and show Peter clearly that the gospel was for everyone. When Peter arrived at Cornelius home he said, "I most certainly understand now that God is not one to show partiality, but in every nation the man who fears Him and does what is right is welcome to Him." It was hard for him to get it. Years later Paul would have to call him out according to Galatians 2 when he came to Antioch and played the hypocrite by separating from the Gentiles to no longer eat with them when Some of the Jewish Christians arrived.

If it took a while for the apostles to learn better and they had been with Jesus all that time and they had the baptism of the Holy Spirit, how crazy it is when we think we have gotten the whole truth by the time we are 25 or 30 years old or by the time we are 68 or 78.

But, doesn't it show disrespect for those who taught us when we say they were wrong about what they taught? I don't know about you but the teachers I have great respect for constantly encouraged me to study and think for myself instead of just taking what they said as the law and gospel.

Don't be afraid to take a fresh look at what the Bible teaches on anything. If what we've said has been wrong then before God, let's change and be right in what we are doing. If you are serious about studying any topic don't be satisfied with just studying from the King James Version of Scripture. It is over 400 years old. The language has changed. There have been tons of things learned about the text and manuscripts discovered that are much older and much better than what the King James was based on. We are trying to get to know God and understand His story from beginning to end. We don't worship the Bible and certainly not some Version of the Bible. We worship the God who gave us the Bible, written through men out of their personality and experience. The Bible wasn't dictated but "Holy men of God spoke as they were carried along by the Holy Spirit." (2 Peter 1:19-21)

LOOK AT ME

Remember those days when your children were small and they seemed constantly to be saying to you, "Look at me, Mommy" or "Look at me, Daddy." There is a fairly short period in a child's life, normally when they seemed to want more than anything to be watched by those of their family. Every deed seems to be a performance and it wouldn't hold its value unless those who are precious in their lives see it.

While most children get past this stage in life and reach a time when they seem instead to be trying to be invisible in the family, some never stop needing the spotlight to be on them. As they get older and it is no longer acceptable for them to say, "Look at me" all the time, they try to gain the attention of their family or loved ones by being outlandish in some way, sometimes even by doing things that they know will bring a rebuke or punishment. During this time it seems that a person's need to be seen or to have your attention runs deeper than any concern for doing what is right.

In most of our lives there came a time when our understanding of God affected the desire to be seen by others. Like Adam and Eve in the Garden of Eden, when we see ourselves as we really are, our motivation is to run and hide from God. Their sense of shame caused them to try to cover their nakedness with fig leaves. We are a whole lot like the child that covers his own eyes so that you can't see them. If they can't see you then they reason that you can't see them. Notice when Adam and Eve hid from the Lord, God's immediate response was, "Who told you that you were naked? Have you eaten of the forbidden tree?"

When we are living in a right relationship with God, the thought that His eye is forever on us is comforting. It means that we are never alone. As the song declares, "His eye is on the Sparrow and I know He watches me." In I Peter 3:12 there is a quote from Psalms 34:12-16 which says, "For the eyes of the Lord are on the righteous and his ears are attentive to their prayers, but the face of the Lord is against those who do evil." Peter quoted from three verses of the Psalm but the song David wrote went on with the following words: "But the face of the Lord is against those who do evil, to blot out their name from the earth. The righteous cry out, and the Lord hears them; he delivers them from all their troubles. The Lord is close to the brokenhearted and saves those who are crushed in spirit. The righteous person may have many troubles but the Lord delivers him from them all; he protects all his bones not one of them will be broken. Evil will slay the wicked; the foes of the righteous will be condemned. The Lord will rescue his servants; no one who takes refuge in him will be condemned."

God's eyes are on us. He watches over us all the time. He isn't watching so he can catch us in some wrong. He watches to give us strength and encouragement, to lessen our fears and to help us know that we are never alone. He not only teaches us to pray, he promises to hear when we pray. Unlike many of us, his hearing never gets bad and his attention is never drawn away from them.

Recently I was visiting with a friend who had gone to see a counselor about some challenges he was facing. I asked how the counseling was going and he said that over all it had been good, but that he felt like he was boring the counselor to death. I asked why he felt that way about the counselor and noted that he was a good person and well qualified as a counselor. He said that he had dozed off one time when he was telling about a particularly trying time in his life. Another time he had kept fooling with his phone, like he was reading something on it. On some occasions he had asked the same question over to him twice in one session.

A person who is living for God need never worry that God has dozed off when they are facing trouble or trials. His eyes are upon us and his ears are open to our cries. The thing that makes this all the more powerful is that even when we don't have the right words to say to God in prayer the Holy Spirit is interceding for us and putting our words in the right form to be presented to the Father. (Romans 8:26) No wonder the writer of Hebrews says that we should come boldly to the throne of grace that we may obtain mercy and find grace to help in time of need (Hebrews 4:16).

Thank you Father for always having your eyes upon and your ears open to our prayers.

LOVE A PHARISEE

You will look in vain to find a time when any of the gospel writers picture Jesus saying of a Pharisee, "Oh how he loved him." Looking at the gospel accounts it is easy for us to develop a pretty hateful attitude toward the Pharisees. As a matter of fact I don't know anyone who wouldn't be offended if you called them Pharisaical. What is amazing is that in that time, among the Jews as a whole, the Pharisees were deeply admired. They were strong in their beliefs. They were devoted to the law or Torah, as they would have referred to it. They tended to be very strict in their efforts to follow the law completely. Why then did Jesus seem to always run counter to them?

I wonder if the beginning of the antagonism wasn't when he preached the Sermon on the Mount and said, "Unless your righteousness exceeds that of the Scribes and Pharisees you can't enter the kingdom of God." Jesus took the two religious groups of the day who were most devoted to the Word of God and said our righteousness had to exceed theirs. Certainly he wasn't saying that our devotion to the word had to exceed theirs. They were completely devoted to what the law said. He actually explained how our righteousness had to exceed theirs in the remainder of chapter five of Matthew. He would say, "You have heard it said…. but I say unto you" with regard to several different important matters of the law. He dealt with murder, adultery, divorce, swearing, punishment, revenge and love and each time referred to how they had interpreted the law of God on these topics and then offered the correct interpretation. Each time he went for the heart instead of just the outward actions that led to the violation of the law.

Instead of just forbidding murder, he challenged us not to be angry and hold on to it. He said to settle problems quickly and not call people by degrading names. Instead of just not committing adultery he challenged us not to look lustfully on another. Instead of just giving the wife a bill of divorcement and putting her away he challenged us to work at keeping their covenant of marriage. All the way through he gave them a whole different view of the Law of God.

There is a major question that should stand out for all people who study God's word and especially the life and teachings of Christ. Does my study of the Bible make me more like Jesus or like the Pharisees? They loved the Word of God, but Jesus loved the God of the Word. I can fall in love with the Bible and studying the Bible and miss the point that the entire Bible is to lead me to a devoted love for God. That really was the point of Jesus saying that the greatest commandment was to love God with all our heart, soul, mind and strength and to love our neighbor as our self was the second greatest.

Can you remember getting love notes or love letters from your wife or husband when you first fell in love? If we had to be away from each other even for a night or two it was difficult and we would write these loving letters and cards to each other to express our love and devotion. It is a good thing to keep those notes and letters and go back at times to rekindle the flame of love that was there. Often when couples come to me saying they have fallen out of love for each other I will ask them to go home and find all those love notes they wrote in days past and have kept somewhere in a box or drawer and reread all those notes. Often the feelings of love begin to burn again as we go back. But it would be completely foolish if one of the couple came back to me later and said, "Leon, Thank you for having me to go back and read all those love notes. I have fallen completely in love with one of the letters that he wrote me back when we were eighteen." I would quickly say, "Look, you missed the point. You were to read those to fall back in love with him, not his letters."

Just as a wife keeps the love notes in the box and treasures those letters we should treasure the word of God, but not to fall in love with the notes but to fall more deeply in love with God who gave us the word. When we fall in love with the word it typically results in our becoming tied to our interpretation of the word and being very judgmental of anyone who sees that passage of Scripture in a different way. The Pharisee attitude was one of enforcement. If you don't follow the law in the way I understand you need to be stoned as with the woman caught in adultery in John 8. Jesus way was to convict them of their sin and to tell the woman, "Neither do I condemn you. Go and sin no more." He was looking for a life change from the woman not a way to punish her for her wrongs. Notice that Jesus didn't say she hadn't done anything wrong or that adultery wasn't so bad after all. He instead challenged her to change and offered her hope.

The great challenge is for us to love God and study His word to learn more of him so I can love and serve him better. Never substitute the things of God for God Himself. He couldn't be contained in a manmade temple and he can't be contained inside the covers of the book that leads us to Him.

MASTERS OF THE INSIGNIFICANT

"Here is the sixty four thousand dollar question." It seems that as far back as I can remember there have been game shows on TV and radio that had contestants to answer questions about things that were of no real consequence and the ones who could answer those questions moved ahead. Because of the use of a phone to call a friend who might help with the answer whole new ideas arose with the game show. What has always amazed me is the amount of people who must have studied to learn all the useless information they could come up with to be contestants on such shows. As a teenager, when $64,000.00 was a huge amount of money, I marveled at one man who remained a contestant on that shows for weeks, never missing a question and defeating one person after another. Back at that time there weren't computers on which you could

Google such information. I suppose he was reading from encyclopedias to remember such.

Can you remember when you were in school and taking test thinking to yourself and probably complaining to whoever would listen, "Why do we need to know this stuff?" For a time I thought if I filled my mind with such trivia there wouldn't be room for all that important material that I wanted to remember. Now we know that the brain is able to handle far more than any of us put into it. Most of us die having used only a small percentage of the capacity of our mind. But, it is true that we often fill our thinking, our time and our energy with things that are useless in the long run.

When Jesus confronted the religious leaders for paying tithes of the herbs in their garden while omitting the more important matters of justice, mercy and faith he was pleading for us to devote ourselves to the things that really mattered. When Paul wrote the Book of Romans in chapter 14 as he dealt with matters of conscience on which people were having disagreements, he noted that foods and drinks were not what mattered in life. He said the kingdom isn't about food and drink but about righteousness, peace and joy in the Holy Spirit. Time and energy do have limits and we can use up our time and energy on things that won't matter within a few days, much less in a few years or in eternity.

When Jesus was going about teaching people in all the different villages he used a phrase often that was intended to call people's attention to what was about to be said. Our KJV of the Bible translates it, "Verily, verily I say to you." Most of the newer translations have it as "Truly, truly I say to you." It probably carries the same point that one saying, "Listen up now" has today. In every case it is an effort to say that here is something that is significant that people ought to hear.

Have you played Bible Trivia before? The name of the game always troubled me to the degree I had trouble even playing it. The notion of information in the Bible just being trivia just didn't seem right to me. I certainly understand that not all matters in Scripture are equal in their importance. If that were the case Jesus couldn't have answered the question "What is the first and great commandment?" as he did. In the love chapter of the Bible, I Corinthians 13, Paul concludes the chapter by saying, "Now abides faith, hope and love, but the greatest of these is love." No wonder David prayed "Lord, open my eyes that I might see wondrous things in your word."

One of the things a parent can do that will make a huge difference in the life of their children is to help them separate the big things in life from the insignificant. When we treat every lesson we teach our children as though they were huge matters we do them a disservice. Determine what really matters in their life and key in on the things that will affect them in life and in eternity and stress them regularly. One day your children will praise your efforts in training them for good.

MOTIVE MATTERS

Jesus and the apostles were in the temple courts, in the area often referred to as the court of the Gentiles or the court of the women. In that area of the temple there were large treasury containers where a worshiper of God could come and put in money as an offering to God and His work. Some of these containers were for specific areas of work that they would support, such as benevolence. In Luke 21:1-4 it sounds as though Jesus and his disciples just happened to be there and Jesus looked up and saw the people putting their gifts into the temple treasury. Mark's account in Mark 12:41-44 it says "Jesus sat down opposite the place where the offerings were put and watched the crowd putting their money into the temple treasury." Either way, he watched them as they gave. Some came with great wealth and put in large amounts of money. A poor widow came and dropped in two pennies. He then offered his commentary on what was happening to the disciples.

"Truly I tell you this poor widow has put in more than all the others. All these people gave their gifts out of their wealth; but she out of her poverty put in all she had to live on."

If you looked at the gifts people were giving it was certainly the case that the wealthy were giving far greater amounts of money. But Jesus looked at their motives. He looked at what they gave in comparison to what they were able to give. He looked at the sacrifice involved. It was a consistent theme with Jesus that heart matters most. He sought from us a love for God with out whole being. He wanted a commitment that puts the kingdom and righteousness first then thinks of matters like food, clothes and shelter. When Jesus told the story of the Pharisee and the tax collector who went down to the temple to pray he demonstrated that heart matters most. The Pharisee certainly had the actions down pat. He gave his tithes regularly. He fasted far more than the tax collector. He had his religious credentials in order. The tax collector was embarrassed to even come before the Lord. He couldn't look up. He couldn't raise his hands or shout an "amen." Instead bowed humbly and struck his chest declaring, "God be merciful to me a sinner." Jesus looked at the heart, the motive of each man and declared it was the tax collector who went down to his house justified that day. Motives matter.

Motives matter even to us. If a husband brings home a dozen red roses each time he messes up, it won't take the wife long to figure out that his motives in bringing the roses is to show penance, not to demonstrate his love and passion toward her. In Philippians 2:3-4 Paul said, "Do nothing out of selfish ambition or vain conceit. Rather, in humility value others above yourselves, not looking to your own interests but each of you to the interests of others."

If we come to God with a pure heart wanting to please him and do what is right but we fail to get it all just right, we are more likely to receive God's blessings and praise than if we come doing everything just right but with a prideful attitude.

But how can we know the motives of another person? I know God knows our hearts and judges those motives, but how can we know? Nothing is more common that having one person question the motives of another and makes strong accusations of some wrongdoing. But are we correct when we say to another person, "I know why you did that or why you said that. In I Corinthians 2:10b-11 it says, "The Spirit searches all things, even the deep things of God. For who knows a person's thoughts except their own spirit within them?" We can see what people do and hear what they say, but only God and His Holy Spirit can know the motives or thoughts the person has when saying what they say or doing what they do.

Imagine how far it would go in helping us to have good relationships with other people if we stopped judging their motives and simply looked at what they said or did as being from a pure heart. Most marriage counselors would be out of business since a huge proportion of what is revealed in such sessions is what one believes is the motives of the other. Usually the other partner will declare that what the person thought they meant wasn't at all what they were thinking. But few are willing to accept the statements of the other because they are sure they know their motives and they aren't good. No matter how well you may have honed your abilities in reading the minds and motives of another person, you can never be sure you are right in your judgments. No one knows the mind of another except his or her spirit within him or her. That is a big truth that it is extremely important for us to learn and believe.

MY FRIENDS

Have you read the Book of Job lately? Job was a really good man who had some devoted friends. I suspect they had enjoyed some wonderful times together in the past, talking about life, family and their work in the world. But things had changed. Job had been recognized as one of the richest, most powerful men in the east. Even God had called attention to his faith and dedication. But life was different for him now. He had lost his wealth all in one day. Storms, thieves and disaster had come upon him suddenly. All ten of his children had been killed in a windstorm on one day. Besides that, his wife had determined that his life of faith and holding on to God was a waste and was encouraging him to curse God and die. But then, his three dearest friends heard of his horrible situation. They left whatever business or family obligations they may have had and came to visit and encourage their friend Job. When they arrived and saw the agony he was in, sitting in a pile of ashes scraping the sores that were all over his body, from the top of his head to the bottom of his feet, they were so moved that they sat down and remained silent for the next week. Can you imagine going to see a hurting friends and being so moved that you just sat down and said nothing for a week?

Were they real friends? I think so. I think they loved Job and wanted to be his closest companion during an extremely hard time. But something happened after that week had passed. Job began to cry out in agony and to declare his innocence and how unfair it was that God was pouring out such punishment on him as a faithful servant. Anything that made God look bad or indicated that he might not be treating a person fairly was offensive to them. They began making their speeches to Job and ultimately to God and anyone else who might listen. It offended them deeply that Job would declare his innocence and it offended them even more that he would even imply that God wasn't treating him fairly.

Because of their faulty belief system, there was only one way for them to react that would seem appropriate. They set out to attack Job and to defend the justice and fairness of God. Since there was no way for them to believe that God would actually bring such disaster on a righteous person and he certainly had faced major disaster, Job must not be righteous. He had seemed so to them all along. They didn't know of any particular sin in his life. But there must be some hidden sin that God knew about that he was punishing. If you take the time to read all the speeches of Job's friends you will hear them accuse his children of living such ungodly lives that God had to destroy them and Job was accused of mistreating the poor, the widow and the orphan. He was accused of not paying his workers fairly thus cheating them. They accused him of looking lustfully on young women. It is even implied that he might have bowed to an idol at some point. Now, Job each time responded to their accusations by denying that he had done anything wrong. They told him if he would just confess the sin in his life and turn from it then God's blessings would again flow for him.

All of the friends were doing what they believed was right. They were being consistent with their understanding of God. Their grasp was that good things happen to good people and bad things happen to bad people. If good things are happening to you, you must be a good person. If bad things are happening to you, you obviously are a bad person. It was far easier and more reasonable to them to attack their friend's integrity than to question their beliefs.

The problem was, they were mistaken in their beliefs. Good things happen to good and bad people and bad things happen to both good and bad people. It took God confronting them and demanding they ask Job to pray for them so they could be forgiven, for them to see the error of their way. In the process of defending himself from their accusations Job also said some foolish things he needed to repent of. But he was still a righteous man, who loved and served God. Ultimately God's blessings again flowed into his life and his family.

If our beliefs lead us to attack good people it may mean we need to question our beliefs instead of the other person's integrity.

There is a local heating and air company that advertises for their services by saying they "are solving problems no one else can, through building science." Every time I hear that advertisement I think to myself that they are a pretty arrogant bunch to think they can do something no one else can do. If the ad just said they could do something no one else in the area could do it would be a little more reasonable. But when you put no such limits on it and simply state that no one else can do what you can it is quite a statement.

I was watching the new TV show "Elementary" that is about Sherlock Holmes the other night. In one of the scenes his helper challenged him for thinking that he was the smartest person in the world. He responded that no he wouldn't say that and she started to compliment him by saying that was the most humble statement she had ever heard him make. He said, "No I wasn't being humble, there was just no way to prove who is the smartest person in the world."

Every person in the world is unique. It is absolutely amazing that each person has a different fingerprint or DNA. You would think that by now there would certainly be several million duplicates. When does God run out of new designs to put into play? Think of the times when phone numbers begin to run out and certain patterns have to be added to keep the system moving forward.

But when it comes to our abilities and understanding of things it is seldom wise to declare that we have answers no one else has or abilities no one else has. When you read the Bible and come to the story of the Pharisee and tax collector going down to the temple to pray, what is your reaction? Remember the Pharisee began to pray and Luke tells us "The Pharisee stood and was praying this to himself: 'God, I thank you that I am not like other people: swindlers, unjust, adulterers, or even like this tax collector. I fast twice a week; I pay tithes of all that I get.' But the tax collector, standing some distance away, was even unwilling to lift up his eyes to heaven, but was beating his breast, saying, 'God be merciful to me, the sinner!' Jesus responded to the story by saying that it was the tax collector that went down to his house justified that day not the religious leader. When you read it, which do you identify with? Which do you come away feeling that you want to be like them? I don't think I've ever met anyone who said, "That Pharisee is my hero."

But in much of life we are arrogant. From childhood we get into the habit of saying, "My dad is better than your dad." "My mom is a better cook than yours." "My car is nicer than yours." "My job is better than yours." Every thing in life seems to be an area for us to compare with each other and think our ways are superior.

Even in spiritual matters we often follow the Pharisee. "My church is better than yours." "I'm more spiritual than you." "I pray more than you do." "I give more than you do."

Think of the apostle Paul in this regard. He marveled that God would accept him and put him into ministry after he had failed him so badly. He didn't point to his many talents or how much he knew. He pointed to his guilt. "I am chief of sinners." "I was before a blasphemer and a persecutor. I was injurious to the cause of Christ."

It is strange how distasteful arrogance is in other people while it seems so reasonable in us. It would be far better for all of us to marvel at how gracious God is to accept and use people like us who have failed him so many times instead of thinking to our selves how fortunate God is to have us as his children. Praise God for his marvelous and overwhelming grace.

NOT FAR AWAY

Try putting yourself into the scene when Jesus was teaching and debating with the teachers of the law. One teacher realizes that Jesus is answering them wisely so he raised the big question. "Of all the commandments, which is the most important?" (Mark 12:28) It is a great question.

How would you have answered the man? I'm sure some would have said, "There are no special commands. Everyone of God's commands are extremely important and to break one is as bad as another." But Jesus didn't respond in that way.

He said, "The most important one is this: "Hear, O Israel: The Lord our God, the Lord is one. Love the Lord your God with all your heart and with all your soul and with your entire mind and with all your strength. The second is this: Love your neighbor as yourself. There is no commandment greater than these." (Mark 12:29-31) Some commands of the Lord are more important than others. There may even be times when it requires me to not obey a lesser command in order to obey the greater one. Jesus went further with the answer than the lawyer had intended. He only asked for the greatest command or most important. Jesus gave him number one and number two.

Can you obey either of these commands without doing anything about your love for God or neighbor? The word used for love in this text involves action. It is a behavioral love. When we love God with all our being we submit to Him in all He asked us to do. When we love our neighbor it will lead to action in helping, serving and blessing the neighbor. If one really loves God he will also love his neighbor. If you were to build a pyramid of love, how would it go?

Love God
Love wife or husband (Ephesians 5:25-27)
Love your children (Titus 2:1-4)
Love fellow Christians (John 13:34-35)
Love self
Love neighbor
Love enemies

All of these forms of love are deeply important but they are not equally important. Imagine a scene in your home this evening. You are there with your wife and children. A person breaks into your home and attacks your wife or child. What should you do as a Christian? You are commanded to love your wife, your children and your enemy. But I'm under obligation to stand by my wife and to protect her and to bring up my children and protect them to the best of my ability. Certainly I'm to love the enemy, but my love for him does not stand on equal ground with love for my wife or children. The loving thing to do is what ever it takes to stop the attack and injury to your wife or children. Someone would say to call 911 and let the police handle it. I'm certainly for calling 911, but what am I to do while I wait for them to arrive? I'm to protect the ones God has given me as a family. If that means shooting the intruder to stop further wrong, then that is what should be done. This point would be equally true if the woman and children were neighbors and I saw them being attacked.

Notice after Jesus answered the lawyer he said, "Well said, teacher, you are right in saying that God is one and there is no other but him. To love him with all your heart, with all your understanding and with all your strength, and to love your neighbor as yourself is more important than all burnt offerings and sacrifices." While other teachers of the law were trying to get rid of Jesus even if it required killing him, here was an honest lawyer to recognized Jesus as correct.

Jesus saw the man had answered wisely and said to the man, "You are not far from the kingdom of God." To be in the kingdom is to be one who has submitted to Christ as the king in ones life. It is to submit to him in everything and seek his kingdom and righteousness before all else (Matthew 6:33). Jesus saw that he was so close to making the big decision that would change his whole life. Who do you know that you could honestly say about them that they aren't far from the kingdom of the Lord?

But notice that one is either in the kingdom or out of the kingdom. To be close means I'm still outside but I know where the door is. I may be thinking seriously about entering the door. But I'm still outside. Many die right at the door of the kingdom of the Lord. They were so close but still outside, unprepared to meet God in judgment. Don't die close!

NOT IN MY BACKYARD

"I'm for a rehab home in a normal neighborhood so that those struggling with addiction may transition to a better life, but not in my neighborhood." "I'm for a halfway house for former prisoners to help them transition to life on the outside, but not in my neighborhood." "I'm for a home for unruly teens that will help troubled families and train troubled teens for a better life, but somewhere other than our area of town." "I'm for increased taxes on the rich as long as the definition of who is rich doesn't include me." "It is all right to mistreat those of another race as long as it isn't my race that is involved." "Why should I care how people treat gays, since I'm not gay?" Does any of that sound familiar? Does it get close to home at all?

The truth is we all tend toward that attitude that as long as it doesn't affect me then I'm not going to get involved or speak up at all. I think Jesus was striking a hard blow against that "Not in my backyard" mentality when he told the story of the man who was traveling from Jerusalem down to Jericho and fell among thieves who robbed him, beat him and left him for dead. The priest came by and saw the situation but he wasn't a priest and it didn't affect him and his work, so he went on. The Levite came by and saw the situation. But he wasn't a Levite and the thieves didn't seem to be attacking Levites, so he went on his way. A Samaritan walked by and saw the situation. The man hurt wasn't a Samaritan, but he was a fellow human. He was hurting and needed help, just like he might on some other occasion. He put himself in the other man's place, and set about to help him. He washed the wounds, poured oil and wine on them and lifted the man onto his donkey to carry him to an inn nearby to take better care for him. When he had to leave, he gave the innkeeper money to continue to take care of him. Even the lawyer wanting to justify himself could see that he was the only one of the three who acted like a neighbor to the one who was hurt.

Every one of us are faced often with those situations where we can think and act only for ourselves or we can think of others and how it will affect them and be a neighbor to the one who is hurting. Not long back I listened to some older followers of Christ talking about how they would vote on the upcoming issue with regard to raising money to improve the schools in their area. One said, "Why would I vote for an increase in my taxes for schools? I don't have children. I'm not going to have any little children so why should I pay for them to have a better school. Let the parents handle that." Thank God there was a widow at the table with a different spirit. With passion she began her speech. "I don't have any children in school anymore either. I certainly don't want my taxes to go up since I'm struggling to pay what I now have. But I care about the future of the generations coming on. To be opposed to building better schools because I don't have children that are school age any more or even family who lives here any more, seems to be extremely selfish. I care about the future of our nation, our state and our city. But most of all I want the children coming on to have at least as good an opportunity, if not better, than we did. I'm for whatever will make things better for the children." I thought to myself, that I had just witnessed the priest and the Samaritan in action.

It may well be the case that the greatest problem we face as a nation isn't political, or even about which party is in control. I suspect the real problem is that selfishness that only considers how any issue that arises will affect me.

One of my heroes in Scripture is Hezekiah. He was a good king and a righteous man. His prayers changed what happened in his life and in the whole country. He became very ill and God sent Isaiah to tell him to set his house in order because he was about to die. He rolled over on his bed to face the wall and cried and prayed. God heard his cry and told Isaiah to go back and tell him he had fifteen more years. News of his recovery spread and the king of Babylon sent messengers to congratulate him for his recovery. Hezekiah was so excited to have them visit he showed them everything he and the kingdom owned. He showed them the treasures of the palace and the treasures in the temple. Isaiah came to ask, "What have you done? What have they seen in your house?" He told the prophet they were from a distant land and that he had showed them everything. Isaiah warned him that Babylon would come and take all the treasures he had shown them back to Babylon. They would kill many of his family and take his sons as prisoners. The kingdom would fall. Hezekiah's response was, "The word of the Lord you have spoken is good.' For he thought, 'There will be peace and security in my lifetime." (Isaiah 39:8) Even great people can have lousy attitudes at times.

"It's only about me" is not a new attitude. God help us!

ONE FLOCK

Words are important. I know the refrain that "One picture is worth a thousand words" but try to get a picture that matches the words of the 23rd Psalm. In studying the Bible it is sometimes the case that translations of particular words lead to wrong thinking and miss the whole point that the writer had in mind and that the people who first heard or read it would have understood. Think with me about a couple of examples where this has happened.

In John 10 Jesus described him self as the Good Shepherd who lays down his life for the sheep. He declared that he had come to give us life and life to the full. He said that as the Good Shepherd he knew his sheep and they know him. In verse 16 he said "Other sheep I have that are not of this flock. I must bring them in also. After this there will be one flock and one shepherd." Earlier translations tended to translate this as "Other sheep I have that are not of this fold" and "Hereafter there will be one fold and one shepherd." The updated NIV follows that notion with "I have other sheep that are not of this sheep pen." But then have "There will be one flock and one shepherd."

Several parts of this passage have been abused such as the "Other Sheep". The point being made by Jesus speaking to a Jewish crowd was that he had other followers who would turn to him who were not Jewish and that he was going to draw people from all ethnic groups, from every nation and all kinds of people. It is certainly not a declaration that some other means of salvation would come to the Native Americans or any other group. Jesus is the Good Shepherd and the only way to salvation is through Him and hearing his voice to follow him.

Jesus wasn't telling them there was going to be one sheep pen or one fold to indicate all who followed him would be kept in one big building or one large pen. The point he was making was that he would draw people from all backgrounds to him and they would all follow him to become ONE FLOCK. Let's face it we can put very different people inside one building or pen that hate each other and can't get along about anything.

This leads to another word that has a very different meaning for us than it did for those who heard it in the first century when Jesus spoke about it. Imagine being there at Caesarea Philippi and hearing Jesus make the promise, "Upon this rock I will build my church and the gates of hades will not be able to stop it." Our immediate thought is that Jesus is building an organization. We think of a place where the people meet to worship and glorify Christ as Lord. It's true that the word generally means, "Called out". But at the time Jesus used the word it generally meant "A gathering, a congregation, a meeting." It was the word used for a town hall meeting or even of a family gathering. If you had a family reunion and all got together to talk about old times and tell old stories that everyone there had already heard a hundred times you would have called that a "church" or "Ecclesia".

Following the mistaken understanding of what Jesus meant in both passages has resulted in organizations being set up calling themselves different brands of churches all over the world. The most common uses of the word "church" today is either of the brand of church I'm a member of or the building where the congregation meets. Both uses are completely mistaken.

Jesus declared he would build a congregation, a flock, a gathering of people who would listen to Him as the Good Shepherd and do what He said. Flocks don't have a brand, they have a Shepherd and they know His voice and follow Him. A gathering of people or a congregation can meet in a building, on the seashore, under a tent or in the park. It isn't about where they meet but that they gather to worship Jesus as the Messiah and to follow His lead to the Father in heaven. I believe that if we focused on the Good Shepherd and following Him, listening to Him and working to get closer to him we would soon forget the brands and the flock would stop noticing all the differences long enough to see what a great Shepherd we have.

ONE OF THE PROPHETS

Why did the people think of Jesus as one of the prophets? When he asked the twelve "Who do people say I am?" their answer was, "Some say you are John the Baptist; others say Elijah; and still others, Jeremiah or one of the prophets." Now Jesus went on to ask who they said he was and Peter rightly answered, "You are the Messiah, the Son of the Living God." (Matthew 16:13-16) Why do you suppose that no one thought of Jesus as one of the priest? So often when people think of Jesus today it is with the image of a meek and mild Savior who never lost his cool and never had any fun. Think of the three men they named that people thought of when they thought of Jesus. John the Baptist wasn't a moderate in much of anything. Elijah was passionate to the degree he took on 400 prophets of Baal at one time and when their god didn't act he made fun of them and their actions. Jeremiah was the weeping prophet. He was a man of passion in his faith, dedication to God and concern for the people.

Jesus would have scoffed at the notion that he was a man of moderation. If we could have seen him when he entered the temple and the rage that burned as he saw they had turned the house of prayer into a den of thieves it would have been a sight to see. He made a whip and began driving out the animals and turning over the tables of the moneychangers. His disciples remembered the phrase, "The zeal for God's house has eaten him up." It was common for the gospel writers to say that Jesus looked around at the religious leaders with anger when they refused to step up and answer him when he asked, if it was right to heal on the Sabbath Day. Not only was he a man of zeal and passion in his anger, he was ready to stand down the crowd when they were ready to throw stones at the woman caught in adultery. When he was healing people and preaching the good news to the poor, giving freedom to captives and sight to the blind the disciples of John arrived to ask if he was really the Messiah or should they look for another. Jesus simply told them to go back and tell John what they had seen and heard. Then he began to describe John. He was a prophet and more than a prophet. Of those born of women there is none greater than John, Jesus told them. But then he made a comparison between him and John and noted that the people weren't happy with either one. He said they were like children playing. Some of them would complain, "We played a happy song and you wouldn't dance." "We played a sad song and you wouldn't mourn." He then compared that to him and John. John the Baptist came to you neither eating nor drinking and you thought he had a demon. Jesus came eating and drinking and you called him a drunk and a glutton.

Why in the world would people think of Jesus as a drunk or a glutton? Probably because he seemed never to be invited to go to a party or a meal in anyone's house that he didn't go. Even if the crowd was a bunch of tax collectors, he was ready to go and spend time with them. He was the friend of tax collectors and sinners. Did Jesus laugh and enjoy life? The evidence is strong that Jesus was a man of joy. When he described the next life in heaven he described it as a wedding feast or as a supper where people would come from the east and west and sit down with him in his kingdom. He chose joyous occasions to describe the ideal life with God. He said there was more joy in heaven over one sinner that repented than over 99 just people who don't need to repent. When the disciples returned from the limited commission he rejoiced with them. In the wonderful story of the Loving Father and prodigal sons, when the younger boy came home the father threw a party with music and dancing that disturbed his uptight brother. Jesus often used humor to make his points with people. When he spoke of his frustration with the religious leaders in Matthew 23 he said they would strain out a gnat and swallow a camel. I would think that everyone there was laughing except the ones he was talking about. His picture of people being judgmental was that it was like a man with a beam in his eye trying to see to get a speck out of his brother's eye. Again, had we been there it would have caused laughter all around. He said it was harder for a rich man to be saved than for a camel to run through the eye of a needle. He used humorous concepts to teach huge lessons that were badly needed.

If you follow Jesus you won't be bland. He wanted us to be salt of the earth and light for the world, to be yeast in the bread to have an affect on the lives of others around us. We need more fire, more vim, vigor and vitality, to be like Him. Some things ought to anger us so much we are ready to turn the tables over and drive the hypocrites out. Instead of just being known for what we don't do or don't think is right, we need to be known as the people who love life and are on fire for God by loving children, caring for the hurting and angry over the sin and hurt in the world. Let's live in a way that someone would say about us, "The zeal for God's house has eaten him up."

OUT OF THE DEPTHS

If your Bible is close by, open it to the Book of Psalms and turn to Psalm 130. It is a short song of only 8 verses. As Israel sang this song in worship to Yahweh it must have been one they went to often. It expresses the heart of all of us at times and for some it lays out their heart most of the time. "Out of the depths I cry to you Lord; Lord, hear my voice. Let your ears be attentive to my cry for mercy. If you, Lord, kept a record of sins, Lord, who could stand? But with you there is forgiveness, so that we can with reverence, serve you. I wait for the Lord, my whole being waits, and in his word I put my hope. I wait for the Lord, more than watchmen wait for the morning, more than watchmen wait for the morning. Israel, put you hope in the Lord, for with the Lord is unfailing love and with him is full redemption. He himself will redeem Israel from all their sins."

We don't know exactly who the writer of the song was. But if we were songwriters we could have penned the sentiments. When was the last time you were struggling with guilt in your life? When we feel the weight of our own sins it is enough to burden us down. Notice how he kept pleading for the Lord to hear and be attentive to his cry for mercy. Perhaps the line that most moves me in the song is "If you, Lord, kept a record of sins, Lord, who could stand?" In I Corinthians 13 as Paul described what real love does in the lives of people, he described the nature of this real love, like God's love for us. In that description of love one of the points he made was, "Love keeps no record of wrongs."

We often have difficulty turning loose of wrongs that we feel have been done to us. The very fact that the one who hurt us has gone on and now has forgotten the things they said or did that hurt us so badly, only adds to our pain. How can they forget something that is still so fresh on our minds all the time? There have been times when someone would tell me of something I said or did that was hurtful to them in years past and that is obviously still very fresh on their minds that I have absolutely no memory of at all. I don't mind asking for forgiveness for such things but it is so often offensive to the other person that I can't remember what they are talking about.

I wish we could all be like God, who forgives sins that we have committed as we turn to him and then wipes out the whole record. He takes it off the hard drive of his computer. It is as if it never had happened at all and we are restored to the relationship we had with him before it ever happened. That is the kind of forgiveness God longs to see in each of us as well. He wants us to have a love that keeps no record of the wrongs done to us.

Notice in the song of Psalm 130, the fact God so fully forgives leads to the psalmist saying, "So that we can, with reverence serve you." God's full forgiveness, allows us to forgive ourselves as well and to serve as though nothing had ever happened to break the relationship. Then he declared that he waited on the Lord like the watchmen waiting for morning. The fact he repeated that statement evidently means he wanted us to notice it.

Throughout the Old Testament God's prophets and teachers emphasized the need to "Wait on the Lord". Isaiah even said that those who wait on the Lord would renew their strength, they would soar on wings like eagles; they would run and not grow weary, they would walk and not be faint. (Isaiah 40:30-31) It is the sure understanding that God has forgiven us of all sins and has wiped our record clean that gets us to the place where we can wait on the Lord and not grow weary.

"Wash your hands before you eat." "Be sure to wash your hands before you come out of the restroom." "Did you shake hands with him? Go wash your hands right now." I suspect that a few hundred years from now some archeologist will dig up ruins from the 21st century and publish their findings that in the early days of the 21st century the number one health advise given to people was, "Wash your hands often." They will likely look at the whole thing and think of what we were doing about like we think of the folks who would put leaches on a person to drain away their toxins from their body or bleed them to help them heal. Someone is likely saying by now, "Leon, don't you think we should wash our hands?" Sure, I wash mine several times a day. But, I can tell you that our biggest problems in life aren't going to be solved with a good hand washing or application of the gooey stuff in the hospital halls or doctors offices.

The whole hand-washing thing isn't new. Remember when the Pharisees and Scribes complained about Jesus and the disciples not washing their hands before they ate in Matthew 15. Their failure violated the traditions of the elders. Jesus challenged them to look at how their trying to find ways around clear teaching from God by some loophole was a much bigger problem than failure to wash their hands. After his dealing with those religious leaders, Jesus called the people to him and said to them, "Hear and understand: it is not what goes into the mouth that defiles a person, but what comes out of the mouth; this defiles a person." Now that is a significant statement that we need now. It seems like every where you go someone is saying that if you will just eat this or not eat that or take this vitamin it will cure what ails you. Jesus disciples approached him after this statement to say, "Do you know that the Pharisees were offended when they heard this saying?" I would have loved to be there when they said this to Jesus. I would like to have seen his expression. If it had been today, I suspect he would have said, "Are you kidding me?" His statements were, "Every plant the Father hasn't planted will be rooted up." And, "If the blind lead the blind, both will fall into the ditch."

What is most intriguing to me is that Peter then came to Jesus to ask him to explain that whole comparison. He didn't get it. I suppose the thinking of the day among the Jews was so attuned to the righteousness of the Pharisees that he just couldn't believe that Jesus would call them blind guides or say that they were plants God hadn't planted and they would be rooted up.

Jesus explained, "Do you not see that whatever goes into the mouth passes into the stomach and is expelled? But what comes out of the mouth proceeds from the heart, and this defiles a person. For out of the heart come evil thoughts, murder, adultery, sexual immorality, theft, false witness, slander. These are what defile a person. But to eat with unwashed hands does not defile anyone." (Matthew 15:17-20) This isn't the time, by the way, to respond, "But Dr. Oz said." It really doesn't matter what anyone says when the one who made our bodies to begin with declares that it isn't what goes in but what comes out that is the problem.

Our real problem in the world isn't our diet. Our real problems are deeper. They have to do with what we have allowed to become our way of seeing things, our values, our dreams and who we are when we don't think anyone is looking. It's a heart problem. The other day I was having lunch with a friend and he, for some reason asked, "Do you have heart problems?" I answered, "Yes, I have some." Later the question came back to mind. It was when I was alone and thinking about our whole conversation that had been very fruitful. But the question wouldn't go away. "Do you have heart problems?" Truthfully, we all have heart problems. No, I'm not talking about the physical kind that leads to taking a handful of pills each day to keep it going. I know I have a bigger heart problem than that.

Look again at Jesus list of what proceeds from the heart. "Out of the heart come evil thoughts, murder, adultery, sexual immorality, theft, false witness and slander." What if we have a heart wash? I wonder if that wasn't at least part of what was on Peter's mind years later when he said; "Baptism also now cleanses us, not the removal of filth from the body but the answer of a good conscience before God." (I Peter 3:21). A good bath makes us feel better and look better. But what is vital is to clean up the heart. If we are filled with the Holy Spirit and allow the Spirit of God to lead and guide us in life we will have something entirely different coming from the heart. "But the fruit of the Spirit is love, joy, peace, patience, kindness, goodness, faithfulness, gentleness, self control; against such things there is no law." (Galatians 5:22-23) Remember the childhood question, "Mary, Mary, quite contrary, how does your garden grow?" It depends on what is planted and on how well you clean out the weeds.

Don't go for the simplistic answers of a fallen society but listen to the voice of the great physician. All our heart problems are curable but it needs a continual cleansing and to be filled, and guided by God's Holy Spirit.

PASTORING

What is the first thing that comes to your mind when you hear the word, "pastor"? In our English Bible it is difficult to find the word at all. In Ephesians 4:11 Paul had quoted the Psalm that "He ascended on high and led captivity captive and gave gifts unto men." Paul's quotation actually differs from the original Psalm. In Psalms 68:18 it says, "When you ascended on high you took many captives; and you received gifts from people, even from the rebellious – that you, Lord God, might dwell there." Notice in the Psalm he received gifts from men and in Paul's quotation he gave gifts to men. Then Paul listed the gifts that had been given. "He gave some to be apostles, some prophets, some evangelists and some pastors and teachers."

The word translated "pastor" is found many times in the Bible but is normally translated "shepherd". Normally, in the New Testament when the word is used it is applied to those who serve as elders in the church rather than to preachers. In Acts 20:28 when Paul met with the elders from Ephesus he challenged them to, "Keep watch over yourselves and all the flock of which the Holy Spirit has made you overseers. Be shepherds of the church of God which he bought with his own blood." These elders were to pastor or shepherd the people who made up the church of God. Notice as Paul used the word it wasn't a title for an office. It was an active word, describing the job to be done. Instead of a title it was a job description. Peter makes a very similar challenge to fellow elders in I Peter 5:1-4.

There is a sense in which every Christian should be a pastor who looks out for the spiritual needs and hurts of other Christians. Our love for one another should keep us thinking of what we can do that will make a difference for good in the life of another. In that sense, it is certainly true that the one who preaches should pastor the people as well as teaching them how to live their life to the full for the Lord.

A preacher who doesn't do any pastoring wouldn't likely be a very good preacher or very effective in helping the church to grow. But notice that the focus of the pastor is primarily on the flock of people that make up the church where they are. It is a work of helping, teaching, encouraging and counseling the members of the body to help them grow in their faith and devotion to God. The work of the Evangelist is to be a carrier of the good news. They certainly have a huge obligation toward those who are in the church. The three times the word "evangelist" is used were all tied to work with the church and its members. In Acts 21:8 Philip is called "the evangelist" and said to have four unmarried daughters who prophesied. In Ephesians 4:11 the evangelist worked alongside the other leaders to equip the saints for the work of ministry to the building up of the body of Christ. In 2 Timothy 4:5 Paul challenged Timothy to "Keep your head in all situations, endure hardship, do the work of an evangelist, discharge all the duties of your ministry." If you go through the book of 2 Timothy most of what was charged to Timothy related to work with the church. But it is true that the primary focus of the evangelist is outside the church toward reaching others for God. He is certainly to have a deep interest in encouraging and building up the church so that it grows through each member developing in his or her faith. But he must always be looking for ways to reach others to bring them to Christ.

It doesn't upset me for someone to refer to me as his or her pastor. I do love and long for each member of the body where I work to grow and develop into all that God wants them to be. But my concern is that as we more and more refer to the preacher as "pastor" that his view will turn altogether toward helping the members to grow instead of on how to reach more people for God. As an evangelist we must be carrying God's good news to the world around us regularly. Let's face the fact that we have so often misused the word "evangelist" by applying it to someone who travels around and doesn't work for any one church, that it is difficult to see the whole idea in it's Biblical way. To be perfectly accurate, I am an evangelist who often does the work of pastoring. In the very same way those who are pastors need to be people who do some evangelizing along the way, since every Christian is to be one that is trying to reach others for the Lord.

If every Christian does some pastoring and every Christian does some evangelizing, what makes some different so that they actually become pastors and evangelist? If one is a pastor it means that is their primary focus. It is who they are and what their job or vocation is in looking after, shepherding and caring for the members of the body. The evangelist is one whose life is centered on carrying the good news of Jesus to other people. He may do many other things but he is an evangelist.

Try this little exercise and see what the results are. Go up to one of the elders or shepherds in the church where you are and call them your pastor. Introduce them to someone as one of the pastors of the church here. See if they are shocked or even try to correct you. Also, go up to the preacher and call him your evangelist. Introduce him to someone who is visiting as the evangelist for the church. See if he goes into shock. It is always good to go back and use words and ideas they way God used them in his word.

PRAY FOR ME

Probably the most common request we hear as Christians both from other Christians and from those who aren't Christians yet is "Please pray for me." It is a great request and I'm certain when we tell someone we are going to be praying for them we have the fullest intent to think of them and their problems when we pray the next time. It is a Biblical thing to ask others to pray for you. In Paul's writings it is quite common for him to get near the end of the book he was writing and request the prayers of the church he is addressing the letter to. Think about it for a moment. When people ask for your prayers what do they normally want you to pray for? When you ask for the prayers of other Christians what is your most common request for the person to pray for you about?

Most likely the most common prayers we are asked to have is prayer for the person who is sick or facing some problem with family or friends who are sick. Occasionally someone will ask that I pray for a child or relative that has gone away from the Lord and from faith in him. But that isn't the norm. I know we need to pray about sicknesses and hurts of all kinds. James said to confess your faults to one another and pray for one another that you may be healed, the effective, fervent prayer of the righteous avails much. John, when writing the beloved Gaius said he was praying that he might be in health and that he might have prosperity just as his soul prospered. So we need to pray for the hurts, sicknesses, and physical problems of each other.

Here is the part of the whole subject that concerns me. Notice two things from the New Testament that stands out. The first is what we are commanded or asked to pray about as Christians and the second is the request in Scripture for the prayers of people. Jesus asked the disciples, after looking out on the crowd and seeing they were like sheep without a shepherd, to pray to the Lord of the Harvest to send out workers into his vineyard. "The Harvest is great but the Laborers are few." When was the last time anyone prayed for more workers in the kingdom of Christ? That isn't a very common prayer even in the assemblies of Christians. Every church I'm aware of has some struggle in finding the workers that are needed. We will make pleas in the bulletin, announcements to the gathering of people and even call people to ask them to work in a given area. But it still is uncommon for us to pray in public for more workers in the vineyard of Christ. The Lord of the Harvest certainly wants the harvest to be great. He has all power. So why don't we ask for the great need for workers to be fulfilled.

In Paul's letters it is common for him to ask the brethren to remember him in their prayers. But most of the time it is that God will open a door for him to preach the gospel of Christ and that he will do so boldly. Many of his letters were written from behind bars in jails and prisons. But we never read of him asking the brethren to pray for his release. Instead he tells of how the word of Christ remains unbound even when he is in trouble.

I certainly understand that our public prayers aren't the same as our private prayers and you can't just look at a person's prayer life based on what you hear from them when they are leading a public prayer. But it does seem to me that our public prayers need to at least contain elements of what God asked for, in our prayers for each other. We are to pray to God about all kinds of things. Instead of worrying about things we should take our request to the throne of God and trust that he will bless in accord with our needs. But I fear that too many of our prayers seem trivial to the God when our constant ask is about things that have to do with our health, wealth and family life.

What if every Christian followed Paul's example when he was in a Roman jail and requested over and over again that God would grant him boldness when they have the opportunity to share the message of the gospel with others. He even told the church at Philippi that his imprisonment had turned out for the furtherance of the gospel of Christ. Many had come to Christ as a result and many of the ones who had been weak were now stronger.

In the next couple of weeks, consider changing your personal prayers. Pray more about the harvest of God and the workers that God will give them the wisdom to see the personal needs of others and to take advantage of every open door they we see in life. I wonder what the results will be for each of us.

PRAYER AND LEADERS

If you can rightly refer to any mortal as a class act, Samuel was a class act. We tend to know more about his boyhood and God's initial call of him as priest and prophet than of his later life. But all through his life he was a dedicated servant of the Lord. After a lifetime of faithful service to Israel as judge, priest and prophet or "Seer" as he was often called in I Samuel, he became old and gray. His two sons were placed into his work as priest, but they weren't of the same character as their dad. They accepted bribes and took advantage of their position instead of serving others. So at this late juncture in life, the people came to Samuel to ask for a king like the nations around them. Their reasons seemed logical. Samuel was old and couldn't continue long and his sons weren't like him, so

"Give us a king." It hurt Samuel deeply, but God reminded him that it wasn't him as judge or priest they were rejecting but God as king over them. God told Samuel to tell the people what it would be like to have a king, but then to give them their request. Samuel, under God's direction, anointed Saul to be the first king over Israel. He did so with the firm instruction that if you stay true to the Lord, God will bless you and make you strong as king and the nation strong as a country. But if you depart from God's teaching and follow the gods around you God will destroy both the king and the nation.

When Samuel installed Saul as king and gave the final warnings to the people and demonstrated to them the power of God by praying for God to send a Thunder storm during the time of harvest to destroy their crops and God responded by sending the storm, the people repented of their sins before God. They pleaded with Samuel to continue to pray for them. In I Samuel 12:22-25 Samuel responded, "For the Lord will not abandon His people on account of His great name, because the Lord has been pleased to make you a people for Himself. Moreover, as for me, far be it from me that I should sin against the Lord by ceasing to pray for you, but I will instruct you in the good and right way. Only fear the Lord and serve Him in truth with all your heart; for consider what great things He has done for you. But if you still do wickedly, both you and your king will be swept away."

Thank about it. Samuel felt rejected. He felt they were turning away from all he had taught them. He was following God's instruction but he felt in his heart that this would lead to more problems for Israel. But in it all he assured them that he would not sin against God by not praying for them and their king.

It didn't take long for Saul to fail as leader of the people. His longing to please the people went deeper than his desire to please God, so when the people became restless he forced himself to make the offering that only the priest should offer. Samuel hurt even more. Then Saul made a foolish vow that almost led to the execution of his son Jonathan until the people intervened for him. God through Samuel gave Saul one more mission. "Go down and completely destroy the Amalekites." Saul took God's army and won a huge victory, but instead of completely destroying them he kept the best of the sheep and cattle and he brought back King Agag to Israel. God sent Samuel to confront Saul for his sin. It was hard to get Saul to see what he had done. In his mind saving the best sheep and cattle to offer them to God and bringing back the king seemed like a good thing even though it wasn't what God had commanded. It was what the people wanted. Samuel's great statement came, "Behold to obey is better than to sacrifice and to listen is better than the fat of rams."

Imagine the dejection Samuel felt as he went home. In chapter 16:1 God again speaks to Samuel, "How long will you grieve over Saul, since I have rejected him from being king over Israel?" It was as though God had moved on, but Samuel was still struggling with grief. God's new mission was to go and anoint David a man after God's own heart as the new king.

I want to have a heart like Samuel's. I want a heart that refuses to quit praying for people even when they have rejected what I think is right. I want a heart that will pray for the one who takes my place even when I think the people have made a bad choice. I want a heart that still breaks for a wandering ruler who has chosen unwisely and refused to follow good advise. Saul's come and go in every country but Samuel's are rare and the nation would be blessed far more by having more Samuel's no matter who the "Saul" may be at the time.

REBUKE?

Is there a time when we should rebuke someone who is either living in some open sin or who is teaching something that is in violation of Scripture? Fifty years ago when I really was beginning to have a deeper interest in pleasing God and following His guide, it was pretty common to hear people who were devoted followers of Jesus rebuke other people. Have times changed so much that rebuking doesn't fit any more?

The Bible still has several passages that command us to rebuke others in given situations. In 2 Timothy 4:2 Paul under the direction of the Holy Spirit told Timothy to "Preach the word; be prepared in season and out of season; correct, rebuke and encourage with great patience and careful instruction." Back in chapter two he had instructed him not to be quarrelsome, but kind to everyone and not be resentful. He said for him to instruct opponents gently so God might grant them repentance. (2 Timothy 2:24-26) In Luke 17:3 Jesus said if someone sinned against you to rebuke them and if they turned to say they repented then forgive them.

It is certainly obvious that Jesus rebuked people who were going in the wrong direction. His rebukes were often for Pharisees, but one must never forget that he rebuked his own apostle Peter as strongly as anyone. How can you get stronger than saying to him "Get behind me Satan? You are not thinking of the things of God but the things of men." He often challenged them strongly as a group for their actions and thoughts. I think if we had been there we would have considered it a rebuke when he said they were of little faith or asked, "Where is your faith?" When James and John wanted the best seats in the house at his right and left hand and he explained to them that such places were reserved for whomever the Father had chosen to be there and the others were angry over their arrogant request, Jesus corrected them all. He told them things among them wouldn't be like it was with the worldly rulers. The greatest among them would be the servant, the one who was last of all.

It is certainly the case that Paul took on that spirit and rebuked some as strongly as one could imagine. He rebuked Peter to his face and called his action hypocritical as recorded in Galatians 2. Think of the way he referred to the teachers trying to convince the churches that they should be observing the law and everyone be circumcised along with being baptized. His rebuke to them that he wished they would emasculate themselves is pretty strong. Or Peter's rebuke of Simon when he wanted to purchase the power to lay his hands on others and give them the miraculous abilities from the Spirit and Peter told him his money would perish with him, was quite a strong rebuke.

So, here is my question. How do we know when and how to rebuke another person? On one occasion the disciples of Jesus rebuked a man whom Jesus told them they shouldn't have done so. James and John seem to have led the way in rebuking a man who was speaking in Jesus name and performing miracles in his name, but wasn't one of their group. They told him to quit. Jesus said not to rebuke him that when he was speaking well of him he couldn't turn quickly and speak evil. "He who is not against us is on our side." First, if people are right around us, be like Aquila and Priscilla and take our Apollos aside to correct his error and then bless his work as he corrects his error. Second, rebuke people to their face as Paul did Peter when possible. His rebuke of the false teachers who were hurting the church wasn't to their face but in writing since it was hurting the church and he wasn't there. Third, don't allow rebuking to become a way of life. Paul told Titus to rebuke those divisive people among them once, then twice and then have nothing to do with them since you can be sure that such people are warped and sinful and self-condemned (Titus 3:10-11). As a rule of life we should "Avoid foolish controversies and genealogies and arguments and quarrels about the law, because these are unprofitable and useless." (Titus 3:9)

Imagine Paul, sitting in the Roman jail, waiting for his appearance before Nero. He knows well the reputation Nero has for insane cruelty. He knows that the lack of evidence of any crime being committed doesn't mean he is going to have a fair trial and be released permanently. He takes time from a busy schedule of talking both to prisoners, guards and anyone who came to visit, about Jesus and His kingdom to write a letter to the church at Philippi. It likely was brought on by the visit from Epaphroditus who brought him a generous gift from the church in Philippi and by the fact that Epaphroditus had gotten ill while there. Paul obviously was concerned that some in the church wouldn't show proper respect for him when he returned due to his illness and his not being able to provide for Paul the comfort and encouragement they had in mind. As was characteristic of Paul, he left nothing to chance and encouraged the church to honor such men and hold them in high esteem.

It's not that part though that seems so out of place. It is the fact that this little letter to Philippians is so filled with "Joy" commands. When he made his first attempt to conclude the letter in what we know as chapter 3, verse 1 he said, "Finally, my brethren, rejoice in the Lord. To write the same thing again is no more trouble to me, and it is a safeguard for you." As he starts to try again to conclude in chapter four he again says, "Rejoice in the Lord always; again I will say, rejoice!" If he had been sitting comfortably in some posh hotel in Rome writing these words it would have seemed somewhat natural. But, had he forgotten where he was and what was going on? Actually it was the perfect setting. When you want to get across the message that our joy as a follower of Christ isn't tied to our wonderful circumstances but to our relationship and hope in Him.

He knew the problems in Philippi. He had just told Clement to help Euodia and Syntyche to solve their disagreement and help them to get along. He had clearly warned in chapter three about the false teachers who were there trying to add to the good news of Jesus and give them a series of laws to live by that didn't come from Jesus at all. He knew that persecution would come to him and them as time went by. He knew the poverty that was going on in that whole area including the church in Philippi (2 Corinthians 8:1-5). But the command that kept driving him was, "Rejoice in the Lord always." Don't get me wrong he had lots of good news to tell the church that had stood with him all the way. He pointed out that the suffering he had gone through had actually turned out for the increase of the gospel. More people were telling the news of Jesus than before he was arrested. Now, it was true that some did so with wrong motives, but still he rejoiced that people were hearing about Jesus. He let them know that some people in Caesar's household had become saints.

But why was this command to "Rejoice" so important to him at this time and why so needed by this church and its members?

It isn't how we rejoice when everything is smooth, sweet and comfortable that shines as a witness for Christ, but how we rejoice in the times of challenge, difficulty, fear and disappointment that demonstrates the difference He makes in our life. When my faith is based on everything going right it isn't at all the faith Jesus longs for. Have you noticed how many times he warned the apostles that following him would lead to persecution in the world? That is the reason the whole "Prosperity gospel" notion is so dangerous and wrong headed. It leads one to believe that if I'm doing right everything in my life will go great. It doesn't and then what?

Jesus is there with us, strengthening us, in all times. He is with us on the really good days and the really awful ones.

He didn't command to rejoice about everything that happens. It is to rejoice "IN THE LORD" always. Because of His presence in life we can face whatever comes and be true to God. With Paul, that would eventually be execution when he appeared Nero the second time. But he felt sure the Lord was there with him each step even in that final hour. Rejoice in the Lord always!

RELEASE FOR CAPTIVES

When Isaiah the prophet looked forward to the coming of the Messiah into the world, one of the promises was that he would bring release for the captives. Tied with that promise was a list of other similar actions He would carry out. He would bring good news to the poor, bind up the broken hearted, open the prison to those who are bound and proclaim the year of the Lord's favor. (Isaiah 61:1-2) When Jesus described what would happen on the day when Jesus comes again and calls all the nations before him to be judged for their actions on the earth, he shocked the crowd with the things he said would be the standard by which he would judge the people. "I was hungry and you fed me. I was thirsty and you gave me a drink. I was a stranger and you took me in. I was naked and you clothed me. I was sick and you visited me. And I was in prison and you came to me. When they couldn't remember doing any of those things for Jesus, he explained, "In that you did it for one of the least of these, my brothers, you did it to me."

Today, I'm going to appear at the sentencing of a young man who is in trouble and messed up his life with crime. I'm to make a plea for mercy from the judge, not for release but for them not to make the sentence so long that it puts him in prison for the rest of his life.

Think of this for moment. We live in a time when most states in this country as well as the local jails and the federal prisons are all facing overcrowding in their prison population. Often the jails are so full that when a person is arrested there is no place to put them because there is no room for another person in the jail. If a person is paroled early, it is all too common that they will be back in prison for some other crime before long. Something is horribly wrong with our system of punishment for crimes as a nation when our only answer is to build more prisons.

Surely, anyone who thinks reasonably or who has ever even known a person who spent time in prison understands that our system doesn't work well for any kind of rehabilitation. Instead, it works against their change, and all too often sets them up to become more hardened as criminals instead of being changed for good. Picture the person who has committed a felony and goes to prison for a year or more. They serve their time and are released from jail to be on parole for another year to 18 months. When they attempt to get a job, they are turned down over and over again because they have a record. Any plea that they have changed tends to fall on deaf ears since the company has a policy not to hire anyone with a record of a felony. If they want to clear their record, it will require a lengthy period of time and usually a good attorney and a healthy amount of money. Since they can't get a job with a record, where is the money to come from to pay an attorney to help them? Unless they are blessed to have a family who is willing and able to help them financially they are out of luck. With no job, no way to get a job and no money to live on, the pressure to turn again to some form of crime becomes huge.

Is this really what we want as a system? Is it punishment and warehousing people that is our goal? Or, should we be like Jesus and want to rehabilitate the prisoner so that they can have release of the captive? There are isolated programs, often associated with religious groups that actually work to give people a new life. Some offer the captive freedom by giving the person who gets out of prison a place to live and a job to go to work in immediately, so that they can rebuild their life and even care for the family that has been hurt as much as the prisoner themselves. What is so out of kilter is that in too many situations, the very programs that have helped many such prisoners by changing their lives, their minds and their goals in life are outlawed because of their association with Christianity. In far too many cases if they are associated with some Muslim group, they are given freedom to have prayer places and times but no such freedom is there for the Christian group.

The longer we allow such a warped system to prevail in this country or any other we put our own eternity in jeopardy. Judgment Day is coming for all of us. When it does one big item on this list will be how we've treated the prisoner and Jesus will identify with that prisoner who has changed their life and committed himself or herself to God. If I really want to be like Jesus and think of the treatment of the prisoner as how I am treating Jesus, I need to get my prayers, my vote and my actions around changing our attitudes and actions toward the prisoner in this country.

RULES OR PERSONALITY

Focus for a moment on the religious atmosphere during the first century when Jesus launched his ministry. The Pharisees were separatist who kept the rules and made lots more rules for others to follow. Jesus epitomized them when he said, "You give a tenth of your spices mint, dill and Cumin but you have neglected the more important matters of the law, justice, mercy and faith." The Sadducees were the educated elitist who rejected much of the Old Testament and denied the existence of hell, of angels, demons and spiritual beings as a whole. The Samaritans were religious but had a mixed bag of faith in that they had taken the first five books of the Bible and tied with it other practices gained from their past. The Essenes aren't mentioned in the Bible but were even more a separatist group than the Pharisees. They had largely left the society to establish their own community of faith. They were legalists to the core. Then John the Baptist came to prepare the way for the Lord. He preached repentance and the coming of the kingdom. He baptized people right and left with a baptism of repentance for the forgiveness of sins. He challenged those who came to him to change their lives and be holy people.

But where did Jesus fit into this mix? It is amazing that he really doesn't fit into any of the different religious camps mentioned. John the Baptist was certainly a godly man doing a great work. But Jesus was so different from him and his work that John questioned whether or not Jesus was really the Messiah before the end of his life. No one ever lived who kept the law of God like Jesus did. He was tempted in every way like we are yet never gave into the temptation so that he sinned. Much of his ministry was given to correcting the wrong headedness of the other religious groups or leaders. It is amazing that these devoted religious leaders looked at Jesus ministry and not only rejected him as the Messiah, but accused him of working under the power of Beelzebub the prince of demons. He declared his mission on several occasions in different ways. He said He came not to do his own will but the will of the Father in heaven. He said he came to seek and save the lost. He came to fulfill the law, not to destroy it. He came to show us the Father. Peter would later say that gave us an example so that we should walk in his footsteps.

If you look at the different religious groups of that day, which one is closest to how you see things today? In reality, people in our own time strive to be Christ followers in each of the different ways that were prevalent when Jesus launched his ministry. Jesus had a plan for those who were his disciples. His followers were to be recognized by the love they had for each other. Jesus declared that he was giving them and us a new commandment that we should love one another as he loved us and it would be by that love that everyone would see and recognize us as His followers (John 13:34-35).

What if we really did learn to love and live like Jesus in our own time? In his love he took a bumbling group of men, who were blue collar to the core and molded them into leaders. He challenged them, corrected them, showed them their lack of faith and he loved to the end. He washed their feet on the night he told them all of them would soon forsake him. He gave them the memorial of the Lord's Supper that night as well. Immediately after saying Peter would deny him three times and all would forsake him he declared, "Let not your heart be troubled. You believe God trust me also. In my Father's house are many rooms. If it were not so I would have told you. I am going to prepare a place for you and if I go and prepare a place for you I will come back and take you to be with me that you also may be where I am." Jesus way was one of service. He came as a servant and told us that the way to greatness as His follower was by being a servant of all. If we follow him we must learn to wash feet even of those who betray us.

The church is the body of Christ. It is Christ in community. Our pattern for living isn't the first century church but the one who built the church and gave himself up for her. When we look, act and smell like Jesus as his church we will bless the world as he did. I pray that we might all live in such a way that the world could see Jesus in us, by the love and grace we demonstrate to all people. Then it will be true that there is neither Jew, nor Greek, neither male nor female, Barbarian or Scythian, slave or free, neither black nor white, neither red nor yellow, neither brown nor tan, but we can all be one in Him. Instead of shouting about what is happening in Ferguson, let the church demonstrate a better way.

SECRET SINS

What is the worst sin that a person can commit? We might answer that it is the blaspheming of the Holy Spirit.

We might go to the greatest command, to Love God with all our heart, soul, mind and strength and say that if this is the greatest command then the greatest sin must be failure to love God with all our being. I suspect that most of us would say that the greatest sins are the ones we don't struggle with. It seems to be part of our human nature to think that the sins we have problems with aren't really all that bad but the sins others around us struggle with are really horrible. David prayed for the Lord to keep him back from "Secret sins." Do you think he was talking about the sins he had hidden from others and were thus secret or did he mean the sins he didn't know about in his own life? It is often the sins we commit that we aren't aware of that are still doing tremendous harm in our life and in the cause of Christ. Quite often it is true that the sins we think are secret from other people are already well known among them. Through the years I've had people come to me to confess some sinful action or relationship they are involved in and ask for me to pray for them about some sin in their life that no one else knows about. Many of those times I had known about the sin they confessed months before they confessed it.

One huge point I need to remember is that no matter how well hidden I may think my sin is, God knows about it. Remember David and what a process he went through trying to hide his sin with Bathsheba. But God knew all along. He sent the prophet Nathan to David to help him see that God knew and that bad things were happening in his life because of the sin. Focus on the words of Hebrews 4:12-13. "For the word of God is living and active and sharper than any two-edged sword, and piercing as far as the division of soul and spirit, of both joints and marrow, and able to judge the thoughts and intents of the heart. And there is no creature hidden from His sight, but all things are open and laid bare to the eyes of Him with whom we have to do."

God's word can reach into the heart of the person and the problem and separate us from the sin or allow us to see that the hidden sin isn't so well hidden after all. Where is your best hiding place? Recently a man contacted me about a sin he had kept hidden from his wife and family for years. Now he is horribly afraid of them finding out because he has a sleep problem and not only snores in his sleep but is quite vocal. He is horribly afraid he will begin talking in his sleep and tell of the secrets that he has kept hidden all this time. I can imagine one of us getting to heaven and standing before the Lord we start to tell him of all the things we have done wrong only to have him say, "I know all about it. I even know of many you have long forgotten. It is all right. They are forgiven." Hebrews 4:13 said, "All things are open and laid bare to the eyes of Him with whom we have to do." Nothing is hidden from his view. Our best hiding place is as open to Him as the things we have sitting on the mantle or the things we have stuck with magnets on our refrigerator. God knows! He knew our sin problems even before He sent Jesus into the world to pay the price for our sins.

Imagine the couple sitting in the counselor's office talking about their lives and problems and seeking her help. He begins to open up and tell her things he has done through the years that he is so ashamed of and needs her to forgive him. She reaches for his hand and looks deeply into his eyes to say, "I know. I've known for years. It's all right. I forgave you years ago." When I've witnessed this kind of thing take place it is absolutely amazing the relief that is felt when the one who thought everything was hidden learns it has been open all along and now they can stop all the efforts to keep it hidden. Whether other people ever know or not isn't the most important matter. God knows. But here is the most amazing part of that. God is waiting, willing and longing to forgive and forget. It is later in this same book of Hebrews that he tells of the New Covenant we have in Jesus where He is our God and we are His children.

He said that when he forgives our sins, they are completely forgotten, and never to be brought up again.

Instead of spending out lives trying to hide the sins that torment us, our need is to commit to a savior, Jesus Christ in faith, repentance and obedience to have even the worst of sins, completely washed away and forgiven by Him. Of course, our sins continue to have consequences in this life, but only in this life. If I got drunk and tried to drive home in that state and ran over a child and killed them, I can repent and be forgiven completely, but the child is still dead and the pain of what I've done won't stop. Isn't it time to be open with the one who already knows it all anyway?

SERVICE AND WORSHIP

We are servants of God Almighty. Paul often even referred to himself as a "Bond slave" of Christ. We emphasize the need for every member of the church to be part of some kind of service to others and thus to the Lord. When we emphasize the different spiritual gifts God has given to us as described in Romans 12:1-9, we stress the fact that whatever the gift may be, it is to be used in service to God. When Paul described the process by which a church is to grow in Ephesians 4:11-16 he noted the gifts of some being apostles, some prophets, some evangelist and some pastors and teachers, "For the work of ministry, for the building up of the body of Christ." The word used for "Ministry" is the same word translated "Service" on numerous occasions. So we are to be servants.

But we are also the bride of Christ on whom He bestowed such amazing love that he willingly gave himself up for the church. His longing for us as his bride is to be a "Glorious church without spot or wrinkle or any such thing." (Ephesians 5:25-27). The church is to be holy and without blame before him in love. Paul gave this love that Christ has for the church as a pattern for the kind of love a husband is to have for his wife. While it is certainly true that both husbands and wives serve each other in the family and marriage relationship, I don't think it would be very smart on the part of a husband to introduce his wife at some function as "His servant". I suspect that if we were out in public somewhere and introduced our wife as our servant we might find that she didn't do much service for us for some time after that.

Service is vital in any relationship and it is certainly extremely important in the life of the church. But I wonder if we don't over emphasize the servant side of our relationship with the Lord to the overlooking of the bride side of the relationship. I certainly believe that I offer service to my wife, children and grandchildren. But if they started treating my like their servant instead of the husband, father and grandfather, I suspect I would be quite frustrated. Yet in church we tend to focus almost all together on the service aspect of our relationship with Christ.

Look closely at John's description of the marriage of the Lamb in Revelation 19:7-10 with me. "Let us rejoice and be glad and give glory to Him, for the marriage of the Lamb has come and His bride has made herself ready. It was given to her to clothe herself in the fine linen, bright and clean; for the fine linen is the righteous acts of the saints. Then he said to me, 'Write, Blessed are those who are invited to the marriage supper of the Lamb.' And he said to me, 'These are the true words of God.' Then I fell at his feet to worship him. But he said to me, 'Do not do that; I am a fellow servant of yours and your brethren who hold the testimony of Jesus; worship God. For the testimony of Jesus is the spirit of prophecy.'"

It was an amazing blessing for one to be invited to the wedding of the Lamb with his bride, the church. The Lord has been working for this marriage from the beginning of time and the bride has made herself ready for the wedding by righteous acts. She is beautifully attired in fine linen that is the prayers of God's people. It is interesting that tied to this whole scene was John's feeling of worship to fall down before the angel showing him the sight. The angel's response was that he needed to worship God.

Here's my point in this whole thing. In church we tend to swing between the emphasis on either service or worship to God. We seem to go from times of thinking that worship is all that matters and service is minor to the times when service is all that matters and worship is a minor sidelight. I think we have moved in the last few years to the side that God's work is all about service. In a husband wife relationship, service matters. But if we don't take the time to demonstrate our devotion and love for each other, the service won't hold the marriage together. If we spend all the time adoring each other and never clean up, mow the yard or cook a meal the adoration may become weak. For the marriage to be strong there must be an emphasis on both the service and the expressions of love and devotion, the romance and enjoyment of each other. In church we must emphasize the service to be done for the Lord all along. But we must also remember that worship is our time to show our love and devotion to the Lord, the husband and Our Father in heaven. Worship doesn't replace service nor does service replace worship. Together they build a marriage and a church.

SO MUCH GOOD IN WORST

"There is so much good in the worst of us and so much evil in the best of us that it ill behooves the rest of us to judge others of us." If you were listing great people who have lived from the past, surely King David would have made the list. He was a man after God's own heart. He felt compassion for those who were hurting. One of my favorite stories of David's life is when he became king after the cruel death of Saul and Jonathan. David sought out any relatives of Saul or Jonathan that he might show them favor in memory of his friend Jonathan. He found a handicapped young man named Mephibosheth, a son of Jonathan. His nurse in trying to help him escape from the Philistines had fallen and left him crippled for life. When David found him, his caretakers were all afraid that it was some plot to get rid of all of Saul's heirs. But David took this young man into his house and he ate at David's table from that day forward. At times like this when I'm reading of David's life I feel great and think what a kind and caring person he was. No wonder God loved David so much and said he was a man with a heart like his.

David did so many things that we can admire about him and about his faith in the Lord. But there was an event near the end of his life that leaves most of us wondering what got into him near the end. In I Kings 2 David was near death and his final official acts had been to set up his son Solomon as the new king over Israel. He offered Solomon a great charge, one like you would have expected or even longed for. "When the time drew near for David to die, he gave a charge to Solomon his son. 'I am about to go the way of all the earth.' He said. 'So be strong, act like a man, and observe what the Lord your God requires: Walk in obedience to him, and keep his decrees and commands, his laws and regulations, as written in the Law of Moses. Do this so that you may prosper in all you do and wherever you go and that the Lord may keep his promise to me: 'If your descendants watch how they live, and if they walk faithfully before me with all their heart and soul, you will never fail to have a successor on the throne of Israel." (Vs. 1-4)

I wish he had stopped at that point and allowed that charge to be his legacy for all time. But he didn't stop. He went on to ask Solomon to get revenge on some of the people whom he was angry toward, some whom he had shown mercy and grace toward during his life. First he reminded him of Joab who had been David's friend and leader of his army through his reign. Joab had been loyal to David in almost every situation. When Absalom rebelled, Joab led the army of David to protect David and kill Absalom. When David committed adultery with Bathsheba and sent word to have Uriah her husband put in the hottest part of the battlefield and withdraw from him so that he would die, Joab carried it out and kept the secret of what had happened. But what David remembered was that Joab had killed Abner and Amasa, so he charged Solomon to "Deal with him according to your wisdom, but do not let his gray head go down to the grave in peace."

He turned to tell him to show kindness to the sons of Barzillai of Gilead who had stood with him during Absalom's rebellion. Then he turned back to the revenge he wished for against Shimei the son of Gera who had cursed him as he ran from Absalom. At the time his loyal servants like Joab wanted to destroy him but David had refused saying the message might be coming from God. But now at the end of his life he asked his son to carry out the revenge he hadn't.

Perhaps David laid these on the heart of Solomon and went to his grave in peace. But two things stand out to me in this whole incident. One is how sad to go to the end of your life and have your mind occupied with ways you have been wronged and how to get revenge. I hope and pray that when that time comes all I will remember is the good people have done in my life and wish for my children to show them kindness for what they did. The second one troubles me even more. He sent his anger into the heart of his son. He tied Solomon's loyalty and love for him to his carrying out revenge against these who David felt had mistreated him. I can't help but wonder if he ever came clean to Solomon about what happened to his mother's first husband. One thing that should amaze us all is the picture of God's grace shown in making Solomon the new king. He was David's child by Bathsheba the one he had committed adultery with and whose husband he had murdered. He wasn't the one born from the adulterous relationship. That child died. Solomon was conceived during the time David and Bathsheba mourned the death of that child. But God chose Solomon to be the new king. God doesn't judge us based on our past or even our parental heritage.

STRAINS ON OUR MARRIAGES

Every time I have a wedding I think of how exciting it is to see a couple, deeply in love, making a life-long commitment to each other to stand by and cherish each other until death. I believe just about every couple that gets married really means it when they make those vows to each other. Even if they have been brought up in a home where they witnessed divorce or unfaithfulness to their vows, they believe it will be different for them and their partner. They really love each other and plan to work at their marriage every day to keep it strong.

The Bible pictures marriage in such beautiful word pictures. Think of Adam with Eve for the first time and saying, that she is bone of his bone and flesh of his flesh. Think of God saying to them, that this is the reason a man will leave father and mother and be joined to their wife and the two will become one flesh. Or imagine Solomon declaring, "He that finds a wife finds a good thing." Perhaps the most beautiful word picture of the all is from Paul in Ephesians 5:25-27. "Husbands love your wives as Christ also loved the church and gave himself for it that he might sanctify and cleanse it by the washing of water by the word that he might present it to himself a glorious church, without spot or blemish or any such thing."

After the wedding when you are working to build a marriage one is faced with life's strains that seem to pull us in every direction. After a long day at work for both husband and wife they come home worn out physically and mentally. Instead of falling into each other's arms to find comfort and relief it is often the reality of mowing the lawn, paying the bills and preparing a meal. The house needs cleaning and the clothes need washing. When all of that is done and you are ready to sit down for a while and talk about life and hold each other, one says, "I'm so tired, I think I'll just go on to bed."

As the years pass the strains tend to become bigger and stronger. We get a house, a car payment, college bills to repay, perhaps a pregnancy and more expenses with it. If we have children the strains grow as the child demands time and attention and the cost of raising a child suddenly becomes real to us. We go to church to be encouraged and built up and have our children in the classes and activities at church and that helps but at the same time it often adds some to the strain because now we are told we need to make time to read our Bible each day, go to a home Bible study and pray about everything. We are also encouraged to give God the first and the best in our life, which includes our time, talent and money. In such strain we can easily forget the wonderful vows we took some years back. The picture of loving and cherishing till death separates us seems like another challenge we can't meet.

In the strains and stresses of life, we have a choice to make. Those strains can either unravel the rope that holds us together in a one flesh relationship or we face the fact that none of these will matter if we lose our marriage in the process. A new job or new car that adds more stress on the marriage is a horrible investment. In those times of stress and strain there is a huge need to sit down together as a couple and place the priorities in our life in proper order. We become stressed mainly because we allow the little pulls to take up the time and energy needed for the vital, the important and the necessary. If God is first in your life, what difference will it make in your daily plans? If God is first, the first question is always, "What does God want us to do about this?" We know that God wants our marriages to work, to be full, happy and encouraging. So if God is first we will work on the marriage. If God is first, we know that He wants us to live without worry. I think money and things are usually the greatest strain on marriage. Here is a simple plan that works if you do. When it comes to finances, learn to live on 80% of your income. That is a huge difference from living on 110% and making up the

10% with credit cards. Stop charging anything that you can't pay off at the end of the month. Of the 20% left, give the first 10% to God by giving to his church. Take the next 10% and save it so that in the future when you need something you don't have to charge but can pay for it. Live on the 80%.

If bills have you where you don't think you can do that now, start a plan today that will get you there. If you need help there are multiple programs available or books written on the topic to help. Don't let debt and stuff run your life and destroy your marriage and family.

STRUGGLING WITH DOUBTS

Doubts are common in life. We doubt all kinds of things. When watching the news and you hear a story about someone or something, if you are like me at all you probably think, "I really doubt that they have the full story." Often I think that they not only don't have the whole story but they have slanted what they do have in a direction to make it seem more sensational. But that is different from the person who looks at life and the problems they face and reacts with doubt that there is a God or that God really loves and cares about them. In many ways it doesn't matter whether my doubt is about God's existence or about His character, it still has the effect on discouragement and pulling me closer to despair. The total unbeliever may feel relief and joy in the supposed freedom they now have. But the doubter seldom feels any such joy, freedom or peace.

Doubting isn't a new 21st century phenomenon. It is one of the most common topics in the Bible. If you read the Psalms it seems that so many of these songs were written out of doubt that God was listening to them and some even question God's care for what is happening to them. John the Baptist was such a great servant of God that Jesus said that of those born of women, there was none greater than John. Yet John faced a time of huge doubt. He was in jail for preaching that Herod was wrong in taking his brother's wife and marrying her so Herod had him arrested. Inside the jail he heard his disciples talk of the work Jesus was doing, he began to question his own witness for Christ. He had powerfully proclaimed that Jesus was the Lamb of God that takes away the sins of the world. But now he is wondering to the degree that he sends his own disciples to Jesus with the question, "Are you the one that should come are should we look for another?" There is no evidence that Jesus was offended by John's question. Instead he told them to go back and tell John what you hear and see: "The blind receive sight and the lame walk, the lepers are cleansed and the deaf hear, the dead are raised up, and the poor have the gospel preached to them. And blessed is he who does not take offense at me." (Matthew 11:5-6)

So, why is it the case that good, godly people face doubts in their life? If we were people of faith and honest students of His word, why would doubt enter our minds? There is no exact answer to that question. But it is usually the case that circumstances in our life have changed and things are now happening that we really thought wouldn't happen to us if we were devoted to God. In the Psalms most of the passages that deal with doubt are about God's silence when they have pleaded to them for answers. They had thought God would quickly come to their aid when the troubled times came even though it was the sin of the nation that had led to the problems. With John, the doubt seemed to arise because he had expectations of Jesus as the Messiah that Jesus wasn't fulfilling. I would guess that he thought Jesus would come to the jail and rescue him from the hands of Herod since he was standing for truth and God when he preached against Herod's marriage. But Jesus hadn't come and hadn't done anything to free him.

In our lives we face the same things. Sometimes it is because of Scriptures we have learned that promise God's presence in our life all the time. He said he would never leave or forsake us. He promised that all things would work together for good for us if we love him and are called according to His purpose. So why does it seem that all my prayers go nowhere? Why does it seem that God is silent when I need desperately to hear his voice? Why doesn't he do the things that I thought for certain He would do if I got into some kind of trouble? Why doesn't he rescue me?

The reality is that God will do what he promises. But we have often applied to the promise things that God never intended. He didn't promise us that everything that happens to us would be good. He didn't promise to always rescue us from our problems even if the problems are there because we were doing right. He promised to be with us all the way through the trials and to bring something good out of all the troubles. Think of the physical fate of the apostles who were so close to Jesus. All but one died a martyr's death. John was exiled to Patmos as an old man for his witness for Jesus. Paul was beheaded and lived most of his later life in jail or prison. Peter was hanged on a cross upside down. Why then would we expect that it would all be smooth for us? Remember Peter said, "Yet if any of you suffer as a Christian, don't be ashamed but glorify God in His name." (I Peter 4:16). Suffering, hurt, problems, fears, tragedy and pain come on followers of Christ just like other people. The difference is that we never face them alone. God promises he will be with us every day of our life for him no matter what happens. When Paul was near death and knew his next appearing before Caesar would be the time for execution said, "At my first defense, all men forsook me, no one stood with me, yet the Lord stood with me and strengthened me." God's presence always helps and His leading will bring us to the right place but it may well go through some tough times getting there.

TAKE IT PERSONALLY

I tend to be good at making some comment to another person only to realize that I've hurt their feelings by what I've said. I've been known to say, "Hey, don't take it so personally. I wasn't talking about you." But as I read the

Bible I become more and more convinced that we don't take it personally enough. We read and think to ourselves how we wish some friend or family member would read this text and think of what it means to them. But too often it seems never to dawn on us that it is about us. Christians too often read and think of how the church they attend should be doing what this passage teaches, but never consider the fact they are the church and the best way to get the church to do what the text says is to begin doing it.

Very little in the Bible is written to the church as a whole. Most everything even addressed to the church turns out to be individual. Consider the letters to the seven churches of Asia in Revelation 2 and 3. He addresses the letter to the angel of the church in each city, which I take to mean the preacher there. But as you proceed in each letter it is obvious that he turns the attention to the individual members of the congregations. No matter how well or how poorly the church may be doing his challenge is to the individual members to be what God calls them to be. He will say things like "Even in Thyatira there are some who have not defiled their garments" and "To him who overcomes will I give the white stone."

Individuals rather than the whole group solve every challenge and problem in the church. We too often forget that we are the church. Someone will talk about what is going on in the church and think of it as the building or the organization or perhaps the leaders of the congregation. But the Bible pictures the church as the people and what they were doing. Even when they met Paul described as when the "Whole church came together in one place." They were no less the church before they came together than when they were all together.

Think of all the ways the Bible describes those who are members of the body of Christ, which is the church. When he described the church as the body of Christ, he called us members of that body in Romans 12:1-8. When he talked about the church as a temple of God he called us priest of the Lord in I Peter 2:5-9. When he referred to the church as a building we are living stones in the building (I Peter 2:5). When he speaks of us as a kingdom, he describes the members as "Kings and priest unto the Lord." (Revelation 1:6). When he described the church as a family the members of the family are brothers and sisters in the Lord. When God looked at the mission of the church in the world in 2 Corinthians 5:17-21 he declared that he had given to us the ministry of reconciliation. "We are therefore Christ's ambassadors, as though God were making his appeal through us. We implore you on Christ's behalf: Be reconciled to God." Think of the significance of being ambassadors for the Lord with the message of reconciliation to the whole world. What an exciting and challenging mission.

The next time you think of criticizing the church where you are a member, think of the fact you are the church and that the church is doing just as well in the world as you are doing as a member of it. If the church is failing to reach its mission of representing Christ in the world or giving to people the message of reconciliation that God wants us to carry it is because we as members aren't fulfilling the mission of being God's ambassadors to the world.

So far as I can tell by reading the Bible the early church didn't have any programs of any sort. Yet they helped the needy, preached the gospel to the lost and carried the saving message of the Lord to the whole world in their time. Since then we have tried to use all kinds of means and methods to reach the whole world again. We've used radio, TV, books, magazines, correspondence courses, and sent thousands of missionaries to the different parts of the world. Yet the world seems less affected by the gospel than ever. I don't think it will ever change until each Christian begins to fill their personal responsibility to be an ambassador for God and reaches out to the people they know each day to influence them and teach them about the Lord. With such influence it won't take long again to reach the world. You never know how far the person you reach for the Lord next door will carry that message to another who will go to whole new realms with the message and reach people that will carry it to different parts of the world until everyone has heard the saving message of the Lord.

THANK YOU LORD

Would you like to improve the atmosphere around your home and place of employment all the time? Would you like to build a stronger relationship with your children and help them to have a better outlook on life? Would you like to improve your relationship with your husband or wife and make it where both of you think more about what is good than what is not so good in the home? Would you like to improve drastically how you feel about the church where you worship and even the preacher that works for the Lord with you? Would you like to become the kind of person that sees God's hand in all the things going on around you and have a clearer grasp of what God wants you to be and do regularly? All these are possible for any one of us. The means of reaching such lofty goals is really such a simple thing that most won't try it because they can't believe that anything so simple could actually have such power.

It is somewhat like going to the doctor to learn how to lose weight. We realize we have put on too much weight and that our clothes are getting entirely too tight. There must be some kind of medical problem that is causing this weight gain. So off to the doctor we go, expecting to hear of some elaborate plan to solve this problem. Most likely we need a prescription that we can take regularly and see our weight come back down to where it was before we started gaining. But how, totally frustrating it is when the doctor says, "What you need to do is cut back on the bread and sweets in your diet, eat more fruit and vegetables and exercise regularly." When we hear this it is amazing where our thoughts usually run. We begin to think that we need to join a gym and have a trainer that gives us a special exercise program instead of thinking we need to get outside the house and walk for thirty minutes each day. The simpler the remedy the less likely we are to believe it will work or to carry it out.

There is an Old Testament story about an army officer named Naaman who had leprosy. A young Jewish maid who had been captured was working for Naaman and his family. One day she told her mistress, "If only my master would see the prophet who is in Samaria! He would cure him of his leprosy." She told Naaman and he told the king, so the king sent gifts and a message to the king of Israel asking that he heal his officer. The king was deeply frustrated wondering why anyone would come to him for healing. Elisha the prophet sent word to the king to send Naaman to him. Naaman and his men went out to the home of Elisha the prophet. Elisha sent a servant out to them and said to Naaman, "Go down to the Jordan River and dip seven times in it and you will be clean." Was he thrilled to have a cure so easily achieved? No, not at all, he was angry and went away in a rage. A fellow soldier said to him, "If he had ask you to do some great thing, would you have done it?" Naaman said, I thought he would come out and wave his arms over it and perform some kind of ritual. His fellow soldier convinced him to try the cure Elisha had given. He went to the Jordan, dipped in it seven times and came out clean from the leprosy. But he almost missed the cure because it was too simple.

What is that simple cure to so many of our down times, discouragement, depression and despair? God's answer to us is, "In everything give thanks, for this is the will of God in Christ Jesus." When we express thanks for everything people do for us or even for others around us it both serves to help us notice more things for which we should be thankful and encourages the one who received the thanks to do more good deeds to hear the thanks expressed. Being thankful and saying thank you to others builds our self-esteem, builds our assessment of others around us and helps us grow in faith in God. In Romans 1:18-32 Paul described how the Gentiles of the day had gone from devoted believers in God to hating God, denying His existence and being given up on by God. Look at where the drift away from God started in verse 21. "For although they knew God, they neither glorified him as God nor gave thanks to him, but their thinking became futile and their foolish hearts were darkened. Although they claimed to be wise, they became fools and exchanged the glory of the immortal God for images made to look like a mortal human being and birds and animals and reptiles." (Romans 1:21-23)

If you were to turn that cup over and start one toward God from unbelief the steps toward faith would be paved with gratitude. The more we thank God for every blessing and opportunity we receive the more blessings and opportunities we notice each day. Our faith grows and our attitude becomes more encouraged and encouraging.

So, have a wonderful Thanksgiving Day but don't let your gratitude be an annual event but a way of life every day.

THAT IS HARD

Not everything, even in the Bible is easy to understand or to apply when we do understand it. In John the sixth chapter, Jesus was teaching the disciples about commitment to him. He made the strange statement that unless one eats of his body and drinks his blood they have no part with him. The reaction of the disciples was, "This is a hard saying. Who can hear it?" From that time many of them turned back to no longer walk with him. It was then that he turned to the twelve and asked, "Do you also want to leave?" Their response was, "Lord, to whom shall we go? You have the words of eternal life." Here the thing that made the statement hard likely had to do both with understanding it and in how to apply it.

In 2 Peter 3:14-18 there is another statement about something being hard. Look closely at this one and think of how to apply it to our time. "Therefore, beloved, since you look for these things, be diligent to be found by Him in peace, spotless and blameless, and regard the patience of our Lord as salvation; just as also our beloved brother Paul, according to the wisdom given him, wrote to you, as also in all his letters, speaking in them of these things in which are some things hard to understand, which the untaught and unstable distort, as they do also the rest of the Scriptures, to their own destruction. You therefore, beloved, knowing this beforehand, be on your guard so that you are not carried away by the error of unprincipled men and fall from your own steadfastness, but grow in the grace and knowledge of our Lord and Savior Jesus Christ. To Him be the glory, both now and to the day of eternity. Amen."

Peter was speaking by inspiration from God. Yet he declared that some of the things Paul had written were hard to understand. Do you suppose Paul might have said the same thing about what Peter had written? It would be very interesting to know what parts of Paul's writings, Peter had been reading when he wrote this statement. It does indicate that even inspired teachers read the writings of others who wrote by inspiration. Earlier Peter said that the Old Testament writers searched their own writings to try to figure out exactly what period of time was involved in the promises of the Messiah coming into the world. He even pictured angels longing to see the message so they could know about the Lord's coming into the world. While it is true that many things in the Bible are simple enough for a child to understand, there are also things in the Bible of such great depth that the wisest scholars struggle to understand them.

How is a person to approach those hard to understand Scriptures so that they don't twist them to their own destruction? First, if a thing is in the Bible, it is meant for us to study and understand. The fact some things are hard to understand doesn't mean they can't be understood correctly. It does mean it requires more effort and deeper care. Second, hard Scriptures should be looked at in light of those, which are easier to understand and apply. Too often people approach Scripture in the opposite way. They begin with the very difficult and come up with a strange or unique interpretation of the difficult and then try to study the easy to understand Scriptures in light of the one that is difficult. The result is just about always disastrous. Third, approach the difficult Scriptures prayerfully. We need to pray for wisdom as we begin looking at God's word, always with the intent to live by what we learn from the word. David prayed, "Lord open my eyes that I might see the wondrous things in your word." That would be a great prayer for us as well. Finally, I need to study without an agenda. When we begin studying the Bible to prove a particular way of seeing things they will begin to fall into place to make the point. The problem is that often such use of Scriptures takes them out of context and has verses saying things that God never intended them to say. The right interpretation of Scripture is what the original writer had in mind and wanted to say from the beginning. Normally, there were problems or concerns being addressed at the time, which must be held in mind as we try to apply it to modern issues and ideas. Once we understand what a passage means and how it applies in the context in which it is written it is then possible to make applications to things that are going on in our own time.

Scriptures can be read and studied correctly to lead to salvation and a right relationship with God or they can be twisted to say what I want them to say and lead to my eternal ruin. Choose wisely how you will study and learn His will.

THE CLIFF

A person would have to be locked up in a sound proof room and not allowed to have any visitors or see any newspapers or news magazines, watch any news on TV or listen to any news on the radio to not hear about the financial cliff we are facing as a nation if Congress and the President can't get together to pass a solution. The image is a vivid one. The very thought of plunging over any kind of cliff doesn't sound like much fun. One would think that surely both our congressmen and our president would see the urgency of getting together and agreeing on a plan that may not be exactly what either wants but keeps the country from going off the cliff.

Thinking about the financial cliff we face as a nation, led to my thinking about another cliff talked about in the Bible. This cliff was also one that needed to be avoided and with God's help it was. The story about this cliff is found in Luke 4:14-30. Jesus had launched his personal ministry as the Messiah by being baptized by John the Baptist in the Jordan River. Immediately, the Voice of the Father came from heaven saying, "This is the Son I love with whom I am well pleased." The Spirit descended on him in the form of a dove. The Spirit then drove Jesus into the wilderness where he would spend forty days in prayer and fasting, being tempted by the devil. After the forty days Satan launched into his three big temptations of Jesus, all of which he overcame. When the temptations were over and Satan left him for a time, Jesus returned to his hometown of Nazareth where he went to the Synagogue on the Sabbath Day. He stood up to read and the scroll of Isaiah was handed to him.

Unrolling the scroll, Jesus found the place where it is written: "The Spirit of the Lord is on me, because he has anointed me to proclaim good news to the poor. He has sent me to proclaim freedom for the prisoners and recovery of sight for the blind, to set the oppressed free, to proclaim the year of the Lord's favor." He then rolled up the scroll and handed it back to the attendant, and sat down. He said to them, "Today this scripture is fulfilled in your hearing." The people were speaking well of him and were amazed at the gracious words he spoke. But someone asked, "Isn't this Joseph's son?" He referred to the proverb "Physician heal yourself!" and "no prophet is accepted in his home town." He then referred to two things that upset his hometown terribly. He mentioned Elijah during the famine in Israel going to a widow in Zarephath in the region of Sidon instead of to a widow in Israel for a place to stay. Then he mentioned Elisha's healing the leper Naaman the Syrian instead of one of the many lepers in Israel. The people in the synagogue became so furious that they got up, drove him out of the town, and took him to the brow of the hill on which the town was built, in order to throw him off the CLIFF. "But he walked right through the crowd and went on the way."

The cliff they wanted to throw Jesus off of wasn't a financial one but a literal cliff. He had dared to upset their whole way of seeing things. That had him pigeon holed as a homeboy who had made good. He was a good speaker and had good things to say. As Joseph's boy, they were proud of him. But when he took a Scripture they had long understood as applying to the Messiah when he came and applied that Scripture to himself, thus making the claim that he is the Messiah, the Christ and the Savior of the world, it just wouldn't fit into their thought processes. The Messiah couldn't be Joseph's son, could he? We've known Jesus since he was a very small boy. We've watched him grow up and work beside his dad as a carpenter.

When we have preconceived ideas about anything, it is close to impossible for us to fit things into our mind that contradict what we have always believed. They knew this Scripture was about the Messiah. But how can it refer to Jesus. This sure didn't seem like the year of the Lord's favor to them. Notice when a person or thought won't fit into the mold we have set for them, it is our natural inclination to get rid of them. Today, we might not try to throw them over the cliff physically. But we will throw them under the bus. Think of all the football coaches being fired in the last few days because they didn't have the season the people felt they should. Think of preachers or teachers that have been cast aside from their job because what they said didn't fit the ideas that were strongly held by some leader or leaders in the church.

Jesus walked right through the crowd and went away. It wasn't in God's plan that he would be killed at this point. That day would come but it wouldn't be by throwing him over the cliff, but on a cross outside of Jerusalem.

I wonder if the financial cliff being faced by this country isn't there because of all the preconceived ideas that people have so that they can't stand to hear anything that won't fit into the square hole in their brain. Cliffs are avoidable. But it requires being willing to see things I never thought were there.

THE GENEROUS HEART

Have you ever noticed that it is often the people who have the least who are willing to give the most? Some years ago Linda and I took a group to Trinidad for a campaign for Christ. The people from the church told us that as we went out to knock doors to be aware that people would want to give you something if you entered their home. We were reminded that we should take caution in the gifts we accepted because it might be the only thing they had for their own lunch or dinner that day. Sure enough wherever we went, people were offering some kind of gift. One man offered a fresh pineapple, another cookies to share with them along with a glass of tea. One day one of the local preachers traveled with me to another city to visit a family who wanted to serve Christ but there was no church in that area. We entered their home and saw a large family all living in this very small house with almost no furniture of any kind. We visited and discussed the Bible for a couple of hours before we started to leave. The mother of the family came out with a beautiful scarf to give me for my wife. I told her I couldn't take the scarf, that it was too much. She seemed hurt and as we left the local preacher said, "You offended the lady by refusing her gift. She was giving what she had and you should have taken it gratefully." I tried to explain to him that it seemed like an expensive gift and she had so little, but he wasn't moved. The trip back to the town where we were campaigning was uncomfortable and extremely quiet. When we finally reached the outskirts of the town, he slowed the car and said what he had obviously been mulling over the last two hours on the road. "We are poor people, but proud. When you come to work among us, we know you have much more than we do. When you refuse our gifts it makes us feel inferior and extremely poor. You came here to share with us the gospel of Christ the greatest treasure in the world. Don't put us down in the process."

In Jesus ministry he told of two women that were each pictured as tremendous examples of generosity. One was wealthy for her time. Her name was Mary the sister of Martha and Lazarus. Her family had provided Jesus a place of refuge when he was in Jerusalem. When the time came for Jesus to face arrest, a mock trial and execution, it was Mary who reached down deep to show her love for the Lord. He was at their home and sharing a meal at which Martha served and Lazarus sat with Jesus at the table. In the midst of it all Mary came in with a jar of very precious perfume, worth about a years wages. It would have been one of the primary treasures of the family. She took the bottle and broke open the flask. She poured the entire bottle of perfume on Jesus and was wiping the excess off with her hair. While the crowd around thought it was a scandalous waste, Jesus recognized it as an act of tremendous faith. "She anointed my for my burial." She did a good and beautiful deed and in doing so did what she could. Jesus even said that wherever the gospel was preached around the world this deed would be told about for a memorial to her. She was a generous wealthy person who gave freely of what she had.

The other generous woman that Jesus told about was not named. Jesus and the disciples were sitting adjacent to the treasury and watching, perhaps through the corner of their eyes, as people put in their contributions. The rich came by and threw in large amounts, making lots of noise as the coins fell to the bottom. But the shock came when Jesus pointed the apostles to a poor widow who had dropped in two small coins worth less than a penny. He said, "She gave more than all the rest. They gave out of their abundance. She gave all she had to live on." This widow wasn't trying to show anyone her sacrifice. But Jesus was alert to her heart. I suspect she shyly gave among the crowd of wealthy people demonstrating their giving. She probably felt how small her gift really was. Satan may have whispered in her ear, "You know this won't help God's cause and you need the money. The rich can handle this. Keep your money." But she gave anyway.

A generous heart is a beautiful sight. We can't impress the Lord with the size of our gifts. After all, he owns it all. "The earth is the Lord's and the fullness thereof." But he is so moved when he sees a generous heart. "Oh God, give me a heart willing to put everything on the line for you."

THE KINGS BUSINESS

How we describe or speak of anything makes a difference. If I explain to a friend who ask what I'm doing that I'm just wasting time with my children it will make a huge difference compared to saying, "I'm loving my children and training them in the Lord's way." We may be describing the same time and events. But if I see my time with my children as a waste of important time then the attitude will rub off on them. They will see time with dad as a waste as well.

Spiritually it matters tremendously how we speak of different things we do. If I look at some form of service I'm doing such as visiting someone who is sick or calling someone who is hurting over the loss of a loved one as "doing church work" it leaves an entirely different feeling and attitude than when I say, "I'm doing the Lord's work" or "I'm doing the king's business." Church programs don't bring much excitement to most of us. But when I think of doing the Lord's work or being about the king's business that is a whole different matter.

Remember when Jesus was just a twelve year old boy and came with Mary and Joseph to Jerusalem to worship. The time came to go home and they were with a large crowd of family and likely had a bunch of other smaller children with them as well. After all we know that Jesus had four brothers and at least two sisters. Whether they had all been born by this time or not, we don't know. But Joseph and Mary started back home thinking that Jesus was in the crowd traveling with them. They had travelled a day's journey when it became obvious Jesus wasn't in the crowd. Joseph and Mary headed back to Jerusalem to find Jesus. It took three days but when they found him he was in the temple sitting with the religious leaders asking them questions and listening to them. Mary began questioning Jesus. "Why did you do this? Didn't you know we would be worried about you?" Jesus responded, "Didn't you know that I must be about my Father's business (or in my Father's House)?" After this he went home with them and was subject to them. It wasn't an act of rebellion against them. It was choosing a priority. Being about the Father's business was more important than anything else.

As a Christ follower, the King is Jesus and His business is representing him in my life and relationships all the time. One of the worst mistakes I can make as one of the Kings followers is to think that doing his business only means a few "Spiritual" things such as going to church to worship him, singing, praying, studying the Bible, preaching His word or giving of my money to the cause of Christ. When I think that fulfills my work for the king, then I go away from the time of worship thinking the rest of the week is my time and I live for myself then.

When Jesus challenged us to "Seek first the kingdom of God and His righteousness and all these things will be added to you" it was in a context of discussing worry over things, security in life and living long on the earth. It was part of the discussion on what really matters in life and what has priority. He said, "No one can serve two masters. He will either love the one and hate the other or he will hold to the one and despise the other. You cannot serve God and money." Kingdom business involves all the actions and affairs of life. It even involves my way of making money, spending money and saving money. No matter how freely I give of my money to the Lord's work or helping other people, if I don't make it in an honest, righteous way I'm not doing the king's business. But when money and things, possessions become the really important things in our lives we aren't about the king's business. We have turned money and things into our god and turned away from the king.

When we are about the king's business we trust the Lord to take care of our future and our present. We devote ourselves to following Christ as husbands and wives in how we treat each other in the home and family. We put the bringing up of our children for God as the primary matter in life. As important as it is to have our children in little league, in drama, dance or whatever else may be the latest trend, it isn't even comparable to having my child in church and teaching them about the Lord and his will for life. What we tell our children matters. But if what I tell them doesn't match what they see in my life, it will be what they see that makes the greatest impression. The king's business involves presenting our bodies as a living sacrifice to God and not conforming to the world but being transformed by the renewing of our minds to prove the good, acceptable and perfect will of God (Romans 12:1-2).

Let's make certain that we are about the king's business today and every day.

I'm thankful we live in a country where people are encouraged to give to all kinds of things. Every time there is a tragedy around the world there is a cry for help and we tend to come through in flying colors. One amazing thing to me is that people don't just give and then walk away but they keep on giving and working until a situation is much improved. Think of how long people continued to go to New Orleans to work after Katrina.

I'm thankful that at Christmas time we think more about giving to someone else. Now I'll be honest I think the giving at this time often goes way beyond reason when people go into debt on their credit cards to the degree they will take most of next year paying it off, if indeed they get it paid off in a year. That is crazy. Gifts don't have to be large and expensive to be meaningful. When parents spoil their children to the degree they are tired of what they get three days later and wanting something else it is ridiculous. Instead of teaching our children to look forward to this time of year because of all they will receive we need to teach them early on that it is about giving to someone else.

We don't know when Jesus said, "It is more blessed to give than to receive." But it should be a rule of life for all of us. Too often when we hear the word "Give" from anyone at church or certainly from a preacher our mind runs immediately to giving to God and his cause at church. But the reality is we need to learn the power of giving all the time in every aspect of life. Remember what Jesus said in the Sermon on the Mount "And if anyone wants to sue you and take your shirt, hand over your coat as well. If anyone forces you to go one mile, go with him or her two miles. Give to the one who asks you, and do not turn away from the one who wants to borrow from you." (Matthew 5:40-42) Now I certainly understand the reaction when we read such verses. "Surely he didn't mean what it sounds like." "I don't want to give to someone who is just going to turn around and blow or use it to buy booze." "Loan money to the one who asked? Who would do that? How would you know if they would ever pay you back? That is no way to run a business." "I want to be sure to use my money wisely and make certain I have enough saved for my retirement."

The list could go on forever. Here is the truth of the matter. If you are stingy with your money and property you can find an excuse to justify it any time you want. Will Jesus be kind and accepting of our excuses? I sincerely doubt it. Another gem to consider is this, if I'm stingy with God in my giving at church, I will be stingy with everyone else except myself. The truth is that stinginess runs deep in our soul. There is no wonder that Paul would say that stinginess or covetousness is idolatry. It is the fact that I've made myself into my God and just don't want to admit it. When stingy people give it is always with view to what they will get back. If they don't get back what they consider to be a good bargain they will cut back on the gift the next time they have a chance.

By now I'm sure that all the spiritually minded folks have started shouting that Paul said, "If a man won't work neither let him eat." For many it has become their favorite verse instead of "It's more blessed to give than to receive." No the Bible doesn't teach that we should become enablers for people to continue in a wrong way of life. The problem is that we often decide without knowing the facts that someone "won't work" and so "shouldn't eat." What if the problem isn't laziness but inability to find a job? What if they never learned how to work since they grew up in an environment where everyone just got welfare and stayed at home? It may well be that the giving they need isn't money but someone to take the time and interest to mentor them toward a better way of life. What if there is sickness I'm not aware of?

The plea is really this; don't allow your excuses to take the place of God's teaching that the better way of life is one of giving rather than one of getting! Be a Giver always!

THE UNVEILING

Have you ever been to an unveiling? It could well have been some new memorial such as the Vietnam Memorial or the opening of a new museum such as Crystal Bridges. But an unveiling is an exciting happening and opens up for us something that has been veiled or closed until now.

The Book of Revelation is intended by God to be an unveiling. The very word "Revelation" means that something is being revealed that has been hidden. It is the idea that people have been confused about something and God is providing something to give them clarity. It is interesting that the very Book that is called a "Revelation" or "unveiling" is often the most difficult to grasp of any of the books of the Bible. Far too often we simply avoid and declare that we can't understand it so why bother. The other extreme that is even worse is to turn the book of unveiling into our own private means of declaring all our pet notions on what will happen in the future.

Remember that the Book of Revelation was written by John the Apostle to the seven churches of Asia that were dealing with problems, challenges and concerns right then. Whatever this book has to say it is obvious that God's intent was that it be an unveiling, a means of making clear some things that were bothering these seven churches and to help them grasp what was going on in their world. We may gain all kinds of principles from the study of the book. But if we are reading it in a way that only makes sense to us in the 20th or 21st centuries then we are misreading it. It was intended to be a local letter written to these seven churches to help them. We are the ones looking into the letter from the outside and seeing things that we can learn.

There was one huge vision that the Lord was trying to get the churches then to see and that we also always need to see. They were struggling under persecution from the Roman Government. At that time the Roman Emperors were claiming deity and demanding worship from their subjects. When the churches and the Christians refused to bow down to the king or to his images they suffered deeply. Throughout the book there are both pictures of the suffering of Christians and references to specific problems that were being faced. Even in the letters to the churches in chapters 2 and 3 he talks about their persecution. One example is in chapter 2 and verses 8-11 as he writes to the church at Smyrna. He told them He knew their tribulation and poverty. He said, "Do not fear what you are about to suffer. Behold the devil is about to cast some of you into prison so that you will be tested, and you will have tribulation for ten days. Be faithful unto death and I will give you the crown of life." They were suffering, being mistreated and in fear of what was coming.

Jesus wrote through John to comfort and encourage them to stay true to the Lord during such times. He kept telling them of His presence with them and how the angels were around them to help and protect. In chapter 6 he pictures a group of saints that had been killed for their faith. They were under the altar crying out "How long O Lord, holy and true, do you not judge and avenge our blood on those who dwell on the earth?" They were given white robes and told to wait a little while until others of their brethren were killed. In chapter 7 he pictures that same group of saints who had been murdered for their faith in Jesus in their white robes and they were being blessed in glory with the Lord leading them by everlasting fountains of water and God wiping away all tears from their eyes. The point was that even though they had suffered and died for their faith here, they were in a great situation with God and Jesus in the heavenly realm.

He tells in this book about how governments of all sorts are under the power of God and that the Roman government will fall. God would bring on natural disasters, there would be enemy nations coming against them and it would ultimately crumble from within.   Their cry for judgment and avenging their death would come.

Revelation is an unveiling to let us know that God is in control and that while horrible, evil things happen in the world and we sometimes suffer for our faith, there is a better world awaiting and God will judge and avenge those who persecute the saints in all ages. Ultimately the point is that if we stay true to the Lord we will have victory in Jesus.

No enemy will stand before Him who reigns as king of kings and Lord of Lords.

TOO MUCH ME

It's a huge challenge when you see someone you love dearly that has either lost all his or her self-confidence or somehow never developed that sense. It takes on an even greater challenge when you are working to help them learn particular skills or show them a better way of doing anything. It often seems that in the very act of pointing out a better way of doing something you injure all the more and they are pushed even further down into the well of despair.

On the other end of the spectrum it is just as great a challenge to deal with someone who is convinced that they are God's answer to every problem in the world. They have no lack of self-confidence. Instead they seem to have a Messiah complex. In this case to try to show them there is a better way to do anything will fall quickly to the ground since it is clear to them they know far more than you could possibly know about anything.

I've been asked at times which of these two situations or types of people had you rather work with and the answer I usually give is "Neither". Both these extremes are far away from the attitude God wants to develop in each of us. Look at Paul's message on this topic in Romans 12:3-6. "For by the grace given me I say to everyone of you: Do not think of yourself more highly than you ought but rather think of your self with sober judgment, in accordance with the faith God has distributed to each of you. For just as each of us has one body with many members, and these members do not all have the same function, so in Christ we, though many, form one body, and each member belongs to all the others. We have different gifts, according to the grace given to each of us."

Lesson one to be learned here is don't think to highly of you and don't think too lowly of yourself. Every one of us is like a different member of our own body. Our different parts aren't equal in value to the body. But it is foolish to the core to compare what my little finger does with what the right eye does. They have very different functions. The only right way to make a comparison is to compare what my little finger does with what a little finger is supposed to do and to compare my right eye with what a right eye is meant to accomplish.

Whether we are in a family, a ball team, a church or even a youth group at church it is common to hear people say, "I just wish I could do like..." I suspect the only parent that has never heard their child compare themselves to older children in the family are the ones who only had one child. I don't think teachers or coaches or even parents have a clue what they are doing to a child's feelings about themselves when they say, "Why can't you be more like your older brother or older sister?"

Lesson two is that no matter who we are or what our abilities are, by God's grace we have a function to carry out in the body. It is God's plan that we operate as members of the body rather than as individual parts trying to make it on our own. If individual members of our physical body tried to set out on their own it would both lead to the destruction of the member since they can't survive apart from the body. But it would also lead either to the death or the decrease of what the body can accomplish. God didn't put in useless parts in our body. In his body the church we all have an important place to fill and we find fullness in life when we find our God intended place and do the very best we can do in that place.

Lesson three is in order to have the right attitude about ourselves we must lose ourselves in a cause much bigger than we are. God made us to operate with a purpose outside of us. If we live all the time thinking about our own feelings, hurts, joys and wants we will be miserable most of the time. But if we live our life bent on serving, helping and doing good for others we find real meaning and purpose in our own lives. One of the results of developing such an attitude is that we can declare with Paul, "I can do all things through Christ who gives me strength." We build the right attitude about self, as we know we are made in God's image, with a purpose from God to be carried out as part of the body of Christ, the church. The vast majority of the work done by the body of Christ isn't done in the public worship of the congregation. Too many people think of themselves as only working in church when they are doing something on Sunday in the worship time. Certainly what is done there is important. But Christians out in the world serving, helping others and doing things in the name of the Lord for someone else are doing God's greatest work. It is for that reason that it is ludicrous for anyone to complain about the church not using him or her in the work. If you are living for Christ in your home, community and world and are serving others on your job or anywhere you find the opportunity you are working in the church. When we do the work God calls on us to do we feel better about the world, better about the church and much better about ourselves.

TRIAL RUNS

Would you buy a car without trying it out? That is the question I've had posed to me almost every time I talk with a couple who are living together and aren't married yet. They usually continue with, "I've seen the marriages of my parents and the misery they've gone through. We are going to make certain we are right for each other before we get married." I've even had parents and grandparents defend the action of co-habitation, as a trial run for marriage. The result of this reasoning is that every year there are more and more people in our circle who are living together without marriage.

May I suggest a few things to consider on this topic before you try to justify the actions that God calls immorality and adultery. First, a husband or wife isn't like a car that you try out for a fifteen-minute trip to determine if it is the car for you. I've never known of a car turning up pregnant during the trial run. Marriage is a covenant between two people for life. A car is something you own and which you intend to trade for a newer model as time moves on. A car is a machine that tends to operate the same way day after day. A wife or husband is a person that thinks, reasons, feels and changes constantly. I've never heard a person say, "I'm getting rid of this car because it has changed since I purchased it."

Playing house or trying to act like married people without being married is not the same thing at all as marriage. During these trial runs it is fine if one decides this isn't for me so I'm moving on. There was no covenant involved. You were simply acting like you were married and taking advantage of the pleasure God placed in the marriage. One of the huge myths that seems to take legs all over again after it has been debunked hundreds or even thousands of times is that if I could just find the right person marriage would be great. We would get along. They would like the same things I do and want to go to the same places as I do. We will always get along and enjoy each other's company. If I'm thinking that marriage is going to be the same beautiful thing every day, I would likely be better off just purchasing a dog. You can pick them at will and get rid of them if they don't fit your wishes. In marriage there is no perfect partner that was just made for you.

The perfect marriage is the one in which the two people love each other, honor each other, and each person works and prays daily to be the best marriage partner they can possibly be. Notice I said they work on themselves to become the best they can be. The natural thing is to start immediately working on the partner to change them and make them into the partner I've always wanted. It is much easier to work on the other person and pretend I don't have any flaws to work on than to face my own problems and work on fixing them.

When God wished to give us a perfect pattern for marriage, look at what he chose as his illustration. In Ephesians 5:21-35 he challenged wives to submit to their husbands as the church submits to Christ. He challenged husbands to love their wives as Christ loved the church and gave himself up for her. He noted that the church belongs to Christ the way a married couple belongs to each other. The married couple becomes one flesh just as Christ and the church are one. So the ideal for a marriage is Christ and the church. I certainly see that Jesus is the perfect husband for the church as His bride, but I'm not able to see the church as the perfect wife. From the very beginning the church has been in a struggle. False teachers, immoral members, people listening to the wrong ideas and going with them or even those in the church making some petty idea or action into a major problem to divide a congregation over.

What if Jesus were looking for that perfect wife, the one made for him, how do you think the church would fare? Thank God our spiritual husband is one who freely forgives and takes us back into his loving arms even when we have failed him horribly. If we can be forgiven, cleaned up and taken back as Jesus wife, don't you think we should learn to do the same thing in our marriage?

Do you remember the vows you made, the covenant you joined? It was to love and to cherish, in sickness and in health, to forsake all others and cleave to this one alone, to remain true to each other in sickness and in health, for richer or poorer, till death we part? That covenant is the heart of a marriage. No pretending we are married to see if we are right for each other can compare with the real thing. Marriage isn't an experiment. It is a covenant relationship! It is for a man and woman to make with each other before God and with His blessing be true to each other for life.

One of those fundamental teachings of the Bible and for us as a church is the intention to be undenominational. In our day saying we are undenominational sends out a very different signal than it once did. It is popular for churches that have long been associated with some denominational group to decide they no longer want to be subject to the organization or carry the name of the group. Often the feeling is that the name is a hindrance to the growth and acceptance of the church. Usually the teachings and beliefs don't change much, if at all but the structure changes a lot. Personally, it is exciting to me for any church to leave the organizational structure and set out to be an undenominational church. It may well lead to growth toward God and toward the New Testament picture of the church.

But what do we mean when we declare that we are an undenominational church? First, we mean that we don't belong to any organization or structure to which we must report and from which we get our teachings. The church in the Bible has only one head and that is Jesus Christ (Colossians 1:18; Ephesians 1:22-23). We have men who meet the standards described by Paul in I Timothy 3 and Titus one who serve as shepherds, elders, and overseers of the local church. These men work entirely in the area of judgment about what is to be done in this church. They have no authority on what is to be taught since we have the word of the Lord that we are commanded to teach and preach (2 Timothy 4:1-5). No one can change the reality that our teaching is to be what God said in His word. But these shepherds have oversight in how we will, as a church carry out the teachings of the Bible in this congregation. For example, the Lord tells us to go into all the world making disciples baptizing them into the name of the Father, the Son and the Holy Spirit, teaching them to observe all things commanded and Jesus promised to be with us to the end of the age. Elders can't decide we won't do what Jesus said. They can decide where we will as a congregation go and support the going into the entire world. We also have men who work as servants or deacons who are put in charge of specific areas of work that fit into the overall plan of the church.

Being undenominational to us means that we have no creed or manual to follow except the Bible, specifically for us the New Testament since it is the covenant we are under today. Being undenominational means that there isn't some set way of understanding everything that we must adhere to all through the ages. We are constantly restudying; rethinking and striving to best understand and apply what the Bible teaches. Sometimes as new translations and new discoveries are made it makes some things clearer from Scripture than has been there before and we must change, as we understand better. It doesn't require the meeting of some board or group to change when we see we've been mistaken in some area. It just means we start teaching it the way we understand the Bible to teach. We are human and our interpretation of Scripture is never perfect. It is the Bible that is the standard, not any particular person or groups interpretation of what that Scripture teaches. When we demand that everyone follow an interpretation of some Scripture we become denominational in the process.

Being undenominational means we are simply Christians, followers of Christ and His disciples. Our loyalty is the Jesus and not any person however great they may be or have been. The Bible doesn't give a specific name for the church. It gives many descriptions such as, "churches of Christ", "church of God", and "house of God", "church of the living God" and "churches of the saints". None of these is the name of the church. Notice in the Bible every one of these descriptions begin with a small letter rather than a capital indicating the translators didn't see them as a proper name. When we turn one of them into THE name for the church we turn it into a denomination.

Being undenominational means we are made up of people who are followers of Christ, who have out of faith turned from sin to God and have been baptized in the name of the Lord to become part of the church. Our job is to teach people what the Bible says to be saved and to live for God. It isn't our job to decide who has done everything to our satisfaction. Jesus is head and he adds people to the church and he takes one's name from the Book of Life if they aren't doing right.

Jesus prayed that all his disciples would be one as he and the Father are one so that the world may believe that He is the Christ. When we turn his church into something that divides every few years over piddling things we defy the head of the church and make it into our own little playhouse. Our desire is to be undenominational and completely loyal to Jesus and His word.

UNDERSTANDING PEOPLE

Do you ever look back on actions in your own life and wonder, "What was I thinking when I did that?" Sometimes we may blame our actions on youth, but that doesn't really cover the wrong because I was certainly old enough to know better. Do you ever become frustrated with your children or grandchildren when they do things that they've been told time and again not to do and do you wonder, "What are they thinking that they would do such things?" Think about it. If I can't even figure out my own actions or the actions of ones I love and have worked to show the right way, why would I ever think I would be able to understand the actions of people who I don't know, have never met, have an entirely different background and a completely different set of standards for right and wrong?

When something happens like the bombing that took place at the finish line of the Boston Marathon, we sit back in amazement. "Why would any sane person want to attack innocent people who were out running?" Normally with any kind of attack that is cowardly, hidden and done from a distance we struggle with understanding it even if the attack is on some government office or building. But an attack on the Pentagon or the White House at least makes some sense if one believes the government is somehow evil and that it is attacking the way of life you believe is right. But the attack on ordinary people out living life each day just doesn't add up.

I feel quite certain that if we could actually engage one of the terrorist or even one of the backers of terrorism, we would get a couple of responses. I suspect that first of all the terrorist would point to the actions of our own country in the use of drones to attack people of other countries. We normally have some definite target in mind that we are trying to eliminate a threat that is waiting just ahead for us. But I feel certain the other side would point out that when we use such attacks it is seldom the case that the only one killed is the enemy we were aiming for. Most of the time there are other people, often wives and children that are either killed or seriously injured in such actions. We can answer that these are the actions of war, but the response will be, "Yes and so are our actions."

The other thing that will come up in such times is for the person to point to the actions of God especially during the Old Testament when He sent the armies of Israel against people such as the Amalekites to completely destroy them. When King Saul refused to kill everything and brought back the king and some of the best of the sheep and goats, God was angered by his disobedience and it cost Saul the throne in Israel. When Joshua led the Israelites into the Promised Land the first city they were to attack was the walled city of Jericho. God told the people to go in and completely destroy everything there except the family of Rahab who had hidden the spies who came to check out the land. If God would have his people kill everyone in a city or country, including the animals and the women and children, how can we condemn the actions of religious people who are, at war with our lifestyles, and us for killing people indiscriminately?

I won't attempt to offer a defense for this country with the drone attacks. And I know that God doesn't need my defense for his actions either in the Old Testament with cases like the ones mentioned or in the New with the punishment of Ananias and Sapphira. But I will point out some things to consider anyway with regard to God's actions. First, we cannot judge the actions of God by the scale of man. To say that God killed the innocent along with the guilty is to assume there were innocent people among them. Think of the fact when God was about to destroy Sodom because of the evil in it, he was ready to spare the entire city if only ten righteous people could be found. In the flood the eight people who were found innocent in the whole crowd were spared by means of the ark. Second, we are limited in what we know of the situations and are trying to judge the actions of God who didn't have such limits. He knew their actions and their thoughts. What we know of the people who were destroyed in these cities or areas is that they were brutal, murderous, incestuous and immoral people. When Jeremiah pictured God looking on people's actions like those just described he pictures God saying, "Such a thing never entered into my mind." Third, we aren't aware of how much time, effort and energy God had put into trying to teach, love and change the lives of the people he ultimately destroyed.

We aren't God and to try to put ourselves into the place of God turns us into people trying to justify actions that are not justifiable. What should we do and how should we think of people who commit atrocities against us? We should pray that God would touch the hearts of these people to bring them to repentance. We should avoid becoming like the very ones that we speak so against. We should look at the actions of our own country to see what among us needs to change and work to see that change as well.

WHAT ABOUT GAY MARRIAGE

With all kinds of turmoil going on with regard to the subject of gay marriage it seems appropriate to take a closer look at the topic. Let me begin with noting that marriage itself was a God thing. It is based on the fact it isn't good for a man to be alone so God made a helper suited for him and had Adam to declare, "This is now bone of my bone and flesh of my flesh. She shall be called woman. For this reason a man will leave his father and mother and be joined to his wife and the two will become one flesh." The distinct thing about marriage from a Biblical point of view is that it is more than a contract, more than a pledge of companionship and more than a legal document. In Malachi chapter two the prophet pictured God saying, "And why did I make the two of you one? So that you might raise up a godly seed." Jesus would add to this point by saying, "What God has joined together let no man separate."

If one goes back into Scripture marriage or even the wedding itself had nothing to do with the state or government. It was a commitment that a man and woman made to each other. They came together with the intent of being husband and wife. When Isaac took Rebekah there was no marriage ceremony. She was brought to him and they went into Sarah's tent to become husband and wife. By the time we reach the New Testament there was an elaborate ceremony described in places like John two when Jesus and his disciples along with his mother went to a wedding feast where the host ran out of wine and Jesus turned the water into wine to save the host embarrassment. Then Jesus used the wedding feast to describe the second coming and judgment in Matthew 25 with the five wise and five foolish virgins. But in both these instances it is a family affair, not a civil affair.

I think I understand how it became a civil matter in our society. Truthfully I think there is not anything that we do that government is looking for a way to tax or get money from by charging some fees. I'm sure there was some more noble reason given as to why the state would begin to give license for weddings.

In truth there seems to be no more intrusion of government into the whole marriage than of church doing so. I'm not opposed to churches having weddings or preachers performing ceremonies. Actually I usually enjoy the whole process. But neither church nor state determine whether a marriage is real, correct or accepted by God. The real question to be raised isn't about whether the state will recognize gay marriages or even whether churches will do so. Both may well accept them as right and good, but it will make absolutely no difference if God doesn't join the two together to make them one flesh. God's joining is between him and the couple. I feel sure he won't change his mind about what to do based on what the church or the government says on the matter.

These truths ought to be kept clearly in mind though. God in giving us marriage determined the helper that was suitable for a man and that was a woman through whom they together might have children, to replenish and multiply on the earth. Even with Malachi's teaching God said he made them one so that they could raise up a godly seed. Marriage was for companionship, but not just companionship. It was to bring children into the world and bring them up for the Lord.

From the beginning God rejected homosexual relationships. It was at least a big part of the downfall of Sodom. Moses in Leviticus states that homosexual relationships are an abomination to God. In the New Testament Paul described the fall of man further and further from him in Romans 1:18-27. He said that God gave the people up because their women were having sex with other women and men were burning in lust for each other rather than for the woman. In I Corinthians 6:9-11 homosexual relationships are listed among the unrighteous deeds that lead to rejection by God. In I Timothy 1:10 it is listed among the sins of lawbreakers and rebels.

Should the state recognize gay marriage? I don't know what the state should do. It should treat all people equally. But what the state does on the matter has little to nothing to do with what really matters. When it comes to human rights I don't believe anyone should be mistreated because of their sexual orientation. State should neither promote marriage or singleness. It should give the same rights to all people. But if the state sanctions gay marriage and it becomes acceptable in the eyes of people, it won't change two things that really matter. First, it won't mean that God joins the two into one flesh. Second, it won't make the gay couple able to produce offspring. Whether we like it or not one of the primary purposes of marriage was and is to produce children. Humans change laws all the time. But God and his creation or his law doesn't change based on what is done by the courts or the legislature.

Having desires for one of the same sex isn't wrong or condemned in Scripture. It is only the sexual relationship that is condemned. Every person has some desires that they have no right to fulfill before God.

WHAT'S THAT SIGN?

One of the favorite phrases of our day is, "Show me." If we are in clothing store and a sales person begins to tell us about some new product or service, our response is "Show me." It is difficult to imagine a hotel or resort area without tons of pictures for you to see on the Internet before you decide if this is the place. Do you remember when there were no such pictures? There weren't any videos to watch to see what the room or area looked like. Instead you had to make the decision based on a description.

The people who came to hear Jesus preach and teach the word of God were a whole lot like us in that they wanted to see the evidence. They were a "Show me" type people who demanded a sign to demonstrate that He really is the

Messiah. In Matthew 16:1-4 it says, "The Pharisees and Sadducees came to Jesus and tested him by asking him to show them a sign from heaven. He replied, 'When evening comes, you say, 'It will be fair weather, for the sky is red,' and in the morning, 'Today it will be stormy, for the sky is red and overcast.' You know how to interpret the appearance of the sky, but you cannot interpret the signs of the times. A wicked and adulterous generation looks for a sign, but none will be given it except the sign of Jonah. Jesus then left them and went away."

I want to focus on one statement Jesus made and that is that no sign would be given except the sign of Jonah. But take a moment first to see the setting of the statement. These religious leaders had followed Jesus and heard his teachings. They had observed him heal all kinds of sick people, cast out demons that changed the whole lives of people, feed 5,000 people with a little boys sack lunch, cause a blind man to see and deaf man to hear and a mute man to speak. So when they asked for a sign it is laughable. It would be like a nurse working in heart surgery unit of a large hospital that had assisted a heart surgeon on over a hundred cases as he did by-pass surgery, replaced valves, and even transplanted hearts from a patient who had died tragically into the body of another person whose heart was at the point of death, who then declared to a group, "If I could just see one of these surgeons do something that really made a difference in someone's life I would feel much better about them and what I do." Don't you think someone would surely stand up and say, "Are you crazy? You've observed all kinds of amazing things happen to change the lives of people from near death to a full life. How can you now say you just want to see them do something that makes a difference in someone's life?"

But for some reason when the religious leaders spoke or asked questions people didn't seem to think it was a crazy question or they didn't have the nerve to stand up and tell them just how crazy their questions really were.

They could read the signs of the clouds and the sky but couldn't read the signs of the Messiah that were marvelous indeed. Do you think we ever find ourselves in the place of these folks? Are we ever the people who see the evidence of God's actions in the world day after day and most of them are far beyond our ability to understand or explain, yet we keep looking for one more sign or evidence that really takes away all of our doubts and fears.

Jesus responded by telling them he wasn't going to be some kind of cheap magician who did one more trick to fool the crowd until they really believed he was great. He wasn't doing miracles just to play some game with them. Every miracle was for the benefit of the people in some way. By far the majority of the miracles he did were to heal some kind of sickness or disease.

But what is the "Sign of Jonah"? Think of some possibilities that it could be. It could be that Jonah was given a mission to people very different from him to carry them the message of repentance. It could be that you can't run away from God. He can prepare a ready-made storm and a big fish to get you when you are thrown into the sea. It could be the deliverance from the big fish after three days. It could be the preaching that he reluctantly did in Nineveh that led to their repentance and forgiveness. It could be his lousy attitude about their forgiveness in which he resented the grace and kindness of God.

Since neither Jesus nor any of the gospel writers ever said exactly what he meant by it we couldn't be certain either. But I suspect it was that God gave Jonah a mission to a foreign, brutal and hated people and that when he fulfilled his mission God brought about a powerful revival that changed their whole future. Jesus came into the world to seek and save the lost, not to get along with the religious leaders of the day. He would send out his disciples on a mission to the world to reach people of every background and problem. We as his followers still are living under that mission to reach people of every kind and every problem to bring them to him. I think that is what he meant by the sign of Jonah.

I sure hope when we fulfill the mission we do it with less reluctance but with the same kind of results on the people.

WHEN NOTHING WORKS RIGHT

"This just isn't working out the way it was supposed to work." How many times have you either said something to this effect or have heard someone else say it? From early in life we learn that if you do certain things it is supposed to have certain results. For example, if you turn the handle on the left side of the sink it will bring hot water to you if you wait for it. What happens if you turn the handle and nothing happens? There is no hot water. There isn't even any water at all. What happened?

The reality is we go through the same education in the emotional and spiritual aspects of life. If you study hard and do well on the test you will get a good grade in school, at least that is what I've heard. If you do well for people they will like you and say good things about you. If you treat a girl with respect and kindness, showing her lots of affection the result is that she will be true to you. If you attend church regularly, give of your income to God and study your Bible prayerfully, you will be a good Christian. If you are a good Christian then things will go well for you. You will make lots of money, build close friendships and have a great life as well as have heaven when this life is over.

The truth is that life can't be manipulated or controlled by our actions. You are certainly more likely to make good grades if you study hard and do well on test but sometimes it doesn't work out that way. You may treat a girl or boy for that matter with the utmost respect, kindness and attention and still have them turn from you to someone else. The Bible does say that we will reap as we sow, but everyone that has ever had a garden knows that you also reap some things you didn't sow.

Focus for a moment on a young man on whom God had bestowed amazing blessings and opportunities. If you had lived in that day and had known Jesse's family you would have thought that David was certainly blessed beyond anything he could have deserved. As a boy out taking care of his father's sheep his dad had such a low opinion of his ability that when Samuel the prophet came to anoint one of the boys as the next king, Jesse didn't even invite David to the party. He never dreamed it could have been David that God had in mind. But Samuel wouldn't allow the party to continue until David came. He was still just a boy when Jesse sent him out to the battlefield to carry supplies to his brothers who were in Saul's army. When the giant, Goliath came out taunting the armies of Israel David was there to hear it all. He was amazed that none of these soldiers, like his brothers were jumping to their feet, grabbing their armor and rushing out to meet this guy. He volunteered for the job. Saul gave him his armor to put on and David tried it on but it just didn't work for him. He went out with what was familiar to him, a sling with five smooth stones. The result was Goliath came tumbling down and David cut off his head with his own sword.

If you could have stopped the clock right there it would have seemed that David had life under his control. He was called to the king's palace to play his harp when Saul had one of his spells. He became a mighty soldier that people sang to when he led the army of Israel in, saying, "Saul has slain his thousands and David his ten thousands." It infuriated Saul. He began a concerted effort to kill David. David escaped the king's palace and went into the hills to live as a fugitive in caves. In time a rag tag group of men came to his side. They were people, like him that had been driven out from the people. Some were debtors; some had other problems with the law. But they developed into a small army. David was on the run, hiding from Saul to save his life. I wonder if you could have sat down with David at this point would he have felt that he was getting what he deserved? He would become king, but it wouldn't be much fun getting there. God was training him for the work he would do as leader of the nation of Israel.

Does God still put us through things that are tough, that we don't think we deserve to prepare us for something important in front of us? Yes, he still does. A few days ago I read the story of a woman who never was able to have children of her own even though she loved and wanted children desperately. When she was in her mid forties, her sister-in-law was murdered and her brother seriously wounded, and later died from the problems of the attack. She took her brother's small children and raised them as her own. As she looked back she said, God had a plan in mind all along and was preparing her for something big. The next time something happens in your life that just doesn't seem fair, think, perhaps this is God preparing me for something important that is coming up. It will help your attitude to be better all along.

WHEN WE ALL GET TO HEAVEN

What is your mental picture when you think about going to heaven? We've heard lots through the last few years about some people who picture heaven where a man will receive 8 or whatever the number virgins for his use. Multiple songs have been written that we have sung through the years about heaven that give all kinds of pictures of heaven for us. But what does Jesus tell us about heaven? He is the one who had lived there through the ages and came down from there to this earth for 33 years and then returned to sit down at the right hand of the Father. What he tells us about heaven certainly should be the standard to go by. Many seem to believe that heaven will be an eternal worship service where we sing praise to God constantly, but I'm not so sure that would be heavenly.

The most well known Scripture in which Jesus talked about heaven is John 14:1-3. He had just pointed out that Peter would deny him and the others would forsake him then he said, "Do not let your heart be troubled. You believe in God, believe me also. In my Father's house are many rooms. If it were not so I would have told you. I go to prepare a place for you if I go to prepare a place for you I will come again to receive you to myself that where I am you may be also." In this picture Jesus drew a comparison everyone there would have been familiar with. It was the wedding picture as a bridegroom told the bride I'm going to prepare a place for us and when I come back we will be married and live there together. He would go back home and build on to his father's house to make room for he and his wife and as the family grew, he would continue to add rooms so there was a place for them. Jesus declared, he was the bridegroom, going to heaven to make a place for us as his bride and he would return for us to take us home with him in his Father's house and there would be plenty of room there. So first, Jesus promises his presence and provision for us in heaven. There is room for all.

In Luke 16 he told the story of the rich man and Lazarus. On earth Lazarus was a beggar lying at the gate of the rich man who had it all but shared nothing. They both died and the rich man lifted up his eyes in the torment of hell. Angels were there to carry Lazarus where he was comforted at Abraham's sode. Heaven then is a place of relationships with God's redeemed of the ages and where we are comforted from the hurts and disappointments of life. In Revelation chapters 6 and 7 John carries this point further when those had been martyred for their faith were crying out to God for vengeance against those who had murdered them. They were told to wait. But then in chapter 7 they are pictured with white robes and are being led by Christ as their shepherd to everlasting fountains of water and God wipes away all their tears. Again the main point is about

God's provision and the comfort offered to those who are redeemed.

Heaven is described as a place of feasting and often as the wedding feast where there was tremendous joy. It likely was pointing to that time when Jesus went with his mother and disciples to the wedding feast and the host ran out of wine. His mother asked him to take care of it and after some resistance he told the servants to fill the water pots outside that were there for purification with water and then dip some out and take it to the host. It was the best wine he had partaken of. Jesus made huge pots full of the wine so the joy could flow fully. In Matthew 25 as he pictured judgment and heaven, the first story was of the wedding feast. Some of the virgins had oil and to spare but others brought only their lamps. When they ran out the bridegroom came and they didn't have the oil of preparation to go with him. They tried to borrow from the wise ones who had plenty but preparation to meet God isn't something you can borrow. They weren't allowed into the wedding feast. Heaven is a place of feasting, of joy and rejoicing. In Luke 14 Jesus pictured heaven in that same way as the master prepared the feast and invited his guest. They had excuses and didn't come so he sent the servants out to the streets and lanes of the city to bring people in and then to the country roads and lanes for more. When the feast comes he said there would be people there from the east and the west to share in the feasting.

In the next story the master gave each of his servants talents of gold for them to use while he was gone, according to their abilities. The one who had five gained five more and there one with two gained two more. For each of them the Master said, "Well done you good and faithful servant. You have been faithful over a few things. I will make you ruler over many. Enter into the joys of your Lord." Heaven is a place where people are rewarded for their faithful service on earth. They enter into the Lord's joy. But note that these who had been faithful here with a few things would then be ruler over many. That doesn't sound like heaven is just a place of singing, worship or resting. There are tasks to be done and the service we render here prepares us to lead in greater things there. In Revelation those in heaven were said to "Serve him day and night."

In the last of the stories in Matthew 25 he said at judgment he would separate us as the shepherd divides the sheep from the goats. To the ones on the right he would say, "Come you blessed of my Father. Inherit the kingdom prepared for you from the foundation of the earth." After telling them why they are on the right he said those in heaven would be with him eternally and those on the left would be in the hell prepared for the devil and his angels eternally. Eternal life or death has more to it that being unending. It has more to do with the quality and fulfilling of all God planned it to be.

So, heaven is a wedding feast. It is a time of joy in fellowship with God and each other. It is a place of comforting and encouragement. It is a place where we enter the Lord's joy and become ones that rule over greater things than ever before. It is a place where we are rewarded for faithful service down here. "Won't it be wonderful there?"

WHERE DO WARS COME FROM

In the words of Rodney King, "Why can't we just get along?" When Jesus said before the end comes there will be wars and rumors of wars he could have been describing just about any period of time that we could consider. It is always amazing that people think that what is going on at any particular time is the worst things have ever been. But you can go back and read things written two thousand or three thousand years ago and find the very same thinking.

Wars don't just happen between countries. Often the wars go on inside the country as we have seen in place after place this year. When you think of Libya, Egypt and Syria it is obvious that the fighting is an inward turmoil. Even in

Iraq and Afghanistan the wars are between religious groups inside the country. Here we tend to think that the Muslim's all want to kill people from the United States but they are just as intent on killing the fellow Muslims who disagree with them on some matter.

But it isn't just in the far away places that wars are common. The most brutal wars are often ones going on inside a family. Many times this is a war of words where each person verbally attacks the other. But there are also the times when the war turns physical and someone is abused or even killed as a result. Family wars leave casualties of all sorts that must be aided by others who love them for anyone to overcome.

Sometimes the wars are between religious groups who all believe in God, Christ and the Holy Spirit and all believe the Bible as His word. But they differ over smaller matters and try to destroy each other, usually with words instead of guns, but not always. But it is even true that the wars may be inside a single congregation of Christ followers. We hear of worship wars going on among Christians who can't agree in particular about the kind of songs they will sing. Sometime you can also add such big issues as whether or not people clap about something they feel good about. Can't you just imagine how thrilled the Lord is with his church when they can't get along because of such trivial matters and end up dividing the church? I feel sure he must see it and weep once again that people care so little about unity even with those who follow Jesus.

Where do all these wars come from? Let's ask the question with James the Lord's half brother who was a leader in the church in Jerusalem and who wrote the Book of James. "What causes fights and quarrels among you? Don't they come from your desires that battle within you? You desire but do not have, so you kill. You covet but you cannot get what you want, so you quarrel and fight. You do not have because you do not ask God. When you ask, you do not receive, because you ask with wrong motives, that you may spend what you get on your pleasures."

I can imagine people reading what James said on the matter and saying, "That isn't why I fight or quarrel with others who follow Christ. My disagreements are all righteous. I'm committed to following exactly what the Bible says. Those who disagree just won't stay with Scripture." But in just about every such disagreement if you talked with those who disagree you will find them equally committed to following Christ and His word. They feel that people are making laws where God hasn't made any and trying to bind their opinions on them.

So where do the wars come from? It really doesn't matter whether you are talking about family wars, wars in different countries or between two countries, wars between different religious groups or even wars inside the local church, the source James says is the same. These wars rise because of our desires or lusts or covetousness. It has to do with what we want and can't get. It happens because people aren't praying and even when they do pray it is selfish prayers about things, as we want them.

Isaiah in prophesying about the establishment of the church said that "They will beat their swords into plowshares and their spears into pruning hooks and none shall study war anymore." (Isaiah 2:1-4) When Micah gave the same prophesy he added one phrase at the end. "But each will sit under his own vine or his own fig tree and none shall make them afraid." The church is to be a place of love, acceptance, healing, grace and unity. It isn't a battlefield with each other. Our wars are with Satan and his demons, not flesh and blood (Ephesians 6:10-16).

WHERE IS YOUR TREASURE

The gospel accounts of Jesus life on this earth picture him often talking about a person's treasures in life. In Matthew 6 during the great Sermon on the Mount he spoke of treasures in connection with our worries in life. Notice some of the things he said. "Do not store up for yourselves treasures on earth, where moths and vermin destroy, and where thieves break in and steal. But store up for yourselves treasures in heaven, where moths and vermin do not destroy and where thieves do not break in or steal. For where your treasure is, there your heart will be also." (Matthew 6:19-21)

The time when Jesus lived on earth wasn't a very prosperous time, especially for the Jews that Jesus worked with on a regular basis. Yet he talked much about our money or treasures in life. Why would Jesus talk about money when most of the people didn't have much money? He knew that whether people had little or much didn't change the fact we could put our trust in the money instead of in Him. The poor person who had received one precious gift from his parents when they died could just as easily place that treasure into too high a place in his life as the one who had much could put his trust in his riches. Now Jesus makes no bones about the fact that it is hard for a rich person to be saved because the more we have the more we worry about making more or not losing what we already have.

God longs for us to find contentment in all aspects of life. But money has a way of taking control. The more we make the more we want to make. The more we have in the bank the more we want to have more in the bank. It is possible for one to find contentment no matter where they are on the wealth scale. Paul said he had learned to be content whether he had much or little in Philippians 4:10-13. It is really about this whole thing of contentment with what we have that led Paul to say to Timothy that the love of money was the root of all kinds of evil. He noted that godliness with contentment is great gain. "We brought nothing into this world and we will carry nothing out of it so having food and clothing we ought to be content." He challenged Timothy by saying, "But you O man of God, flee from all this, and pursue righteousness, godliness, faith, love, endurance and gentleness. Fight the good fight of faith. Take hold of the eternal life to which you were called when you made your good confession in the presence of many witnesses." (I Timothy 6:11-12)

Focus on one statement Jesus made that we have a hard time believing in our day. "Where your treasure is there will your heart be also." We desperately want to believe that we can treasure both the things we have in this life, the money we make and the amount we have in savings and still have our treasure and heart in heaven. Jesus in Luke 12 illustrates the difficulty of doing this when the man came to him wanting him to tell his brother to divide the inheritance with him. That would seem like a fair request to make. But Jesus took the opportunity to warn the man about covetousness. He told him the story of a rich farmer who had a great harvest and didn't have the barn space to store the whole harvest so he decided to tear down his old barns and build bigger barns and he said to his soul, "Soul take your ease. Eat, drink and be merry for you have much goods laid up for many days." God responded to him by saying, "You fool. Tonight I will require your soul of you and then whose will these things be?" Jesus draws this conclusion from that story. "So is everyone who is rich in this world but is not rich toward God."

Think of Jesus challenge to us to make certain we have our treasure in heaven. First don't worry about food, clothes and shelter. That is what the unbelievers worry about. Second, "Seek first the kingdom of God and his righteousness and all these things will be added to you." Third, "Don't worry about tomorrow for tomorrow will worry about itself. There is enough evil in today to concern yourself with." So we are to put the priorities of life on the kingdom and living right with God and on living one day at a time.

Perhaps the primary reason God taught his people to be generous with their money both to the church and in helping others was to help us keep our heart where it ought to be. Stingy givers never have their whole heart in the kingdom of God. We can come up with a thousand excuses not to give freely. We can say it is because the church isn't doing what we want it to do. But the truth is we aren't giving, as we should because the devil has convinced us that we can do better with the treasure than God can. When we say, "I'll give this but only if you use it as I tell you," it really isn't a gift at all since we are demanding the control. Where is your treasure?

WHILE WE STAND AND SING

How many invitation songs have you sung, heard or participated in? For me it has been a bunch. I remember those invitations when I was a boy and often felt guilty for something I had done in the last week and would either respond to the invitation to be prayed for or would leave feeling more guilty than ever. There were lots of preachers that I heard in that time that were really powerful in extending the invitation. They could run through the sins we were guilty of and the impression was left on me that if I didn't come down to the front of the building and confess all the wrongs to be prayed for then I couldn't be forgiven of the sins. It was some time later that I began to understand from Scripture that as a follower of Christ I could pray to God anytime, anywhere and have God's forgiveness for my wrongs (I John 1:8-10). Certainly there are times when I need to go to another that I've wronged and make it right and there are times when I need to confess my sins to another to have them pray for me as described in James 5:16. But I've never seen anything in Scripture that even approximates the form of invitation and response we have become accustomed to in the church world today.

I think the whole invitation song and pleading for people to come originated more in the revivals of the 19th century and the first half of the 20th century. I suspect it has been patterned more after the Billy Graham campaigns than anything relating to Scripture. Focus on two things for a moment. First notice the Book of Acts and the sermons recorded in it. On Pentecost in Acts 2 Peter preached to the multitudes about Jesus. As he talked about how they had crucified and slain the Son of God but God had raised him from the dead and he was now reigning at God's right hand, he was interrupted by the people who were cut to he heart with the question, "Men and brothers, what shall we do?" There was no invitation song or pleading to come. He told them to repent and be baptized into the name of Jesus Christ and their sins would be forgiven. Luke tells us that with many other words he testified and exhorted them to save yourselves from this crooked generation and 3,000 of them were baptized that day and added to their number. I suspect we read that and imagine Peter with tears in his eyes talking about how horrible hell is and with soft music and dimmed lights he is telling them to bow their heads and while their heads are bowed if you know you need to give your life to Christ then raise your hand. But that would be our putting what we've seen back into the text rather than taking from the text what happened. When Peter preached in Acts 10 to Cornelius and family his sermon was interrupted with God sending the Holy Spirit on the people and their speaking in tongues praising God. He then turned to the people with him to ask, "Can anyone forbid water that these should be baptized that have received the Holy Spirit just as we did in the beginning?" He then baptized the family of Cornelius.

But didn't Jesus extend an invitation? He said to the people, "Come unto me all who are weary and burdened and I will give you rest...." But there wasn't the follow up of here is how to do it or anything like that. In Revelation 22:17 it says that "The Spirit and the bride say come and let him who hears come and take of the water of life freely." So the Spirit and the church are to extend the invitation to people, but there isn't an explanation of when or how. I would suggest this is the open invitation that is there at all times for people to come to the Lord. It is when we talk to friends, family or a questioner and tell them of God's love and how they can be saved and they determine to obey the Lord to become a Christian.

Are invitations like we've become used to wrong? No, I don't think so. I think they could be wrong when it leaves wrong ideas in the minds of people such as that one can't make their life right with God when they have failed unless they are at the building, sitting on the front pew during a service time. It would be wrong if someone got the notion that to be baptized there had to be a service time. But when we begin to think that we haven't had a proper worship time unless the sermon concludes with an invitation song and a plea to come, then it is wrong. Tradition must never be placed on the par with Scripture. Something that is "A right way" must never be pictured as "The right way."

What if we stopped having an invitation at the conclusion of each sermon? What if we extended such an invitation only once in a while? Would such a change in pattern lead to more thought of what is involved instead of looking for the point in the sermon when the preacher starts to wind down so I can see it is almost time to "Stand and sing?" I'm just wondering.

WHO IS FAMILY?

How do you think of the people who belong to God? Especially, how do you think of the different people who worship God alongside you each week in the same church building? Are they family, friends, and fellow members of the same club, different parts in the same body or citizens of the same kingdom? There is definitely a sense in which all of these are correct. But each image has some parts to it that make it seem like a round peg in a square hole.

Focus on the family image for God's people for a moment. As a family we share the same Father. We enter the family by means of the new birth and by being adopted into the family. "Because you are sons, God has sent forth the Spirit of His Son into your heart, by which we cry Abba

Father." Being in God's Family is an amazing thought. No wonder John would say, "Behold what manner of love the Father has given to us that we should be called the sons of God. It does not yet appear what we shall be but we know that when he appears we will be like him for we shall see him as he is." To think of God's family as the whole body of disciples, around the world in all ages of time seems mind-boggling.

But that isn't the only picture of God's family. I'm not even certain it is the main one on which we should focus. When we think of the church as a whole we have a way of seeing things through very different colored glasses. Some of those are rose colored so that everything looks great and some are obviously cloudy so that nothing seems great. When Paul wrote to Timothy and said, "These things I've written to you intending to come to see you soon, but so that you will know how to conduct yourself in the family of God, which is the church of the Living God, the pillar and foundation of the truth" I don't think he was so much thinking about how Timothy was to conduct himself in the church around the world as he was on how to handle things in the church at Ephesus where Paul had left him and was asking him to stay. When you look at the context of these verses, he has just told him the kind of people to look for to set apart as elders and deacons in the church.

In that family of God's people there were members who had to be withdrawn from because they were teaching that the resurrection was already past. There were challenges going on with regard to what God's woman could and should do in the church and what they shouldn't do. There were challenges in the leadership of the body. The church in Ephesus had been established several years back and had elders for a long time. Paul had met with those elders in Acts 20 on his way to Jerusalem. He had written them and talked about their work alongside the evangelist, apostles, and prophets while in his first Roman imprisonment. Now he is writing to Timothy who is preaching for them during his second imprisonment in Rome. But there were still challenges in leadership and Timothy needed to set apart new people who met the qualities he had given. There were those among them spreading false teachings. There were problems with regard to materialism or coveting. All of this was going on yet God had Paul to describe them as His family. It was also in writing Timothy that Paul said that God knew those who were His. We may not be sure who is in or out of the family of the Lord, but God knows and that is the one who matters.

Families have problems. The best families you know of still have problems. Most of them have far more problems than you know anything about. Yet they love each other and even enjoy being with each other. One thing that all of us need to remember when we become critical of the family and are sure that some in-law is the real problem in the group; most likely there is someone else in the family that believes we are the problem. In good families, there is an acceptance of the fact that we don't have a perfect family, yet we love each other and accept each other for who we are. Can you imagine having a family meeting to vote some out that you think are causing problems in the group? No, we tend to look at the in-law or out-law in the family and laugh about some of their antics but think that they add color and flavor to the whole group.

When we can look at the church family in that same light and realize that some folks are the peculiar sisters or odd in-laws and enjoy the differences we will be seeing it as the family of God. We have a perfect father in God and a perfect older brother in Jesus. We have a perfect Spirit to guide and bless us. But after that, the family tree is full of knots and dead limbs. But it is a great family tree so enjoy it.

WHOSE RUNNING THINGS?

Some questions just seem to rattle around in the rafters to return ever so often. During the days when I was on the school board in North Little Rock if something was done that people didn't like they wanted to know who was running things, was it the board or the Central office or in particular the Superintendent? When I ran a Real Estate office if the sales people were upset about something they wanted to know who was running things, was it I as the broker or was it the owners of the company? And in church it works the same way. Any time anything happens which someone doesn't like the question begins to arise "Who is running things here?"

When thinking of the church in any place, the right answer first of all is that the Lord is running things here. He is the head of the church, which is his body, the fullness of him who fills all and in all (Ephesians 1:22-23). The church is not some corporate body that is run by a board of directors or has a CEO. It is under the directions of the Lord as to what can and cannot be done. All authority in the church is in Christ (Matthew 28:18). In the local church God has set up the elders, pastors or shepherds to have the oversight of the people or flock. In Acts 20:28 Paul encouraged the elders at Ephesus to focus on each other and to shepherd the flock of God that was among them taking the oversight of the body. In I Peter 5:1-4 Peter, a fellow elder charged the elders to shepherd the flock as overseers but to be careful not to lord it over God's heritage. In Hebrews 13:17 leaders are told to be watchmen for the souls of the people. So when we are talking about the care and oversight of the people at church the elders are charged with that duty. When it comes to the preaching of the word and what is preached, Paul charged the preacher to "Preach and rebuke with all authority." (Titus 2:15) He is to preach the word of the Lord with clarity and boldness without regard to who may like it or not. When it relates to ministries in the church the deacons were put "over this business." (Acts 6:1-7) That indicates that the deacons are running the different ministries of the church. In I Corinthians 16:15-16 Paul said the family of Stephanas had appointed themselves to take on the ministry to the saints. So members and families are often over some work or ministry in the church that they have taken on. Teachers run the different classes they teach week after week.

So when you think of the church as the community of believers that belongs to the Lord the question of who is running things really depends on what things you are talking about. When different staff members are assigned work to do and they take the responsibility for that work, they run the ministry they are assigned to do. Would you really want the elders trying to run the nursery, the children's classes or the children's worship time? What about the work with the teens, who is running things there? The elders hired the youth minister to work with the young people or have appointed other people to lead in that work. Would you really think it was best for the elders to be there telling them every class to teach and every activity to plan? There are all kinds of areas of the work of the church that the elders do their job when they choose a person to lead that ministry and get out of the way and allow them to do the job they have been asked to do. Who runs the work? The person who has been given the responsibility runs it.

Members on an individual basis do most of the work of the church as they live the Christian life in their home, on the job or in school or in any other realm of life. They personally decide how they will do the job and how they will direct their families or their personal efforts to do what God calls them to do. The truth is we only worry about "who is running things" when we don't like the direction it is going. The Lord runs the church. He has delegated elders to oversee the work in the local congregation. In most churches the elders choose people to run the particular aspects of that work. Each person runs their own life and ministry as they try to please God.

I think a better question would be "Who in the church is running to do what God calls each of us to do?" (Hebrews 12:1-2)

Do you remember when your parents thought you were a crazy kid? Do you remember when they said about you and your peers, "I just can't understand what they are thinking."? I suspect it has been going on since Adam and Eve had kids. As long as I can remember in preaching I've been hearing folks say things like, "There is no telling what the church will be like in 50 years. It is for certain our young folks can't see things the way we've been doing them up until now." Should there be concern from one generation to the next of what will take place? Of course there should be concern. After all if you read the Bible there is nothing more common in the Old Testament than to see people turn from their roots with God to their own ways as one generation died and another came on.

Think of the message from Joshua 24:31, "Israel served the Lord throughout the lifetime of Joshua and of the elders who outlived him and who had experienced everything the Lord had done in Israel."

Will there be changes in the church in the next thirty years to the degree many things won't look the same as they do now? Answer that question by answering another. Have things changed in the church over the last thirty years so that the ones who were of my parent's generation would be amazed to see what has happened? The real concern isn't about whether or not there will be change in the church and in the world in the coming days. The real question is about what will change. If we are talking about changes as to incidentals in how we do things then change and go on. Those things should change in every generation. When Paul described the church in Ephesians 5:27-29 as not having spot or wrinkle or any such thing, at least one point was that the church wouldn't get old. Think of when a person starts having spots and wrinkles in their life. It isn't during our youth or teen years. It is when years have passed and we are getting older ourselves. The point is that

234

the church is to be refreshed and young in each generation. Some have said that if the church marries any one-generation it is sure to be a widow in the next generation.

The world changes all along. You change. How many of us go anywhere today that we don't carry our cell phone with us? Yet a generation ago they were highly unusual and most of us were saying we didn't want that kind of thing that made it possible for people to reach us anytime they wanted. We are changing all the time. Just sit down in most new cars today and see the things that our fathers or grandfathers would have been overwhelmed by.

It isn't about whether there will be change, there always will be. The question is what will change. If we change the fundamentals of the gospel then we are in deep trouble. Praise God if the next generation restudies the things that troubled us in the past generation. Praise God if they see places and things where we reasoned incorrectly and change that to make what we teach more accurate with the Bible.

Many years ago when I had just started preaching I was introduced to Brother Gus Nichols at his home in Jasper, Alabama. One of the things I remember him saying to me that day was, "Be a real student of the Bible. Don't just accept what anyone else tells you about what the Bible teaches. Be one that refuses to believe anything just because someone says it. Learn what applies to now and what is just passing. Stand for what you believe the Bible teaches no matter who or what you stand against."

The Gospel doesn't change. It will always be the case that the church is the place where we are to glorify God (Ephesians 3:21). The kingdom of the Lord is unshakable (Hebrews 12:28-29). But worlds of things will change all along just as it has between the time when your parents and grandparents became members and today. Let's just be certain that what changes is what ought to change and not that we change the very things that are essential to being the church Jesus built.

It is certainly easy to turn to Hebrews 10:24-25 and say, you should go to church every time the doors open because the Bible tells us not to forsake the assembly. What does that Scripture actually say, anyway? "Let us consider how to stimulate one another to love and good deeds, nor forsaking our own assembling together, as is the habit of some, but encouraging one another and all the more as you see the day drawing near." It is certainly true that the Spirit led the writer to say not to forsake the assembling together. But there is a context to that command that gives it a deeper meaning than just that I must be in a church service each Sunday or each time we meet.

Personally, I never want to miss a church service. If I'm sick and must stay at home it seems like the whole week is missing something. But I must, at the same time admit that I have never thought to myself that I shouldn't be in the church service today because God commanded for me to be there. I don't want to miss because of the blessings I receive by being there. When we are out of town for some reason other than my preaching for another church on Sunday's I would never consider sleeping in that day and not finding a church to attend. In truth if we are going some place on vacation, one of the first things I do is look up what churches are in the area and how to get to one of them for worship that day. Why go to all that trouble? I go because I want to be with my fellow Christians. Because I believe that when we take communion that we are in fellowship with Jesus and I don't want to miss that opportunity. Because I will hear someone preach and teach the word of God and usually feel challenged by something that is said or done. Sometimes I will see things we can do better in or sometimes I see things that I want to make certain we avoid as a church.

Look more closely at the Scripture in Hebrews 10:24-25. It is characteristic of this book that the writer says, "Let us" at the beginning of any challenge. He doesn't' say to them, "This is what you should be doing." He puts himself right into the mix each time and that is powerful. Let us consider one another. In a world of selfishness, "Meism" and "Selfie's" it is a challenge to consider one another and not just self. We must think of our influence on others and how we may help another person. Church gatherings aren't just about what we can get out of it. They are about how we can encourage someone else and demonstrate for them devotion to God. Consider how we may stimulate others to love and good deeds. If I'm a parent or grandparent I certainly want to stimulate my children for love and good works. If I treat the church assembly as a matter of choice each week depending on how we feel or what is going on or even where we are, I'm telling them church attendance isn't all that important. No wonder so many grow up deciding it was all a waste of time anyway. I must demonstrate to them my excitement for gathering with others to worship the God of the universe. When we sing songs of praise to God and spiritual songs that encourage us to grow and serve we are fulfilling the point of this text. When we pray for each other and teach God's word on how to live we are doing so as well.

Don't forsake the gathering but encourage one another. Some were already choosing other things to do and places to go instead of assembling. But don't follow that. Be there to build up each other. The day of trial is always approaching. It is important to know that forsaking the assembly and missing church may be entirely different things. It would seem to me to be the same difference as missing supper with my family as compared to leaving them for six months to go and do my own thing in the mountains somewhere. We may miss a service due to illness or caring for someone who is ill or a multitude of other situations that may arise. But that is different from forsaking the gathering. To forsake is to intentionally determine I'm not going to the church gathering for a few weeks or months while I do my own thing. If we say we are going to the lake for the summer and don't plan to gather with the Christians during that time, we are forsaking the assembly. The result will always be that we declare by our influence on our children, family or anyone else that worship to God comes somewhere below my own enjoyment. It leaves me without the benefit of the encouragement of fellow Christians. It leaves me out of communing with the Lord. It takes away everything I might have done to build up, stimulate and encourage someone else who is struggling.

I know the cry, "I don't get anything out of it." It is appropriate to ask, "What are you putting into it?" If we put our heart into singing praise to God, praying with others, communing with Jesus, studying God's word and giving of our money, we will get something out of it because we will be putting something worthwhile into it.

WHY NOT LORD?

Jesus was tempted in every way like we are; yet he never gave in to the temptations that Satan hurled at him. Focus for a moment on the three big temptations Satan attacked Him with immediately after his baptism and 40 days of fasting and prayer. Each temptation challenged his own image of who he was. Satan said, "If you are the Christ, command these stones to be made into bread." It really seems like a good move for Jesus. He was certainly hungry after a month and a half of doing without food or drink. He had the power to turn the rocks into a loaf of bread. If he performed the miracle it would demonstrate his deity and take care of his need for food. So, why not command these stones to become bread? Because it is written "Man shall not live by bread alone but by every word that proceeds from God's mouth." Although Jesus had the power, there was a purpose for his power and that purpose wasn't to satisfy his own needs or desires. He didn't come to do his own will but the will of Him who sent him.

Luke records his second shot at Jesus as being that of taking him to a high mountain and showing him all the kingdoms of the world and saying, "If you will just bow down and worship me, I will give you all the kingdoms of the world. The power to give them has been given to me." It seemed like a small thing. It would allow Jesus to receive these kingdoms without going through the suffering, rejection and agony of the cross. He wouldn't face the feelings of being forsaken by God the Father. It must have entered his mind that if I give into this temptation I will have the blessings without the pain, the problems or the rejection. So Why not Lord? Thank God Jesus didn't take the easy way out because it would have cost him the pleasure of being in complete unity with the Father and his Holy Spirit. It would have shouted the message for eternity that it is good to look for the short cuts, the easy way out and to refuse the pain that comes through facing our temptations and trials head on and growing through them.

In Luke's account the temptation he puts third is the one that Matthew has as the second. Satan took Jesus to the highest point in the temple. As they stood there Satan demonstrated some things about himself that we need to learn. First, he is willing to quote Scripture to us when it serves his purpose. Jesus had faced the temptations with the common phrase, "It is written." Satan picks up the line and even gives a pretty good application of what the Psalmist said. "For it is written: He will command his angels concerning you to guard you carefully; they will lift you up in their hands, so that you will not strike your foot against a stone." Did the Psalmist actually say this? Yes it is from Psalms 91:11-12. So if Scripture said it, why wouldn't Jesus be willing to obey it? Notice his response was "It is said: 'do not put the Lord your God to the test." He was quoting from Deuteronomy 6:16. So if both these were Scripture how can one be used to explain why Jesus wouldn't follow the other one? What if Jesus had jumped down from the highest point on the temple and the angels had caught him and made him have a smooth landing? Would it have led people to believe in him? Perhaps for a little while it would. But there is a huge lesson in this. The things that bring a person to the Lord are generally the same things that keep them there. If people came to faith due to some amazing feat Jesus performed, it would require a little bit bigger feats the next time.

Besides that, the miracles of Jesus were not intended for personal use or simply to demonstrate his power. He was given miraculous abilities to help the people. He wasn't some magician always trying to come up with a better trick. He healed the sick, raised the dead, fed the hungry, and stopped the storms. But he never performed a miracle just to show what he could do.

Jesus demonstrated in all these that the end doesn't justify the means. In the first he could have satisfied a forty-day hunger. In the second he could have escaped the cross and its agony while taking the blessings of having all the kingdoms under his control. In the third he could have saved himself and showed how much power he had. He could even have used a Scripture to justify his actions. But he chose to reject Satan's advances in order to be the Son of God and to be the messiah who would offer freedom from sin and freedom from Satan's control. He demonstrated to us that quoting Scripture doesn't always mean one is right. Satan can quote Scripture with the best of them. Are they obedient to Scripture as a whole? Does the interpretation of Scripture match what God said elsewhere? Will my actions glorify God or will they please mankind? Will my actions leave me stronger in faith and devotion to God or weaker and more in line with Satan and his demons? Praise God Jesus rejected all the temptations and submitted to God in it all.

WITHOUT LOVE

Have you ever tried cooking a cake or pie and left out one ingredient? With some things it won't matter much if they are in the cake or pie or not. But there are other things that if left out the taste is completely changed and often not fit to eat. In our life for God there are some things that aren't all that significant and if left out aren't deadly for the church or the Christian. But there are things, such as love, that if left out, nothing else really matters. In I Corinthians 13:1-3 the Holy Spirit through Paul said, "If I speak in the tongues of men and of angels, but do not have love, I am only a resounding gong or a clanging cymbal. If I have the gift of prophecy and can fathom all mysteries and all knowledge, and if I have a faith that can move mountains, but do not have love, I am nothing. If I give over my body to hardship that I may boast, but do not have love, I gain nothing."

In this God was pointing to all the things that the people in the church at Corinth had thought of as being vital. Speaking in tongues had become their test of one's spirituality. Prophecy was the main item of worship and what built people up. Having faith to do miraculous things seemed to them to be at the heart of their faith. It was their means of demonstrating to others that God was truly among them. Having miraculous knowledge set them apart from others and gave them a sense of significance. Yet God wanted them to see that all these things they had seen as the essence of their faith and service to God had no meaning at all if they weren't grounded in love.

I wonder if he were writing to a present day church to tell us the things that we place so much emphasis on to be a great church don't really matter at all if love isn't at the heart of what is being done. I suspect he might say things like the following: "Even if you have the largest and most beautiful church building in the city and have the largest crowds come to worship each Sunday, if you don't have love it isn't worth anything. If your worship is powerful, singing with excitement and enthusiasm and your preaching is eloquent and grounded in Scripture and you don't have love it is meaningless. If you Bible classes are well taught and well attended and people invite all their friends to come and share in the classes, but you don't have love it has no benefit at all. If your benevolent program is so good that you have no one among you or around the city that is in need and their needs aren't being met by the church, but you don't have love you are nothing."

The Bible uses different words that are translated love but I'm not sure that all the distinctions between their meanings are warranted. But it is certain that the word used here (agape) is love in action. It isn't about a warm feeling or a falling in love or out of love with another person. This is the active, beneficial and unconditional good will and service to another. It is this love that describes how God loves us so much that he gave his one and only son for us (John 3:16). It is this love that Jesus talked about when he said to "Love your enemies and pray for those who persecute you, that you may be children of your Father in Heaven. He causes his sun to rise on the evil and the good and sends rain on the righteous and the unrighteous." (Matthew 5:44-45) It is the love Jesus talked about when he said, "A new command I give you: Love one another. As I have loved you, so you must love one another. By this everyone will know that you are my disciples, if you love one another." (John 13:34-35)

We sometimes talk about identifying marks of the church that you read about in the Bible. But I've seldom heard anyone list love for each other as one of those fundamental marks. Why is the world is that the case? Without doubt Jesus placed love as the primary mark one should use in measuring their Christianity and the essence of the church. Let's be perfectly clear that if you get everything else right and miss out on love for the Lord and for each other you have missed it entirely. Once in listening to a group of men discuss a sermon they had all heard on hell. One of the men who weren't a part of the church there made this comment. "I don't mind someone telling me I'm going to hell if I don't' change some things, if they do so with tears in their eyes showing it hurts them to think of me being lost. What I can't stand is a person preaching on hell and telling me I'm lost in a way that seems like they are happy about it."

It is a good day to check our love levels. If we are running low on love, it is time to add some before the engine of Christianity is destroyed.

WINE, WHIP, WATER, WOMAN

God obviously loves a good story. So much of the Bible is given to stories about God's dealings with people. In the four gospel accounts, that focus turns to God's work through Jesus with people. In John's Gospel, chapter 2-4 there is a series of stories of Jesus dealing with very different people from very different backgrounds and with extremely different problems. Yet he deals with each problem in exactly the right way. It reminds us that life with and for the Lord will take one into a wide variety of places, situations and with very different people, we can represent God well in each case.

In John 2 we are first introduced to Jesus along with his mother and a few of the early disciples at a wedding feast. We don't know who was getting married but Jesus and his mother were invited to the feast. Somewhere during the week of celebration the host ran out of wine and Mary learned of the problem. She brought the problem to Jesus who seemed to be frustrated that she brought it to him. There must be something big missed in the translation from Greek to English because what Jesus is recorded as saying and Mary's response just don't seem to add up. He seemed to chastise her for asking him with "Woman, what does that have to do with me? My hour has not yet come." She responded by saying to the servants, "Whatever he tells you to do it." He told them to fill the water pots with water, then draw some water out and take it to the leader of the feast. They did it, knowing that they were taking him water from the purifying pots. He took a drink of it and called for the groom. They probably thought the poor groom was about to be called on the carpet, but he said to the groom, "Others serve the best wine first and after people have had too much to drink they give them the poorer wine when they won't know the difference. But you've saved the best wine for last." I don't know if the groom was in on the whole miracle or not. But Jesus saved a host from embarrassment and provided the best wine of the feast by means of his first miracle.

Later in John 2 Jesus and the disciples go down to Jerusalem to the temple. When they go inside and Jesus saw the people selling animals, exchanging money and carrying on all kinds of commerce, he became livid. He made a whip and began driving out the animals and the moneychangers saying, "You've turned my father's house into a den of thieves" or a place of merchandise. The disciples saw it and remembered the Psalm, "Zeal for God's house has eaten me up."

Then in John 3 a Religious leader, member of the Sanhedrin and a Pharisee, came to Jesus one night. He said, "Teacher we know that you are a teacher from God since no one can do these signs that you are doing unless God is with him." Jesus looked deeply into the heart of the religious leader and declared, "Except a man is born again, he cannot see the kingdom of God." The man was confused. What do you mean? How can a grown man be born again? He can't crawl back into his mother's womb and be born again, can he? Jesus said, "Except a man is born of the water and the Spirit he cannot enter the kingdom of God." He went on to lay before him the greatest of all verses in the Bible. "For God so loved the world that he gave his one and only son that whoever believes in him should not perish but have eternal life." He treated the religious leader as one who didn't know God, didn't know the will of God and one who desperately needed a major overhaul in his life instead of a minor tune-up.

Finally, in John 4 he was traveling through Samaria as he went from Judea to Galilee. Being tired he sat down by the well outside of town while the disciples went into town to get supplies. A woman with a poor reputation and likely the attitude to go with it came to draw water. Her life had been drained with five different marriages and now just living with a guy she hadn't even bothered to marry. Jesus, a Jewish man, asked her for a drink. She was amazed. "What are you a Jewish man doing asking me a Samaritan woman for a drink?" Jesus shook her mind-set even more when he said, "If you knew who I was, you would ask me and I would give you living water. You can drink over and over of this water and just get thirsty again and have to come back to draw more. The one who drinks from the water I give will never thirst again. He will have the springs of water springing up in him to produce overflowing water. She wanted that water. But Jesus messed with her mind again when he said, "Go call you husband and return." "I don't have a husband," she said. Jesus said, "You are right about that. You've had five and the man you now live with isn't your husband. He went into her mind from being a strange Jewish man to a prophet of God very quickly. He wasn't satisfied with that jump and led her to a deeper faith in him as the messiah, the Son of God. Then she wanted to know about worship and he told her that God is spirit and those who worship him must worship him in Spirit and in truth.

How to reach out lovingly to all four groups Three chapters, four situations, four very different kinds of people and backgrounds yet Jesus is right at home with them all. Yet Jesus knew or individuals. He could easily use, wine, a whip, water or even living water to reach out to a Samaritan woman. Would you have fit into each of these situations and had an answer for the crisis? Most people could pick one or two that they might work with and feel all right about. The church as the body of Christ must be able to go

where Jesus went and fit where Jesus fit to reach the people Jesus does reach or that we reach for him.
THAT'S ALL!

<u>CLOSING REMARKS:</u> I certainly hope and pray that the things in this book have been a blessing to you and have encouraged you to grow in God's service. I would be encouraged to know that it also led to your questioning some things in what you have always believed and thought always being dedicated to allowing God to lead you in every aspect of your study of his word. Please pray regularly with me: Oh God, our father please open my eyes that I might see the wondrous things of your word and on seeing them willingly share them with others and devote myself fully to being and doing what you teach in your word. Through Jesus we pray, amen.

Leon Barnes

19388513R00142

Made in the USA
Middletown, DE
18 April 2015